'A scholar's eye for backgrour
tion to meaning, a pastor's ap
contemporary context. All th̶ ̶.̶.̶.̶.̶.̶.̶.̶.̶.̶ ̶i̶n̶ ̶t̶h̶i̶s̶ clear-minded
and warm-hearted exposition of 1 Corinthians, to make Paul's
great letter come alive with sparkling insights and pressing
relevance.'

David Jackman
Proclamation Trust, London

Dedicated to

Marcus Loane KBE (1911-2009)
Archbishop

1 CORINTHIANS

Holiness and Hope of a Rescued People

Paul Barnett

CHRISTIAN
FOCUS

Paul Barnett is the retired Bishop of North Sydney, Visiting Fellow in History at Macquarie University, Senior Fellow in the Ancient History Documentary Research Centre, Macquarie University, Teaching Fellow at Regent College, Vancouver and Faculty Member, Moore Theological College, Sydney. He was also Head of Robert Menzies College, Macquarie University.

Copyright © Paul W. Barnett 2011

ISBN 978-1-84550-721-3

First published in 2000 (ISBN 1-85792- 598-X)
Reprinted in 2004, 2011 and 2018
by Christian Focus Publications
Geanies House, Fearn, Ross-shire,
IV20 1TW, Scotland

www.christianfocus.com

Cover design by Moose77.com

Printed by
Bell and Bain, Glasgow

CONTENTS

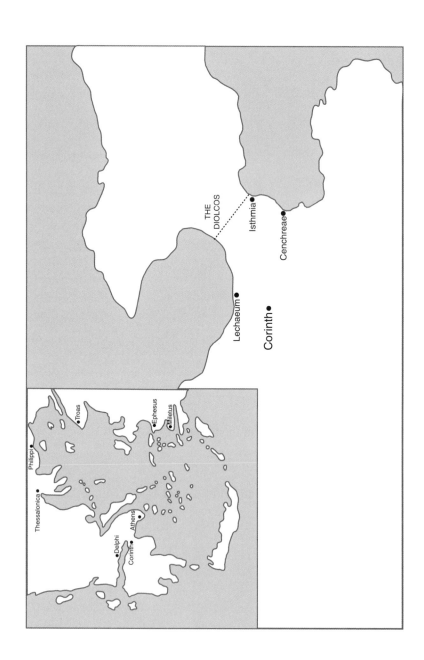

Introduction

1. Paul's Story so far

It was only a matter of months after the crucifixion of Jesus that the young Saul of Tarsus launched his attacks on the church of God in Jerusalem. To survive the fury of his onslaught a few (the apostles) hid in the Holy City, but most fled to other places of refuge, including Damascus just beyond the historic borders of the land of Israel. The young zealot must pursue these 'Nazarenes' to that city and bring them back for trial in Jerusalem.

What happened next is so well known that a 'Damascus Road' experience is part of worldwide speech. Blinded by the bright light, the young rabbi stumbled into Damascus into the care of local believers, where he was baptized. It was then and there, apparently, that Saul 'received' the oral traditions about Christ, formulated a few months earlier in Jerusalem, and which, in turn, he was to 'deliver' to churches he established, which included Corinth sixteen years later. Two of these oral traditions regarding the Lord's supper (11:23-26) and the outline of the gospel (15:1-7) will figure prominently in First Corinthians.

During those sixteen years Saul/Paul was to preach that Jesus crucified and risen was the Messiah of God, in fulfilment of the promises of the law and the prophets in Damascus, Nabataea, Jerusalem, Cilicia, Syria, Phrygian Galatia, northern Asia, Macedonia and Achaia. He arrived in Corinth in late AD 49.

2. Roman Corinth

Paul the Roman citizen appears to have set his sights on Roman provinces, usually concentrating on the leading cities from which the gospel would spread throughout the province. Corinth was capital of the province of Achaia.

7

In classical times Corinth had been a rival of Athens. The Roman invasion of Greece, however, reduced the city to rubble in 146 BC. About a century later Julius Caesar re-established the city, but as a Roman colony. The city became a melting pot for Greeks, Syrians, Jews and resettled Roman veterans. There were numerous slaves as well as freedmen (former slaves) in Corinth, as there were in other cities of this size.

Corinth's geographical position on the narrow 'land bridge' between the Greek peninsula and the Peloponnese was crossed by many people. Sea travellers and mercantile goods passed both ways across the Corinthian isthmus through the ports of Lechaeum and Cenchreae; the seas to the south of the Peloponnese were dangerous to shipping. Every two years the Isthmian games brought competitors and multitudes of spectators to Corinth. Furthermore, Corinth was noted for its manufacture of bronzes according to a secret formula. This city was famous for its prosperity.

Corinth, however, was not without its difficulties. While it was known for its wealth, there were also many impoverished people in the city, as well as slaves and those who had recently emerged from slavery. One visitor wrote of the 'sordidness of the rich and the misery of the poor', a place 'abounding in luxuries but inhabited by ungracious people'.[1]

There is evidence of grave food shortages throughout the eastern Mediterranean during the later forties and early fifties resulting from crop failures in Egypt. Infrastructure for grain storage was lacking, so that times of famine meant soaring prices and rioting. Claudius made special provision for grain distribution in Greece during the years of Paul's association with Corinth. Possibly this helps explain Paul's reference to this 'present crisis' (7:26) and to his sense of outrage that the wealthy ate and drank to their fill at the Lord's supper while those who 'have not' were hungry (11:21-22).

Corinth appears to have been an exceptionally 'religious' city. Thanks to the travel writer Pausanias who came to Corinth a few years after Paul, we know of many temples for the gods, shrines for the Roman imperial family and mystery cults. Paul's pithy reference to 'many gods and many lords' (8:5) was true

---

1   Alciphron, *Letters of Parasites* 3.60, writing a century and a half later than Paul.

of the Achaian capital. This presented a grave problem for the members of the church in Corinth, many of whom remained enmeshed in 'temple culture'. This is evident throughout chapters 8-10, where Paul refers to 'an idol' (8:4,7; 10:19), the 'idol house' (8:10), 'the worship of idols' (10:14), 'idol-sacrificed meat' (8:1, 4, 7, 10; 10:19) and 'temple-sacrificed' meat (10:28).

Religion and politics were inextricably linked. All the cults of the gods and the mysteries expressed solidarity with local civic life and reverence towards the Roman emperors upon whom all provincial life depended. Only the Jews were excused from participating in the sacrifices. At the beginning the Christians may also have enjoyed this liberty since officially they were viewed as part of Judaism (Acts 18:12-16). Some scholars have suggested that this immunity began to be lost in the aftermath of Paul's departure from Corinth in AD 51. It appears possible that a cult for the Roman emperor may have been established in Corinth at that time, bringing sharply increased pressure on the new church.

By the time of Paul's visit, about a hundred years after its re-foundation, Corinth was a bustling port city, a dazzling Roman city of cosmopolitan character and brash manner. Its vigorous cultic life, however, was an ever present threat to those Gentiles who as Christians must turn their backs on the gods, the temples and their priests. Paul's arrival in Corinth coincided with times of great hardship for the poor due to the widespread effects of famine.

3. Paul in Corinth (AD 50-51)

Paul's initial ministry in Corinth occupied about a year and a half. On his arrival from Athens he stayed with Aquila and Priscilla, who were fellow-Jews, fellow-tentmakers and, most likely, fellow-believers. During this period Paul taught the gospel to Jews and God-fearers[2] in the synagogue (Acts 18:1-4). When he was rejoined from Macedonia by Silas/Silvanus and Timothy, Paul intensified his ministry in Corinth which now extended to the Gentile population of Corinth. The book of Acts comments that, 'Many of the Corinthians hearing Paul believed and were baptized' (Acts 18:8).

---

2   Gentiles who attended the synagogues, whose males were as yet uncircumcised.

4. Paul in Ephesus (AD 52-55)

It was probably soon after the middle of A.D. 51 that Paul left Corinth.[3] With Priscilla and Aquila Paul visited Ephesus and, leaving his companions there, journeyed alone via Caesarea 'up to' Jerusalem where he greeted the church (Acts 18:22). From Jerusalem he revisited the churches from Antioch in Syria through Cilicia and southern Galatia back to Ephesus.

For the next three years (52–55) Paul taught the gospel in Ephesus. For the first three months he taught in the synagogue on the Sabbath. Thereafter he taught daily for two years publicly in 'the hall of Tyrannus'. Many people from the province came to hear Paul speak the word of the Lord. As well Paul proclaimed the gospel in the various house churches and to the gatherings of the wider community of believers.

Towards the latter part of Paul's ministry in Ephesus opposition to the apostle appears to have increased.[4] At the same time Paul heard of problems back in Corinth.

5. Corinth: After Paul Left

5:1 Visiting Leaders

Silas/Silvanus and Timothy remained in Corinth when Paul left in A.D. 51, though it is not clear how long they remained. We lose track of Silvanus for the next dozen or so years until he appears in Rome as Peter's amanuensis (1 Pet. 5:12). Some time after Paul came to Ephesus Timothy rejoined him from Corinth (1 Cor. 16:10; Acts 19:22).[5]

A sequence of Christian leaders visited Corinth during Paul's stay in Ephesus. First came Apollos, the Jew from Alexandria. Apollos had heard about the preaching of John the Baptist and it is possible that Apollos had been baptized by John in the Jordan two decades earlier. Apollos did not grasp that Christ was the fulfilment of John's preaching and baptizing until he came to the synagogue in Ephesus where Priscilla

---

3   A proconsul held office for a year from 1 July until 30 June. Having been acquitted by Gallio (Acts 18:12-16) Paul may have timed his departure to avoid a re-trial by an incoming pronconsul.

4   1 Cor. 15:30-32; 16:8; 2 Cor. 1:8-10; Acts 19:23-27.

5   It is possible that Timothy suffered a period of imprisonment in Corinth (Heb. 13:23).

and Aquila 'showed him the way of God more accurately' (Acts 18:26). Apollos created a great impression when he came to Corinth, both for his eloquence and the power of his spiritual fervour (Acts 18:24-25, 28). In 1 Corinthians Paul addresses the new fascinations of the Corinthians in rhetoric, wisdom and 'spiritual' ministry. It is possible that Apollos' ministry had unintentionally inflamed these expressions of ministry in Corinth and made the local people somewhat dissatisfied with Paul's less spectacular approach. Paul must address the issues of wisdom and rhetoric in chapters 1–4 and 'spiritual' ministry in chapters 12–14. While Paul writes positively of Apollos, the Corinthians' request for a return visit by him does not seem to have the apostle's support at that time (16:12).

Some time later Corinth was favoured by a visit from Cephas/Peter and his wife (9:5). Peter had been a disciple of John the Baptist before becoming a disciple of Jesus. Peter was, historically, the first witness of the resurrection. From A.D.33-49 Peter had been the apostle to the land of Israel, proclaiming the gospel in Jerusalem, Judaea, Samaria and Galilee. After the Jerusalem Council in c. A.D. 49 Peter began to travel outside the land of Israel. He probably revisited churches in Palestine and most likely came once more to Antioch. It is possible that he travelled through Asia Minor before coming to Corinth some time after 52. It is possible that Peter's visit, like Apollos', also unsettled the Corinthians in regard to Paul, though in different ways. Peter may have created the impression that since Paul had not been a disciple of the historical Jesus he was not fully an apostle. This would explain why Paul needed to insist on his genuine apostleship (9:1-3; 15:8-11).

Barnabas, too, may have come to Corinth. A Cypriot Jew and an early member in the Jerusalem church, Barnabas had been sent to check on the new church in Antioch. Barnabas was senior partner to Paul in the missionary journey from Antioch to Cyprus and southern Galatia. Thereafter Barnabas and Paul parted company and Barnabas went to Cyprus. Again, Barnabas' visit may have unsettled the Corinthians.

The coming of Apollos, Peter and Barnabas showed the Corinthians that Paul was by no means the only preacher or Christian leader.

5:2 Local Leaders

It also appears that a local leader or leaders had arisen who were taking the church in a rather different direction from the founding apostle (3:10, 18; 4:18-19). These have created their own loyal followings, against one another and against Paul (4:6). These new leaders are teaching a wisdom-based message, not Christ crucified and risen. But this would be a different superstructure from the foundation Paul laid, that is, the preaching of Christ (3:10-11). The aspirations of these local usurpers has issued in arrogance and envy. Paul's famous teaching on 'love' is addressed to leaders like these who are 'envious' and 'puffed up' (13:4-5).

Paul faces these troublemakers with his admonitions in the letter, but also by urging the Corinthians to recognise responsible local people like Stephanas (16:15-18) and welcoming warmly Timothy when he comes (16:10-11). It is understandable that Paul is not too keen about Apollos returning to Corinth in the immediate future (16:12).

5.3 Issues

This is a long letter, with a number of major topics to be covered, but with many twists and turns. Is it possible to identify Paul's underlying but ultimate concerns for this church?

a. *Apostolic authority.* The most basic problem was the opposition to Paul's authority as an apostle. In his absence various unnamed persons have arisen to seize control of the church. These are rejecting the authority of Paul as an apostle of Christ to direct their thinking and behaviour. Paul responds to this challenge throughout the letter.[6]

b. *Eschatology.* In the past three years a rather different eschatology from that which Paul taught has come to the surface in Corinth. We are able to know Paul's eschatological perspectives when present in Corinth since these may be seen in First and Second Thessalonians, which were written from Corinth. But the Corinthians appear to have switched their focus from the future to the present. For the Corinthians 'wisdom' had come to be associated with power and the appearance of things. Paul

---

6   1:1; 2:10-16; 3:10; 4:8-16; 9:1-3; 14:36-38; 15:8-11.

must remind them that the believers' hope is directed to the future, to glorious things which eye has not seen nor ear heard, nor the human heart imagined (2:6-9).

Paul must remind them that 'Christ crucified' is the 'wisdom and power of God' that overturns all human ideas of wisdom and power and which (1:17–2:5), when apprehended, opens the way to God's coming glorious kingdom.

Related to this, it seems, are the doubts of 'some' in regard to the future resurrection of the body (15:12), doubts which are corrupting the church (15:33-34) and shaking their foundations (cf. 15:58). Possibly these doubts about the future resurrection stemmed from a combination of Greek skepticism about the resurrection of the body and the Corinthians' new sense that in their new experience of the Spirit, God's purposes were for now, not later (over-realized eschatology cf. 4:8; 14:36).

If there is no resurrection of the body there will be no judgement of God in the end. If there is no judgement of God then there is no reason not to engage in bad behaviour. The members of the church could, therefore, adopt an easy-going attitude to adultery and visiting prostitutes (5:1-2; 6:9-20). Furthermore, continued involvement in the temples and partaking of idol-sacrificed meat is not a problem (chapters 8–10) if there is no divine judgement.

Since the kingdom has come in the full flood of the Spirit, the 'sign' of marriage is dispensable since there is no marriage in the kingdom. Some wives who prophesied have removed the sign of their marital submission to their husbands (11:2-16). Other women believe that the arrival of the new age means that sexual relationships (and childbearing) should be set aside while those who are married to unbelievers are free to leave them (7:1-2, 10-11).

c. Worldliness and Individualism. Arising from their flawed eschatology is their worldliness and individualism. Paul confronts them with these twin evils at many points. They are seen in the arrogance of upstart leaders and in the parading of 'gifts' of wisdom, knowledge and eloquence (1:5; 8:1-3, 10; 10:12). Their enhanced sense of knowledge and wisdom blinded them to the effects their liberty (in attending temples) was having on weaker Christians. Yet they appeared not to care about the impact of their behaviour on others. The preoccupation with 'spiritual gifts' that enhance the ego of the one who speaks demonstrates well the individualism of the Corinthians. Paul must teach them that the true evidence of the Spirit is conversion and that 'gifts' are given for the upbuilding of the 'body' of believers; if they are not used in 'love' for them they are quite valueless.

d. Scandal in Corinth. The church in Corinth was a new social grouping and Paul was concerned lest it create a bad impression in the city. There were quite a number of aspects of the life of the Corinthians that would have provoked negative comment locally. One example is the adultery of a man with his stepmother, a sin not found even among pagans (5:1). A second is the practice of church members taking one another to the public courts. This told the wider community that these Christians were a disorderly lot! (6:1-8). A third example is the women prophets who are casting off the 'sign' of their submission in marriage (11:13-14). A fourth is the factions apparent at the Lord's supper (11:17-22), especially at a time of food shortage. A fifth is the chaos in the meetings with the babble of tongues, prophets talking over the top of one another and wives calling out questions across the meeting (14:26-40).

Such behaviour would have attracted serious criticism in a city like Corinth, where good order in cult groups was important. Surviving rules governing mystery cults reveal that disorder was unacceptable. These groups governed themselves strictly so as to avoid scandal in the community. The Bacchic society insisted that, 'No one shall deliver a speech without recognition by the priest or vice-priest'.[7] The Cult of Zeus Most High decreed that, 'It shall not be permissible...to make factions (*schismata*)...to abuse one another or to chatter or to indict or accuse...'[8] We note that Paul accuses the Corinthians of creating 'schisms' (*schismata* 1:10; 11:18; 12:25), chattering (14:26-40) and 'indicting and accusing'!

These and other examples from the period cast light on much of this letter and indicate that Paul was sensitive to the church developing a bad reputation. Many of Paul's concerns found in

---

7   Cited in J. Harrison, 'Paul's House Churches and the Cultic Associations,' *Reformed Theological Review* 58 (1999), p. 40.

8   Harrison, 'House Churches,' p. 41.

First Corinthians arise from his awareness that the behaviour of the Corinthians may have fallen below the standards that applied to other groups at that time.

This is relevant. Modern societies are deeply conscious of ethical issues. Professional associations adopt strong moral codes and discipline their members where necessary. It is a scandal when standards of behaviour in the church fall below those of the community. Believers must not allow their standards to be less than the standards of various groups within the community.

6. Paul's Literary Genius

Hints scattered throughout the letter help us understand how the letter came to be written. First, reports of problems were brought from Corinth to Ephesus by Chloe's retainers and Stephanas and his assistants. These told of factions, adultery, wives casting off their hair covering when prophesying, selfish actions at the Lord's supper and doubts about the future resurrection.

At about the same time a letter had also been sent from Corinth apparently seeking Paul's clarification on six questions. For the most part, however, these questions are couched in argumentative tones. Surely it is right for women to abstain from sexual relations (7:1)? Has a father really done wrong in betrothing his older-than-usual daughter for marriage (7:25)? Surely it is acceptable to dine in an idol-house (8:1)? Surely 'tongues-speaking' is the true sign of the Spirit (12:1)? How long must we put money aside for this collection (16:1)? Surely Apollos will come back to us soon (16:12)?

Paul could have dealt with the reports, then answered the questions. He might have done this in a few pages. Rather, he analyses these reports and questions and finds five broad topics. These he presents as a sequence of pastoral sermons for the upbuilding of the church in Corinth and elsewhere. Paul takes his readers through each topic with meticulous care. It is important they know his teachings, yet in such a way that they learn to think in a Christian way.

	Chapter
True wisdom and false	1–4
Holiness in sexuality	5–7

In chapter sixteen Paul outlines his future plans and finishes with words of strong encouragement.

This is a truly great letter. Careful attention to its message, but also its method of Christian reasoning, will bring the blessings of God to those who patiently work through it.

1

Contention in the Church
(1 Cor. 1:1-17)

In his opening greeting to the Corinthians Paul introduces the theme which will dominate the remainder of the letter, that is, God has called the Corinthians to be his 'holy ones' (vv. 1-3). To be sure, in the 'thanksgiving' he reassures them that through the gospel God has placed a firm foundation under their feet (vv. 4-9). Yet there is much that needs their attention in terms of 'holiness'. To begin with, they are quarrelling among themselves as to their preferred minister Paul, Apollos or Cephas/Peter. The super-spiritual ones say they belong to Christ, while others do not! (vv. 10-17).

1. Greeting (1:1-3)
Letters then had a very simple format: A to B, greetings followed by the body of the letter. Such letters were more practical than ours today where we have to go to the end to find out the sender of the letter. First Corinthians is no mere personal letter, however. Paul says that he is 'called to be an apostle of Jesus Christ by the will of God', which is pretty heavy. The sender is the 'official delegate of the Messiah, Jesus' and note this carefully he holds this office 'by the will of God'. The reader, past and present, ought to listen carefully.

By contrast, Sosthenes, the co-sender, is merely Paul's 'brother', a fellow-Christian who was with him at the time of writing. Lack of further identification suggests that Sosthenes was the former ruler of the synagogue of Corinth who was beaten up in the presence of Gallio the proconsul (Acts 18:17) and who must have been converted in the meantime and become a co-worker of Paul's in Ephesus. We know nothing further of this Sosthenes.

Paul's letter is addressed to 'the church of God' or more literally, 'God's assembly', which was 'in Corinth' (v. 2). Here the emphasis is on the 'gathered people of God' who have met together, for example, to remember Jesus' death in the Lord's Supper (11:17, 33) or for word ministry to one another as 'a whole church' (14:23). Usually the believers met in smaller house groups but they also met as a plenary assembly (11:18; 14:23), though we do not know whether this was weekly, monthly, or only occasionally. It was at such a gathering of the 'whole' Christian community in Corinth (in the house of Gaius? Rom. 16:23) that the letter would have been read aloud to the people. (All reading was then aural and Bible writers wrote their words to be listened to; it was more like a cassette than our idea of a letter.)

The 'church' is a living 'body', as Paul will say later (12:12-27), not a dead institution or a lifeless pile of bricks. But this 'body' does not belongs to any local leader or minister but to *God* himself for he 'bought' the church and its individual members with the precious blood of his own Son (Acts 20:28; 1 Cor. 6:19-20).

One of Paul's methods as a letter writer is to signal in his opening words an important theme or themes which will be developed throughout the letter. In this letter it is the theme of 'holiness' which is critical because of the *unholiness* of some of the Corinthian believers, both in their lovelessness and crass individualism within the congregation and their ongoing compromise with pagan idolatry and sexual practices in the wider community of pagan Corinth.

It has been a universal human failing throughout history to think of special places ('temples'), special people ('priests') and special times ('holy' days) as sacred. Nothing could be further from the truth. It is the gathered *people* who are 'sanctified in Christ Jesus...called to be saints'. It is *they* who are 'set apart' in God's sight as his people because they belong to 'Christ

Jesus'. But this 'sanctification' of status is accompanied by God's insistence (his 'call') that they also *be*, in practical terms, his 'saints' or 'holy ones'.

As Christians today God calls us to *become* and *be* by his strength what he mercifully sees us to be in Christ, that is, morally 'blameless' (1:8). This 'holiness' is not merely outward reverence, however, but practical obedience to God's revealed will. This will mean, on one hand, our separation from sexual impurity, false worship, lying and cheating (6:9-11), and on the other hand, our love of one another (13:1-13) and of the Lord Jesus (16:22; cf. Eph. 6:24). In short, God through his apostle, is calling us to a life of holiness. That, in a nutshell, is the message of Paul to the Corinthians and to us.

Paul also addresses his letter to 'all those everywhere who call on the name of the Lord Jesus Christ, their Lord and ours', a probable reference to other centres of Christian fellowship in the province of Achaia (cf. 2 Cor. 1:1). In passing, this implies that this letter will be copied for other churches, explaining how in time the letters of Paul were made available throughout all his churches (cf. Col. 4:16). Paul established churches in major cities like Corinth and Ephesus, with one of his aims being for local evangelists to establish a cluster of satellite churches in the region (Phil. 4:2-3; Col. 1:6-7). This was Paul's strategy for the rapid spread of the gospel.

It is evident from these opening words that these men and women of Corinth had been profoundly converted, even though as new believers some of their number continued to wrestle with various expressions of unholiness. Previously, as temple-going idolaters, they had worshipped 'many "gods" and many "lords"' (8:5-6). But now, through the gospel, they have come to acknowledge from their hearts, instead, Jesus as 'Christ' (that is, as 'king') and 'Lord' (that is, as a divine 'master') and the one true God as their own 'Father'. This is the experience of all true Christians in response to the faithful teaching of the gospel.

Paul concludes his opening formalities with the prayer that the readers may know the 'grace' and 'peace' from their Father and the Lord (v. 3). 'Grace' is God's unexpected and undeserved mercy shown in the death of Christ for our salvation (Eph. 2:8) which has made possible 'peace with God' (Rom. 5:1) and its consequence, the 'peace of God' in formerly troubled hearts (John 14:27; Phil. 4:7). The Corinthians in the assembly had come to know these blessings of 'grace and peace' in recent days through the preaching of the gospel by Paul and his colleagues (2 Cor. 1:19-22).

2. Paul's Thanksgiving for Them (1:4-9)

In Greek letters of that time a thanksgiving to the gods followed the opening address and greeting. Once again Paul follows that convention, though his thanksgiving is addressed to 'my God' (v. 4). In Paul's case it was no empty formality, however, but heartfelt. How could he forget the former evil lifestyle of so many of his readers (see on 6:11)? Previously they had attended the local temples for the worship of 'many gods and many lords' (8:5). As members of a port city like Corinth, with more than its share of rogues, many of Paul's readers had previously been involved in sexual immorality (both heterosexual and homosexual), thievery, drunkenness, loutishness and extortion (see on 6:9-10). But they had been converted from idolatry to the service of the living God and the risen Lord and they had turned their backs on sexual impurity and other moral wickedness (see on 6:11). This was no merely human moral turnaround, however, but one empowered by the grace of God, 'grace given to [them] in Christ Jesus'.

This 'grace of God' which had been 'given them' was no merely invisible thing. Rather it had been made evident in the life of the congregation in Christian 'speech' and 'knowledge' (v. 5). Here Paul is referring to 'gifts' of speaking like teaching, prophecy and 'speaking in tongues' which arise from their new 'knowledge', that is, of their 'Father' and their 'Lord'. This is not merely the activity of 'speaking' and 'knowing', however, but of *what* is 'spoken' and 'known,' the confession of the Lord Jesus Christ in contrast to their former worship of 'many gods and many lords' (see on 12:1-3). In other words, Paul is pointing to the manifest fact of their conversion from pagan idolatry, to the confession that '*Jesus* is Lord' as expressed in the assembly in teaching, prophecy and 'different kinds of tongues' (see on 12:3-11).

Paul sees this 'speaking' and 'knowing' as a sign that his 'testimony about Christ' has been 'confirmed' in the life of their

congregation in Corinth, 'placed under them as a firm foundation', as it were (v. 6). That 'testimony' was the gospel which
he had preached in the city of Corinth. 'Testimony' was a witness' sworn evidence in a court, based on what he or she had
seen and heard. In Paul's case it referred to the gospel which
had come to him so personally on the road to Damascus. But
the same principle applies to us. The gospel we give to others,
whether as preachers or as individuals, must always be *our*
testimony, words about things that are deeply true in our own
experience. The light of the word of God must have shone in
our hearts before we are able to shine it into the hearts of others (2 Cor. 4:5-6).

In their 'speaking' and 'knowing' the Corinthians did not fall
behind any other church (v. 7). This is probably Paul's way of
telling them that, in fact, they *exceeded* other churches in these
things (cf. 2 Cor. 8:7). But while Paul genuinely wishes to encourage them, there is also an 'edge' to his words. What if their
'speaking' and 'knowing' were not matched by 'love' within
their community of faith? As the letter proceeds it will become
clear that this is precisely their problem (see on 8:1-3; 13:1-3).

Nonetheless, he encourages them in such 'speaking' and
'knowing' as they 'await the revelation of our Lord Jesus Christ'.
Right 'knowledge' and faithful 'speaking' will help sustain
them as they, with others, look for the coming of Jesus. While
Paul and his churches eagerly anticipated the return of Jesus,
this was not something they thought would necessarily occur
immediately. As he explains elsewhere, other events must first
intervene, including the appearance of the mysterious 'man of
lawlessness' (2 Thess. 2:3-4).

Mention of the return of Christ naturally prompts Paul to
reassure the readers about their ongoing spiritual security. The
Lord Jesus will continue to 'confirm' them, that is, 'place a solid
floor under' them 'until the end' (v. 8). *Bebaioun* literally means
'to lay a foundation'. Therefore, let them be assured that in 'the
day of the Lord' God will continue to hold them to be 'blameless', as indeed they are now already 'in Christ'.

Many hazards face Christians throughout their lives, as
well as numerous temptations, not all of which are successfully resisted. Sin will be a present reality until the onset of the
coming age. Until that time God's 'holy ones' will periodically

succumb to unholy behaviour. Nothing could be clearer than this from the letters of Paul and the other apostles. Yet we are called to holiness in the knowledge of God's loving forgiveness through the sacrifice of Jesus on the cross for us. By no means least is Paul's assurance given here that 'God is faithful' to us in spite of our many failures (10:13; 2 Cor. 1:18; cf. Deut. 7:9). In his grace God is always reliable, always true to his people (2 Thess. 2:13-14). Having 'called us into the fellowship of his Son' we may be assured that God will remain 'faithful' in 'keeping' us, enabling us to be 'more than conquerors' in whatever comes against us (Rom. 8:37; cf. 8:28-30).

Very striking, indeed, are Paul's words, '[God has] called us into fellowship with his Son' (v. 9). Through his word, the gospel, spoken by men and women, God 'calls' fellow humans 'into his Son', that is, into a relationship of faith in Christ in which we are 'reckoned' to be 'righteous' by God, reconciled to him, through the death and resurrection of Christ. This is as true for us as individuals, as it is for us as the family of faith, though it is easy enough to forget the latter. Not only the individual but also the church is 'in Christ'. Thus the church is 'the fellowship of his Son'. It is quite astonishing that this 'body' of people, unworthy as we more often than not are, should be called the 'sharers' or 'stakeholders' *of* or *in* the Son of God. Yet this is quite consistent with the Gospels, where we read of 'sinners' who clustered around Christ (cf. Luke 15:1-2), whose 'friend' he was (Matt. 11:19).

Historically and theologically, Paul's reference to Jesus as God's 'Son' in a letter written *c.* A.D. 55 is extraordinarily important. In recent times many have attempted to play down or even deny Jesus' deity, including, for example, the Jesus Seminar. They argue that Jesus was merely some kind of prophet or sage whose life and teaching may be bracketed with Socrates or Buddha as casting moral light on our path.

Paul's letters, however, are critical for two reasons. Firstly, as the earliest written part of the New Testament they speak of Jesus as 'the Son of God' who died for our sins and who was raised again (Gal. 1:1-4; 4:4; 1 Thess. 1:9-10). Galatians, Paul's earliest surviving letter, was written *c.* 48, a mere decade and a half after the life span of Jesus of Nazareth. Secondly, Paul quotes teaching from those who were apostles before him, which had been formulated in the immediate aftermath of the resurrection, on which he was dependent (see on 15:3-5). Paul did not invent these confessions. He was not the second founder of Christianity, as is often claimed. Rather, before his conversion he was a persecutor of earliest Christianity, seeking to 'destroy the church of God' and its 'faith' which were already in place (Gal. 1:13, 17, 23). Paul's innocent and passing reference here to Jesus as God's Son is powerful evidence of the truth of historic and orthodox Christianity.

In this 'thanksgiving' Paul, as a consummate pastor, has 'placed a floor under' his readers' feet, the sure foundation of God's faithfulness in calling them and keeping them. Certainly he will challenge them and rebuke them in what follows. But first let them be assured that they are secure in God's love and care.

3. 'Quarrels' in Corinth (1:10-17)

1. Factions (1:10-12)
Paul now introduces the body of the letter with his immediate and urgent concern for the unity of the church. In verses 10-12 Paul does three things: (1) he appeals to them to be united, (2) explaining that a report has come to him about contention in the church, which (3) he amplifies that 'each' member says he 'belongs' to Paul, or to Apollos, or to Cephas or to Christ.

Paul's 'I appeal' (*parakalō*, v. 10) is one of his favourite ministry words to his churches. It is not a military 'command' to be dumbly obeyed, but a warm encouragement to be acted on, that is, 'be united'. By this approach Paul, like a wise parent, puts before them (and us) an important principle of Christian behaviour, which is the need for unity within the congregation, but in such a way that its fulfilment will prove to be a 'growing experience' for the readers.

Nonetheless, his 'appeal' is 'through the name of our Lord Jesus Christ'. His invocation of that great 'name' signals how important the issue of the moment is. It amounts to this. They are 'all' to 'speak the same things', that is, about their core be-liefs, rather than '*each* saying I belong to' a, b or c. Paul is calling for unity in Christ in place of factious individualism. Here Paul uses a metaphor from clothing. There are to be no 'schisms' or ripping apart of the fabric of their community. Rather, they are to be 'knit together' in 'mind' and 'opinion' in the one garment. Interestingly, Paul's verb *katartizō* was used of the fishermen 'mending' their nets (Mark 1:19). Such a 'knit together' 'mind' and 'opinion' concerns their commonly held commitment to the Lord Jesus Christ. It does not mean that Christians must have identical musical tastes or political loyalties. But they are to be so solidly united about Jesus that there will be no room for minister-based factions.

The report came from Corinth through members of Chloe's household (v. 11). This woman was so concerned about the 'quarrels' in the congregation that at some expense she sent associates or family members to inform Paul, a journey of several days across the Aegean Sea. The word 'household' (NIV) does not appear in the original Greek text, though it is a reasonable inference, indicating that Chloe was a woman of means, perhaps a trader. Her name given on its own suggests that she was a widow. The name 'Chloe' is drawn from Greek mythology and implies that she was not a Jewess, though she may have been a Gentile 'God-fearer' who had previously attended the synagogue in Corinth before her conversion to Christ. Her initiative in sending her people to Paul probably means that she was an early convert in Corinth and one who had valued Paul's ministry in the city three years earlier.

Paul expands on Chloe's report (v. 12). The 'quarrels' in the church were due to factionalism as the members identified themselves with the minister who had baptized them (see vv. 14-16), whether Paul, Apollos or Cephas /Peter. Paul, the founding apostle, spent a year and a half in Corinth (Acts 18:1-18). Doubtless many members continued to look to his leadership. But it was now three years since he had left and in the meantime other ministers had visited the city. First came Apollos, the brilliant Jewish scholar and preacher from Alexandria (Acts 18:24-26) and he, too, had his admirers (cf. 16:12), most likely among the better educated members who prized rhetorical speechmaking. Next came Cephas/Peter, the spokesman of the Twelve and the leader for twenty years of the mission to the Jews in Palestine (Gal. 2:7-9; cf. Acts 1-5; 8:14-25; 9:32–11:18; 12:1-17; 15:6-11). This eminent leader doubtless had many supporters, especially, we imagine, among the Jews in the congregation.

Many members divided themselves into supporters of one or other of these leaders. Some, however, said they 'belonged to Christ'. This intriguing group may have been those we encounter later in the letter who prized 'spiritual gifts', in particular 'speaking in other tongues', which they may have claimed as coming to them from the risen Christ, setting them apart as an elite group (see on 4:7-8; 14:6-25, 36-37). It is possible we meet the same faction in the Second Letter as those who declare themselves to 'belong to Christ' but question whether Paul does (2 Cor. 10:7).

These words written so long ago continue to be painfully relevant. Churches and denominations continue to be hotbeds of factionalism. Members very readily cluster exclusively around one minister or elder against others, whether current or previous leaders of the congregation. And, it must be said, ministers themselves are not always innocent of cultivating factious support, to the division of the body of Christ.

2. Three Critical Questions (1:13-16)

Paul now fires three rhetorical questions at the Corinthians, each based on the foundation of the Christian church in Corinth. First, he asks, 'Is Christ divided up' among you? Later in the Letter Paul makes this striking statement:

For just as		the body is one
and has	many members,	
and all	the members of the body,	
though many,		are one body,
so it is		with *Christ* (12:12, RSV).

The human body, though of many parts and organs, is a single entity. We expect Paul to say, 'So, too, is the church as the body of Christ, multi-membered yet one'. But to our surprise he says, 'So, too, is *Christ*'. '*Christ* is multi-membered yet one.' In other words, Paul makes the astonishing statement that (somehow) Christ *is* the church. What does he mean? Paul is saying that, through his ascension, Christ is in heaven, no longer physically present on earth, but that by the Holy Spirit Christ is active in the church, the local 'body' of believers. Just as the church is now 'in Christ' in heaven (Eph. 1:3; 2:6; Col. 3:1-3) so, too, Christ is now 'in the church' on earth. So let the Corinthians understand that Christ has not been 'parcelled out' only to some with obvious spiritual gifts (v. 13a). In the 'body' of the congregation Christ is co-terminous with all and belongs to all who belong to him.

Secondly, he asks, 'Was Paul crucified for you?' (v. 13b). How foolish even to ask the question! Only Christ was or could be crucified 'for' and 'in place of' (*hyper*) his people. This question is as impossible as its predecessor, 'Is Christ divided up' and present with only some of you? Christ has died for *all*, belongs to *all* and is in *all* (cf. Col. 3:11). Only of God's Messiah, his Christ, could this be true. By contrast, Paul is merely his apostle, sent by him (v. 17), one of a number of his servants through whom they had come to believe (see on 3:5).

Paul's oblique reference to '[Christ] crucified' introduces a subject which was evidently an embarrassment to some within the church (see on 1:18-25). Suffice here to reflect that it was by that monstrous death that Christ provided 'for' the salvation of his people and indeed of all people at all times and places (2 Cor. 5:14-15,19).

His third question, 'Were you baptized into the name of Paul?' (v. 13c) must also be answered 'no'. Because Christ was 'crucified for you', only in *Christ's* 'name' could a believer be baptized. Certainly not in the name of the baptizer Paul who, as a matter of fact, had only baptized Crispus, Gaius and the members of the household of Stephanas from the total congregation.

These questions, with his assertion, 'Christ...sent me to preach the gospel', are closely connected. Together they form a window through which we glimpse the initial missionary penetration of Paul in Corinth, and we suppose of other places as well. First, he preached the gospel, a message which focused on Christ crucified for their sins (see on 15:3). Then, as they received the gospel they were baptized 'in the name of Christ'. Third, baptism 'incorporated' them fully into the body of believers, notwithstanding the divergent nature of their ministry 'gifts'. The preaching of Christ crucified, the opened heart of faith expressed in submission to baptism in the name of Christ, followed by membership in his body, all belong together and provide an instructive pattern for the ongoing work of evangelism.

The names and associated details are also helpful for our understanding of Paul's mission work. The three persons he baptized were each significant in some way. Crispus was a Jew, in fact the ruler of the synagogue in Corinth (Acts 18:8), and therefore a man of wealth and high standing. Gaius is mentioned in Romans 16:23 as '[Paul's] host and of the whole church' in Corinth (Romans was written from Corinth cf. Acts 20:3). The book of Acts, however, says that Paul stayed with a 'God-fearer' named Titius Justus (Acts 18:7). Most likely this is one and the same man, a Roman whose full name was 'Gaius Titius Justus'. He, too, was a man of prominence whose home was sufficiently spacious to accommodate a meeting of the 'whole church'. Reference to the '*household* of Stephanas', with its implications of retainers and servants, also signals material prosperity. Indeed, this man's household were Paul's first converts in Achaia, and he has ministered materially to the saints in Corinth (see on 16:15). Stephanas, with his (probable) retainers Fortunatus and Achaicus (whose names 'Lucky' and 'Achaian' suggest that they were nicknamed slaves), have now visited Paul in Ephesus and are probably the bearers of this letter back to Corinth. These three, with Chloe (as noted above) and, for example, Erastus the director of city works (Rom. 16:23), give the impression that Paul found significant support among people of wealth in Corinth, though probably these were in a minority within the total congregation (see on 1:26).

3. Sent to Evangelize (1:17)

To return more directly to the passage, Paul insists that Christ did not send him to baptize but to evangelize. This is not to say that Paul dismisses the importance of baptizing but to insist that it is ancillary to his prior and overarching calling to proclaim the gospel of Christ crucified and risen. Baptizing is entirely dependent on and subsidiary to preaching the gospel. That calling had come from Christ himself, an allusion to the encounter of the Risen One with the persecutor as he journeyed to Damascus (see on 9:1; 15:8-11; Gal. 1:15-17; Acts 26:15-18).

Paul now lays the groundwork for what he will say immediately about his evangelizing (1:18-2:5). In Paul's case it was not with words of wisdom, lest 'the cross of Christ' be emptied of its content. Something is in the wind here, about which from this distance we can only guess. It seems that the Corinthians had become interested in and diverted by somebody preaching with 'words of wisdom'. Most probably this person or persons had so preached as to place the spotlight on the speaker, rather than the message itself. Thus the attention of the hearer had been diverted from Christ crucified to the 'wise' preacher. But what can a preacher accomplish if he fails to draw attention to Christ? Nothing. Only one person could be crucified for others, for their forgiveness, and that person was the Messiah, Jesus.

SOME QUESTIONS FOR PERSONAL REFLECTION:

1. Am I, perhaps, prone to thinking as an individual rather than as a member of the body of Christ? Am I and others at this time rather individualistic, as the Corinthians had been?

2. To what extent is my faith bound up in a particular minister? If that person was not my minister would it affect my relationship with Christ?

STUDY QUESTIONS:

1. In Paul's greeting what does he mean in calling the Corinthians, 'Holy Ones'?

2. Is this sanctification something which they manufacture? How is it produced?

3. How was the grace of God evidenced in their lives?

4. In spite of their sin, how does Paul answer his readers that they are 'called and kept' by God?

5. What are the three main concerns which Paul addresses in the beginning of this letter?

6. What is at the heart of Paul's three critical questions?

2

The Word of the Cross
(1 Cor. 1:18-2:5)

Often in Paul's letters he takes his readers in the churches back to the fundamentals of his initial message to them. Perhaps new members had been added to the church in the three years since he had left and didn't understand his teachings, not having heard them from his own lips. Among them, we may also suppose, were those who had in recent times risen to prominence, but whose grasp of the gospel was defective and who appeared to be taking over the intellectual and spiritual leadership from the founding apostle of the church. Paul will later hint at the influence of these teachers within the church in Corinth (3:10,17; 4:18-19).

So what was their message? In a word, 'wisdom'. At the time Corinth was the greatest of the cities of Greece, so it comes as no surprise that the members of the church there might be interested in Greece's most characteristic intellectual pursuit, 'wisdom'.

'Wisdom' as used by Paul may mean more than an intellectual pursuit. More broadly, that one word may capture what we may call a 'world view'. In that world view 'man' is at the centre and God is at the margin. Such 'wisdom' from the Greeks is a celebration of the subtlety of Socrates, the elegance of Aphrodite in marble, and the athleticism of Olympic competitors portrayed in red on an amphora. In a few words it is about 'cleverness', 'power' and 'style', things so important to the Greeks, but expressed in every society where those values become dominant.

How might this 'wisdom' have found expression among the Corinthians in the several years since Paul left them? I say 'might' because we do not certainly know the precise form this 'wisdom' took within the church in Corinth. Perhaps it included the glib mottoes like 'all things are lawful' and 'food for the stomach and the stomach for food' which Paul echoes only in order to rebut (see on 6:12, 13). Most probably, too, it was found in their inflated estimate of their 'speech' and 'knowledge', which were so in evidence that Paul acknowledges these 'gifts' in both surviving letters to this church (see on 1:5; 12:8; 13:2a; cf. 2 Cor. 8:7). 'Speech' and 'knowledge' exercised haughtily for self-aggrandizement and not for the good of others is probably what Paul more briefly calls 'the wisdom of this age and of the rulers of this age' (see on 2:6).

How does Paul respond to this worrying pastoral situation? First, he states that the word of the *cross* is 'foolishness' to those who are perishing, but 'wisdom and power' to those who are being saved (1:18, 21). Only through the message of the crucified One are people able to be saved. Second, through the preaching of 'Christ crucified', God is overturning currently held human values of 'wisdom' and 'foolishness' (1:20, 25). In the coming age all present values will be reversed (see on 7:29-31). Third, this is confirmed by looking around at the undistinguished members sitting in the assembly of believers (1:26-31). Fourth, consistent with that, as he reminds them in 2:1-5, his initial preaching concentrated on 'Jesus Christ and him crucified' proclaimed in plain words, not 'in lofty words of wisdom'.

1. The Word of the Cross (1:18-25)

Paul now explains the divisive impact of 'the word (*logos*) of the cross'. No doubt this reflects his experience of twenty years in ministry to Jews and Greeks in the eastern Mediterranean. He points out that God's scale of values is opposite to man's scale of values. Thus the 'wisdom' of man is 'foolishness' with God and the 'foolishness' of God, as man judges it, is true 'wisdom' and true 'power'.

Two words that keep appearing in this passage are 'weakness' and 'foolishness' and their opposites 'power' and 'wisdom'. The opposites 'the wise' and 'the fool' abound throughout the 'Wisdom' literature of the Old Testament, especially in the book of Proverbs. Sometimes 'the wise' and 'the fool' are contrasted within the same sentence:

A fool's talk brings a rod to his back,
but the lips of the wise protect them.[1]

Jesus, too, stood in the tradition of the 'wise' teacher of godly proverbs. Remember his parable of the wise man who built his house on the rock and the fool who built his on the sand (Matt. 7:24-27)? Paul's contrasts between 'wisdom' and 'foolishness' in this passage place him in the same tradition.

Evidently Paul is engaged in a dispute with a section of the church in Corinth who were preoccupied with 'the wisdom of words' (v. 17) which was not 'wise' at all. As he will show true 'wisdom', that is, God's 'wisdom', is found in 'the word of the cross' (v. 18). As best as we can recapture the situation, these persons were now saying that Paul's 'word of the cross', his message of 'Christ crucified', was 'weak' and 'foolish'. It must be improved, made more acceptable, by dressing it up differently, using 'words of wisdom'.

1. The Great Reversal: Wisdom is Foolishness (vv. 18-21)

In verse 18 Paul none too subtly contrasts 'the word of the cross' with 'the wisdom of words' (v. 17). The latter are just 'words' which only appear to be 'wise', whereas 'the word of the cross' is a content-laden 'word', a message about 'the cross' on which the Messiah met his awful death. Paul's message was solid in content, though not 'flowery' in its presentation (see on 2:1-5), whereas the message of those he criticizes was empty of content though impressively eloquent in delivery.

Paul's 'word' had devastatingly opposite effects on its hearers, as Paul knew well from his many years of preaching it. To people in general who are 'perishing' because they belong to the 'present age' which is 'passing away' (7:31; cf. 2:6), 'the word of the cross' is 'foolishness' (*mōria* 'moronic'). But 'to us' who receive that 'word', who are 'being saved' by it, it is 'the power of God'.

---

1   Proverbs 14:3; cf. 3:35; 14:1, etc.

We ask, 'being saved' for *what*? Paul has in mind the coming age of God, for which this present age is a temporary and transient anticipation. Thus those who are 'perishing' in this age will 'perish' absolutely and eternally in the coming age, and those who are 'being saved' in this age will be 'saved' absolutely and eternally in that age. And the 'word of the cross' is the instrument of salvation for the coming age.

At the onset of the coming age God will 'destroy the wisdom of the wise', as Paul observes, quoting Isaiah 29:14. The 'wisdom' of the present age regards the 'word of the cross' as 'moronic'. But that 'wisdom' will be seen for what it is, 'moronic', and what is currently dismissed as 'moronic' will be seen to be profoundly 'wise'.

Reflecting on twenty years of debating unbelievers Paul asks, 'Where is the wise man' (of the Greek academy)?, and 'Where is the scribe' (of the Jewish synagogue)? These unbelievers, whether Greek or Jewish, are 'disputers of this age' with minds closed to 'the word of the cross'. In the coming age their 'wisdom' will be recognised as 'foolishness'. So he asks, 'Surely God has made foolish the wisdom of the world?' By 'world' Paul means 'human history and culture' which is dominated by sin and death, from the time of Adam's rebellion.

Paul offers a 'proverb-like' observation. 'Wisdom' has failed. God in his kindness has provided another way to know him.

> For since in the wisdom of God
> the world through its wisdom did not know him,
> God was pleased
> through the foolishness of what was preached
> to save those who believe.

In the depths of God's wisdom, he did not allow the 'wise' of Greece or the 'scribes' of Israel to know him through *their* 'wisdom'. God knew that human arrogance would be intolerable if people from this corrupt 'age' could reach up with their intellects and say, 'There is God, *we* have found him'. Truly, God eternally eludes such people. They never find him for he hides himself from them (Matt. 11:25-27; Ps. 89:46). Because God was unreachable through human 'wisdom' he was 'pleased' to make himself known. How did he do this? It is 'through the foolishness' the *mōria* of the preached message, that is, 'the word of the cross'. As this 'word' is proclaimed God 'saves' those who believe it, saves them for his coming age.

Thus this 'word of the cross' divides those who are 'being saved' from those who are 'perishing'. Those who are 'saved' have 'life' in this age through the Spirit, whereas those who are 'perishing' in this age face eternal 'death' in the next (2 Cor. 2:15-16).

2. The Great Reversal: Foolishness is Wisdom (vv. 22-25)

Why are the efforts of the Greek 'wise' and the Jewish 'scribe' doomed to futility? It is 'because Jews seek signs' and 'Greeks seek wisdom'. The gospels amply demonstrate Jewish blindness. The Pharisees were preoccupied with 'miracle signs' (Mark 8:11-13), often of a grotesque and freakish kind (e.g., a cow giving birth to a lamb in the Temple[2]) which they saw as pointers to the coming Messianic age. Yet the 'signs' of Jesus, which were truly miraculous, were not understood, because they were not self-serving, done quietly for the relief of human misery (cf. John 6:26). The 'signs' of Jesus were evidence that the kingdom of God stood in their midst in the person of Jesus, but they had no eyes for it (Luke 17:21).

The blindness of the Greeks to God was, in Paul's experience, due to their preoccupation with 'wisdom'. The Greek city states were the home of philosophy as is evident in the respective contributions of Socrates, Plato, Aristotle, Zeno (founder of Stoicism) and Epicurus (founder of the Epicureanism). Following Alexander's conquests of Asia Minor, Syria, Palestine, Egypt and Mesopotamia in the fourth century BC, schools of philosophy were transplanted from Athens to the conquered regions, including the Greek cities that ringed Israel itself in Paul's day (e.g., Gadara in the Decapolis). It cannot be denied, however, that many of the intellectual achievements of modern times flow from the Greeks, as the writings of their philosophers were re-examined during and after the Middle Ages.

Is Paul, then, attacking 'wisdom' or the 'mind' *per se*? By no means! Paul frequently urges his readers to think (see, e.g., on 14:20) and his own letters are argued with a lawyer's logic. Paul is not against 'wisdom', since this is God's gift to understand

---

2   Josephus, *Jewish War* vi. 292.

his world and its workings. A whole body of literature in the Bible is 'wisdom' literature, much of it quite down-to-earth. Rather, Paul is opposed to 'the wisdom of the world', that is, of this fallen and corrupt age, as it applies to just one subject, man's attempt to find God by that 'wisdom'. The early Christian writer Tertullian (*c*. 160-220) said there was no common ground 'between a philosopher and a Christian, between a disciple of Hellas and a disciple of heaven', or historically speaking, between 'Athens and Jerusalem, Academy and church'.[3]

In contrast to those who fruitlessly seek God by 'wisdom' Paul declares that he and other Christians 'preach Christ crucified', which is another way of referring to 'the word of the cross' (v. 18). For us crucifixion is quite remote. It has not been practised since its prohibition by the Emperor Constantine in the fourth century. Furthermore, 'Christ crucified' has become for us either a preacher's slogan, a theological topic or a religious ornament. But in Paul's world it was the most horrific method of execution known, reserved as a deterrent to keep slaves and provincials in their place. According to Cicero it was so unspeakably ugly as to be 'off limits' in polite conversation. 'The very word cross,' he wrote, 'should be far removed not only from the person of a Roman citizen but from his thoughts, his eyes and his ears' (*Pro Rabiro* v. 16).

When, therefore, Paul 'preached Christ crucified' in Corinth in *c*. AD 50 he was speaking of Jesus' gruesome death twenty years earlier. There was an immediacy of time, a horror of detail and a depth of humiliation for the crucified that today we cannot imagine. Reading Paul's words we capture something of the shock and distaste experienced by the original hearers.

To preach that God's uniquely anointed king, the Messiah, had been crucified was to invite scorn from every quarter (v. 23). For Jews their Messiah was to be *powerful*, a victor, spattered with blood, perhaps, but with the blood of enemies he had vanquished. To contemplate a Messiah who was *powerless*, bloodied with his own blood, humiliated as he hung naked impaled on a stake by the hated Romans, was 'a stumbling block' (*skandalon*) to Jews, something utterly unthinkable, a massive barrier to belief.

---

3   Tertullian, Apology 46.18; *Prescription Against Heretics* 7.9.

For their part, Greeks cherished the tradition of Socrates of the philosopher king,[4] a ruler who was *wise*, one who was loftily above human passions and pain. Paul's announcement that God's king, who made claims on their loyalties, had been *crucified* was *moria*, 'foolishness'. The reaction of Greeks to the message of the cross is captured in a rough drawing on the wall on the Palatine Hill in Rome in the third century. A foolish looking youth is worshipping a crucified man with an ass's head. The crudely written graffiti reads, 'Alexamenos worships his god'. Here is a fool worshipping a crucified ass-man!

But not all Jews and Greeks have rejected 'the word of the cross'. To '*those* who have been called' whether Jews or Greeks, 'Christ [crucified]' is 'the power of God and the wisdom of God'. Those who are 'called' (cf. 1:2) are '*us* who are being saved' and '*those* who believe' (vv. 18, 21). How does God 'call' his people? There are two steps in Paul's sequence of thought. First, there is the preaching of 'the word of the cross'. In consequence, second, the hearers, when they 'believe' this 'word', are 'saved' for the coming age. Thus 'the called ones' are those summoned by God to his kingdom, by the preaching of Christ crucified.

We must note Paul's interchangeable way of speaking of 'Christ crucified' (v. 23) or simply of 'Christ' (v. 24). The former represents his 'work' of salvation achieved for us on the cross, the latter simply to his 'person' or identity as the Messiah of God, his Son (cf. 1:9). Theologically 'Christ' and 'Christ crucified' must not be separated. On the one hand, we must declare that Jesus *is* the Christ, but that he is the Christ who was *crucified*. But on the other hand, in declaring his crucifixion for our justification, we must not separate this blessing from the *person* who was crucified. There must be neither a cross-less Christ nor a Christ-less cross.

Contradicting the 'wisdom of the world' and 'of this age', Paul declares 'Christ crucified' to be 'the power of God' and 'the wisdom of God'. Christ is the 'power' because only he makes possible forgiveness of sins (see on 15:3; cf. Rom. 1:16) and 'righteousness' from God (see on 1:30). Christ is that 'wisdom' given by God, by which those who previously did not know God at last know him (see on v. 21). Joined inseparably are God-given reconciliation with God and God-given knowledge of God.

---

4   Plato, *The Republic*, books v-vii.

Greeks attempted to find God and know him by climbing a ladder called 'philosophy'. They found no one there but themselves, no matter how high they climbed. It is only as God reaches *down* in 'the word of the cross' and offers us forgiveness of sins that his hidden identity is at last revealed. Our only action is to receive God's mercy with open hands at the foot of the cross of Christ. Here God proves to be deeply personal, a Father, merciful beyond imagination, who draws those who did not know him into a living relationship as his own dear children. But the proud intellectual will live and die not knowing him.

Paul concludes with a proverb-like statement of God's great reversal of this age's values as expressed in the 'word of the cross'. Paul remains astonished at God's ways. He speaks of the crucifixion of Christ as 'the foolishness of God' and 'the weakness of God'. It is as if Paul, the former persecutor, with tear stained face was pondering Christ on Pilate's cross, and asking, 'God, what were *you* doing there?' 'Was there no other way?' Yet Paul knew well there was no other way of dealing with human sin and human arrogance. 'Far be it from me to glory,' he told the Galatians, 'except in the cross of our Lord Jesus Christ by which the world has been crucified to me and I to the world' (Gal. 6:14, RSV).

But these words, 'foolishness' and 'weakness,' though ironic, are a window into the mind of God which we now know from 'the word of the cross'. The crucifixion of Christ reveals just who the Master of the universe is, humble, self-giving, tender-hearted, suffering for and therefore with creatures made in his image. Proud Jews and high-minded Greeks scoffed at the very idea that God could be like that. Muslims express outrage that God could be humble-hearted, as revealed in the crucifixion of his Son. The cross continues to be regarded by many as 'offensive' and 'stupid'. Yet in reaching down to save and reveal himself in the crucified One, God has identified with sufferers and suffering in the world. The Creator of the universe is no stranger to suffering, weakness and humiliation.

Paul concludes that the 'foolishness' and 'weakness' of God is 'wiser' and 'stronger' than men, for in that 'foolishness' and 'weakness' human salvation was won for those who will receive it.

Inscribed upon the cross we see
In shining letters God is love:
He bears our sins upon the tree;
He brings us mercy from above.[5]

2. The Great Reversal: The Redemption of Nobodies (1:26-31)

Paul invites the Corinthians to look around at the members of the congregation in Corinth. They are the fruits of 'the word of the cross' Paul preached in the Achaian capital five years earlier, together with others who have been added since. Picking up the categories of 'wisdom' and 'power' from the previous section he asks them to take note of their 'calling'. He observes that 'not many' are 'wise', 'not many' are 'powerful'. To be sure, there were *some* who were, as noted above (see on 1:13-16); but 'not many'. To these he adds, 'not many were of noble birth'. In other words, the predominantly ordinary and undistinguished character of the church's membership was exactly in line with the 'foolishness' and 'weakness' of the message of 'Christ crucified', 'the word of the cross' by which they had become its members.

'But', writes Paul, using the strongest adversative available (*alla*), God chose 'the foolish things of the world', speaking of 'foolish *people*', to shame the 'wise'. He is thinking of that Great Day when all true values will be revealed, the Great Reversal of God, when he will lower the lofty and exalt the lowly (cf. Luke 1:51-52). Likewise, God chose the 'weak of the world' to 'shame the strong'. Paul continues in this vein. God chose the 'low-born', and the 'despised nobodies', and 'things that is, people that are not', that he might 'bring to nothing the things that are'. How relatively undistinguished were these Corinthians assembled in the house of Gaius Titius Justus in comparison to the dazzling wealth and power of the brilliant elite from a Corinth shimmering in white marble in the Mediterranean sun.

And the reason for the divine choice of such ordinary persons for the kingdom? It is, literally, 'So that no *flesh* may boast before him'. Paul's word 'flesh' catches the idea of human effort independent of God, picking up from verse 26 the 'wise... powerful...noble born' which these things are, 'according to the

---

5   T. Kelly (1815), quoted from *The Anglican Hymn Book* (162), (Church Book Room Press, 1965).

flesh'. But 'flesh' also means weakness, transience, in contrast with God's power and eternity.

The words 'before [God]' (cf. Rom. 3:19-20; 14:22; 2 Cor. 4:2; 7:12) means 'in the presence of [God]' or, more literally, 'in the eyes of God'. It is a reference to the Last Judgement. On that Great Day no man or woman will be able to point to his or her 'wisdom', 'power', or 'nobility' as the basis of acceptance with God in his kingdom. Rather, God will point to the inconsequential people who have heeded 'the word of the cross', to shame the 'beautiful people', the rich and famous who scorned 'Christ crucified'.

The third century writer Origen echoes the surprise of the pagan philosopher Celsus at the type of people attracted to Christianity. Those who joined the mystery religions were pure and wise, but those attracted to Christianity were despicable.

> Those who summon people to the other mysteries make this preliminary proclamation, 'Whoever has pure hands and a wise tongue.' And again, others say, 'Whosoever is pure from all defilement, and whose soul knows nothing of evil, and who has lived well and righteously.' Such are the preliminary exhortations of those who promise purification from sins. But let us hear what these Christians call. 'Whoever is a sinner,' they say, 'whoever is unwise, whoever is a child, and in a word, whoever is a wretch, the kingdom of God will receive him.'[6]

This is similar to Paul's observations about the character of the church in Corinth.

A lady told me how she had made a 'decision for Christ' at the preaching of Dr. Billy Graham when she was a teenager forty years earlier. Her mother did the 'follow up' homework because she was intellectually disabled and could neither read nor write. Despite her problems she remained a firm disciple of Jesus. The brilliant and the strong who reject Christ crucified stand humbled in the face of the faith of one of these 'little ones'.

Paul now makes a huge contrast between 'no flesh' of verse 29 and Christian believers. He writes, 'but of [God] *you* are in Christ Jesus...' Nobody stands 'in the presence of God', either now or then, as *flesh*, as persons unaided and alone, but

---

only 'in Christ Jesus'. Those who are 'in Christ' are in the kingdom, for Christ is the king of God's kingdom. How do people
come to be 'in Christ'? It is because they are 'of God', that is,
by means of God's 'call' or summons to them by 'the word of
the cross'. Here, though, there is the mystery that only some
heed God's call while others reject it. Why are Chloe, Crispus,
Gaius, Stephanas, for example, believers while others in Corinth
are not, despite having heard Paul preach 'Christ crucified'?
The answer is that their positive response was the outworking
in time of God's election of them before they were born (cf.
2 Thess. 2:13-15). This, too, is what Paul means by 'you are *of
God* in Christ Jesus'.

As individuals who have heeded and accepted 'the word
of the cross' they have become members of a congregation
of Christ's people. It is easy to assume now, as it was then
in Corinth, that by 'in Christ' Paul was speaking only about
individuals. To be sure, response to 'the word of the cross' is
personal. No one can make that decision on behalf of someone
else, by proxy as it were. Yet once my personal decision has been
made it means that I am now a member of a *people*. Everything
I do as an individual must be in terms of its effect on the fellow-
members of that 'body' of people. So *I* am 'in Christ', but I am
at the same time 'in Christ' with *others* who are 'in Christ'. It is
a modern failing not to recognise this, as it was among those
Corinthians.

In Paul's focus on Christ it must not be forgotten that he is
thinking of 'Christ *crucified*'. In his death Christ was 'made for
us' (*by God*) 'wisdom from God, righteousness [from God], sanctification [from God] and redemption [from God]'. The words
'from God', though only attached to 'wisdom', are intended to
be joined to the other words as well.

Each word is full of meaning. 'Christ crucified' is '*wisdom
from God*', that is, God giving us true knowledge of who he is
and the means to knowing him, as against 'the world's wisdom'
which left us ignorant of the Creator of the universe.

'Christ crucified' is '*righteousness* [from God]', God's pro-
nouncement that we are now acceptable to him, vindicated
by him (as in a court of law). But this was on account of the
divine transaction that occurred when Christ was crucified, as

2 Corinthians 5:21 explains. God 'made' the crucified One to 'be sin', to be the bearer of the punishment of the sins of others, to be the Suffering Servant prophesied by Isaiah 52:13-53:12. His sinlessness in life was his qualification in death to be the sin-bearer for others. In consequence, those who are 'in Christ' through 'the word of the cross' are dedicated 'righteous' to God. They 'have become the righteousness of God in him'.

'Christ crucified' is *holiness* [from God]'. Christ is the 'holy one of God' (John 6:69; Acts 3:14; Rev. 3:7), so that those who are 'in Christ' are the 'holy ones of God', his 'saints'. 'Holiness' means God's total distinctiveness from us. We are God's 'holy ones' because of God's gift of 'righteousness' to us in 'Christ crucified' and because he gives us his *Holy* Spirit. Believers, whether as individuals (see on 6:19) or as the congregation (3:16), are the 'temple of the Holy Spirit'. God lives in his people, walks among them in his Holy Spirit (2 Cor. 6:16).

'Holiness' calls for separation from 'unholiness', which was an ongoing issue in pagan Corinth. The individual believer was to have no union with a prostitute (see on 6:12-17) nor involvement in idolatry by temple attendance (see on 10:14-22). In his Second Letter Paul exhorts, 'let us purify ourselves from everything that contaminates body and spirit, perfecting *holiness* out of reverence for God' (2 Cor. 7:1). There is much that is 'unholy' in the modern western world, especially through various forms of entertainment. Furthermore, the paganisms of other lands have now come to formerly Christian societies in the temples which now sit side by side with churches.

Finally, 'Christ crucified' is '*redemption* [from God]'. Societies of that time were based on slavery, as most societies have been throughout the greater part of history. Men and women and children were taken as booty through military conquest. Prisoners of war became slaves in perpetuity, bought and sold like other merchandise or property. It was not unheard, however, for a slave to be 'redeemed', that is, set free upon the payment of money.

> I free Helen, a slave born in my house, and I receive for her ransom two thousand two hundred drachmas.

This was an owner's receipt for the manumission of his slave woman.[7] The language of redemption must have been overwhelmingly potent at that time, since almost everybody either was a slave or owned slaves.

The theological background to this 'redemption' was Israel's slavery in Egypt from which the Lord redeemed his people (Exod. 6:6). In New Testament times the people were looking for a new redemption, the liberation of God's people enslaved through Roman occupation of their land (Luke 24:21). Jesus promised redemption, but redemption from their sins and from the power of unclean spirits, not from their political oppressors. 'The Son of Man came...to give his life a *ransom* for many', he said (Mark 10:45; cf. 1 Tim. 2:6). Through the preaching of 'the word of the cross' slaves to sin and the power of dark forces of idolatry find deliverance (cf. Gal. 4:8-9). Christ's death brings forgiveness of sins (see on 15:3) and freedom from slavery to those sins (see on 6:9-11). Because the ransom price for spiritual freedom was paid for by 'Christ crucified', those who have been set free are said to have been 'bought with a price' (see on 6:20). Jews, too, have been 'redeemed', from slavery to the yoke of endless law-keeping as a futile way of knowing God (Gal. 3:13; 4:5). In Corinth then and throughout history since, those who are 'in Christ', both Gentiles and Jews, know the meaning of God's 'redemption'.

God had a reason for choosing and calling undistinguished persons to find their 'wisdom', 'righteousness', 'holiness' and 'redemption' only 'in Christ'. In the Great Day of God's Reversal the only boast able to be made will be 'in the Lord'. No pride will be possible arising out of our 'wisdom', our 'power', or our 'nobility' of birth.

Paul is quoting Jeremiah 9:23-24 where the 'Lord' is Yahweh, God of Israel. But here the 'Lord' is Christ Jesus, as verse 30 shows. Thus Paul makes an identification between Yahweh and Christ Jesus. The deity of Christ is established by this passing reference.

3. Not in Lofty Words of Wisdom (2:1-5)
Paul continues to address the problem of 'wisdom' preaching in Corinth. Some person (or persons) was placing too much

---

7   Quoted in C. Spicq, *Theological Lexicon of the New Testament* (Peabody, Mass: Hendrickson, 1994), II, p. 426.

emphasis on the 'wisdom' of the Greeks, expressed as this was in fulsome rhetoric. Speechmaking was highly developed and prized among the Greeks. It was even a form of popular entertainment, with speakers using various verbal skills to win the applause of crowds. Public speaking competitions were held throughout the Greek cities and were probably part of the local games held every two years at nearby Isthmia.

Paul's first sentence in this section shows that he is contrasting himself with another preacher or preachers within the Corinthian church. His opening words, literally, '*I* for *my* part' (*kagō*), are contrastive, 'as opposed to *him* for *his* part'. Another hint is found in Paul's daring use of the words 'proclaiming the *mystery* (*mystērion*) of God'.[8] Greek 'mystery' religions each had a mysthrion, by which only the initiated came to know the 'hidden secret' of eternal life, which he was forbidden to reveal. Apparently a preacher of 'wisdom' in the church was interested in the Greek 'mysteries', since Paul, continuing to speak against him, connects 'wisdom' and 'mystery' in verse 7: 'we speak the *wisdom* of God in a *mystery*'. Paul may have felt justified in taking over this word since it was also used in Jewish apocalyptic literature for 'God's transcendence'. Paul often uses 'mystery' in his new sense elsewhere in First Corinthians (4:1; 13:2; 14:2; 15:51) and in later letters (Rom. 11:25; 16:25; Eph. 1:9; 3:3,4,9; 5:32; 6:19; Col. 1:26, 27; 2:2; 4:3).

Who was the culprit responsible for 'wisdom' and 'mystery' preaching within the church at Corinth? Was Paul obliquely criticizing the brilliant orator Apollos (cf. Acts 18:24-26), who had come to Corinth on the heels of Paul? This is unlikely since Paul speaks warmly of the Alexandrian later in the letter (see on 16:12). Moreover, there is no suggestion that Apollos preached about 'wisdom' or 'mystery'. But it is possible that Apollos' eloquence made Paul's more mundane presentation (cf. 2 Cor. 10:10; 11:5) appear inferior. Perhaps these Greek believers were given a taste for 'words of wisdom' from local

---

8   RSV and NIV have 'testimony of God' (so, too, Fee, First Corinthians, p. 88). But early manuscripts have 'mystery of God'. The words *martyrion* and *mysthrion* have the same number of letters and are very similar. Perhaps an early Christian copyist could not believe Paul would use the word 'mystery' because of the 'mystery religions' and changed three letters.

Corinthian preachers as a result of Apollos' visit and had become unsure about Paul's credentials.

So what is 'the mystery of God' which Paul came to 'proclaim' in Corinth? Was it a collection of coded words or magic numbers or an enigmatic mathematical formula so favoured at this time? Was the 'mystery of God' a highly secret ritual involving hooded priests, flickering candles and burning incense, and performed behind the high walls of an enclosed temple? The 'mystery of God' is none of these things. Astonishingly and unimaginably it is 'Jesus Christ and him crucified' (v. 2). The previously 'hidden' plan of God for human salvation was now 'an open secret' in the preaching of 'Christ crucified'. That message is the death knell to all mystical and magical forms of the divine 'mystery' so favoured in antiquity, and also in the resurgence of paganism in modern times.

Consistent with the message of 'Christ crucified', his manner of delivery of that message when he was initially present with them five years earlier was not 'in lofty words or wisdom' (v. 1). In brief, he is saying that, just as the church is composed of mostly ordinary members (1:26-31), consistent with the humbling message of 'Jesus Christ and him crucified' (1:18-25), so too his preaching was not contrived, but direct and plain. 'Thus, not only the means (the cross) and the people (the church in Corinth), but also the preacher (Paul), declare that God is in the process of overturning the world's systems.'[9]

Further, not only did Paul preach simply and directly, consistent with the message of the crucified One, he came originally 'in weakness, in fear, and with trembling' (v. 3), 'crucified', as it were. He arrived in the Achaian capital after being mocked in the Areopagus of Athens, a body equivalent to a university senate (Acts 17:18, 32). Moreover, he arrived in the great city of Corinth alone. Only later did Timothy and Silvanus arrive to assist and support the apostle. So anxious was Paul when he first arrived that the Lord appeared in a vision at night encouraging him 'not to be afraid' (Acts 18:9).

How could Paul forget the 'weakness, fear and trembling' (v. 3) he felt, which drove him to depend on God who did not fail his servant. Nor could he forget that his preaching was 'in

---

9   Fee, *First Corinthians*, p. 89.

demonstration of the Spirit and of power'. Only here is the word 'demonstration' (*apodeixis*) used. Ordinarily used in rhetoric it meant 'a compelling conclusion' to a well-argued case. Here it should be understood as a 'revelation' from God following the preaching of the cross, showing God's otherwise hidden power. That 'demonstration' is the morally changed lives of the people (6:9-11) with accompanying 'gifts' of the Spirit for ministry to others in the church (1:4-7).

We must not read contemporary theological debates into Paul's statements. It is sometimes said that 'straight' evangelical preaching is what Paul dismisses here as 'lofty words of wisdom' and 'persuasive words of wisdom' but that his own preaching was, by contrast, Spirit-anointed, Spirit-empowered and miraculous in its effects. But this misses the flow of Paul's letter to this point. What Paul is dismissing is *Greek* rhetorical speechmaking with its 'lofty words of wisdom' and 'persuasive words of wisdom' in comparison with his own plain speaking of 'the word of the cross', dependent on God in his 'weakness and fear'.

To be sure, Paul recognizes that his preaching was 'in demonstration of the Spirit and of power'. But this was not derived from some special 'anointing' but from his focused preaching of 'Christ crucified', delivered out of 'weakness, fear and trembling' in Corinth, in dependence on God. Paul is not contrasting 'anointed' versus 'unanointed' Christian preaching, but Christian preaching versus preaching that was compromised both in its avoidance of the cross and by a pretentious style of delivery which was a denial of the message of 'Christ crucified'.

Indeed, a single-eyed focus on 'the word of the cross' delivered in simplicity but with passion is fundamental to establishing the hearers truly in 'the faith' (v. 5). The 'wisdom of men' delivered with showy rhetorical flourishes will never achieve that. The medium must be appropriate to the message or the message is actually compromised by the medium.

The values of this age may be likened to a pyramid. In Egypt this massive structure existed exclusively for the Pharaoh, specifically for his after-life. The history of Egypt as we have it is almost entirely the history of these oppressive rulers. Few others are mentioned in the hieroglyphs. Each Pharaoh sat at the pinnacle of the 'pyramid' of society with all others underneath supporting him (or her, in the case of the woman Pharaoh, Hatshepsut), there merely for his benefit. But this has been true of other rulers regardless of the culture or their span within history.

But the dispensation of the Creator of the universe has upended all this in the 'word of the cross'. The Crucified One is now, through his resurrection, at the top, as 'Lord of all'. With him there will be the downtrodden nobodies who came to belong to him through the message of the word of God. All existing values are now overturned and stand judged, in advance, for the Day of God.

Some questions for personal reflection:

1. How might modern Christians slip into a preoccupation with 'wisdom' or 'mysteries'?

2. How does 'Christ crucified' reveal God to you? What does it imply for our lifestyle?

Study questions:

1. What was the 'wisdom' which the church at Corinth may have been listening to?

2. What does the 'foolishness of the cross' do for those who hear its message?

3. What does the 'foolishness of the cross' do for those who refuse to hear it?

4. Why are the efforts of the Greek 'wise' and the Jewish 'scribe' doomed to futility?

5. Why would the message of the 'cross' be so offensive to Jews and Greeks?

6. What is the meaning of 'Christ Crucified'?

3

Wisdom Among the Mature
(1 Cor. 2:6–3:23)

This passage is part of Paul's meticulously organised presentation in the four opening chapters of the letter. He begins by stating that as an apostle he has been given 'the mind of Christ' to understand the previously hidden plan of God. The Corinthians have not shown themselves to have understood this, but to be 'babyish' and 'fleshly', as revealed in their factionalism. So Paul must teach them about the respective roles of himself and Apollos in particular.

This reference to Apollos is a form of a literary and rhetorical device (see on 4:6-7). In the three years since Paul left them a teacher or teachers of 'wisdom' have risen up within the church, building a superstructure on to Paul's foundation which is quite different from Jesus Christ and him crucified (2:2). It is 'wood, hay and straw', a teaching of some kind of 'wisdom'. Paul points to Apollos as 'waterer' of the seed Paul 'planted'. But Paul has no argument with Apollos; he is merely named as a 'device' to save naming the real offenders in the church which would be a terrible 'loss of face' for them in that culture. Paul's real target is the unnamed teacher or teachers of 'this worldly wisdom'.

Through his carefully and sensitively written, yet powerful, early chapters Paul is seeking to re-connect with the Corinthians as their apostle and to reinstate the cross of Christ, rather than the 'wisdom of this world', in the mind of the Christians in Corinth.

1. Wisdom Among the Mature (2:6-9)

This passage gives us an insight into the mind of Paul, as inspired by the Spirit of God. Paul begins by stating that he 'speaks wisdom', which he clarifies first negatively then positively before making a critical amplification which he substantiates from the Old Testament scriptures. The keyword in this passage is 'glory'.

a. Initial assertion (v. 6a):	Paul 'speaks wisdom among the mature'.
b. Negative clarification (v. 6b):	This is not the 'wisdom of this age'.
c. Positive clarification (v. 7a):	Rather, Paul 'speaks wisdom *in a mystery*'.
d. Amplification (v. 7b-8):	God destined this beforehand 'for our glory'.
e. Scriptural substantiation (v. 9):	'Eye has not seen,' etc. (Isa. 64:4; 65:17).

In essence Paul declares that he speaks 'wisdom among the mature' (v. 6), which he clarifies as 'spoken in a mystery' about a 'glory' beyond our imagination, which God has ordained before history for his people. In effect, then, this passage is about the Christian's sure and indescribable *hope* in the coming age. This present age is 'passing away'; there is no future here.

In these verses Paul boldly uses the language of his opponents, but so as to overturn their teachings. Thus Paul 'speaks the wisdom of God in a *mystery*', wisdom that had been '*hidden*' which he spoke 'among the *mature*'. But Paul is using these terms deliberately. God's 'wisdom' was 'hidden' because it had been pre-ordained by him; it was only now revealed in the preaching of the gospel. This 'wisdom' was a 'mystery' because it turned out to be something utterly unexpected, the crucifixion of the 'Lord of glory'. It was spoken 'among the mature' because they discerned that the coming age of God was where their hope lay.

But this is not at all 'the wisdom of this age', nor what was understood by its intellectual and political 'rulers', for whom the present age is all there is. How blind were Herod the Tetrarch of Galilee, Caiaphas the High Priest of the Temple and Pontius Pilate the Roman Prefect of Judaea. Had they eyes to see the coming glory of God they would not have crucified its Lord, the man Jesus of Nazareth who stood before them, 'the Lord of glory'. Jesus is the glorious Lord of the coming age, the age of God's glory or brightness. Irony underlies Paul's words, for how utterly '*un*-wise' it was for those so-called 'rulers' to '*crucify* the Lord of *glory*'. In their crucifixion of 'the Lord of glory' this present age and its rulers with their twisted 'wisdom' are self-judged and self-'crucified', metaphorically speaking, and brought to nothing.

But the age to come is glorious beyond what any eye has seen, or any ear heard, or any thought of the human heart. Yet these are the very things 'God has prepared for those who love him'. This is 'the wisdom' Paul spoke 'among the mature' when he had been with them three years earlier.

2. Revelation to the Apostles (2:10-16)

Paul continues to speak about the unimaginable 'glory' of the coming age. The new emphasis now, however, is on the insight into that hope uniquely given to Paul as an apostle. This is immediately established in the opening words, '*But to us...*' The 'rulers of this world' are blind, deaf and of darkened understanding in regard to God's glorious future. '*But to us* [apostles] God has revealed it through the Spirit...' Paul repeats and reinforces this contrast between himself and these 'rulers' throughout the passage. He writes, '*But we* have not received the Spirit of the world, but the Spirit which is from God' (v. 12), and '*but we* have the mind of Christ' (v. 16).

Throughout these verses the apostle uses the analogy of a person's mind. Mind reading is a party trick, but it does not work in real life situations. My thoughts are private to me. No one really knows what I am thinking. A secret 'password' given to the bank guarantees the security of my savings; it cannot be guessed. My 'spirit' or 'mind' knows my innermost thoughts, but they are not able to be known to anyone else unless I speak of them (v. 11a). This is true of God, too. Only 'the Spirit of God searches out the deep things of God' (v. 10), 'knows the thoughts of God' (v. 11b).

But Paul has 'received the Spirit from God so that he might know what has been freely given to him by God' (v. 12), that is, the glorious and untold hope of God's coming kingdom. This has not come to Paul from 'the spirit which is from the world', otherwise Paul would have been as preoccupied with this age as its 'rulers' continue to be.

Paul speaks about this 'glory' not in words 'instructed by human wisdom' but instead in words 'instructed by the Spirit', that is, God's Spirit who alone knows God's mind. Only by this means does Paul 'express spiritual truths in spiritual words' (v. 13). There is 'human wisdom' which is useful for day-to-day decision making in this life throughout this age. But this 'wisdom' sheds no light on God's coming kingdom. That kingdom and its 'glory' are known only to God, and his innermost thoughts are revealed by his Spirit. Paul knows what is in God's mind, but only through the Spirit he has received.

In contrast with the apostle's insight into the mind of God is the 'psycikos man', as Paul calls him (v. 14). The word psycikos, which occurs in Paul's writings only in this letter (see on 15:44, 46), has been translated as 'natural man' (RV), 'unspiritual man' (RSV) and 'man without the Spirit' (NIV). Who is this 'man'[1]? He is the opposite to Paul, the 'spiritual man', to whom God has given insight into his glorious future. The 'psycikos man' is the typical man and woman of this age who, like the 'rulers of this age' (v. 7), can neither see nor hear nor know of 'the good things God has for those who love him' (v. 9). The people of this present time, unaided by God's word and Spirit, simply do not 'see' the coming glory of God. Spiritually speaking the 'psycikos man' is like the tone deaf unable to hear the beauty of the music of Mozart, or is like the colour blind unable to appreciate the artistry of Monet.

Paul, however, is the 'spiritual man' who judges or discerns all things, that is, in relationship with the kingdom of God (v. 15; cf. 2 Cor. 5:15a). Paul does not claim to be all-knowing. His comment is limited to 'wisdom in a mystery', previously 'hidden' but now revealed in 'the word of the cross'. Paul attributes this 'wisdom' to the Spirit whom God has given to him. In his judgement of 'all things' he is not subject to the judgement of others, that is, the 'wisdom'-preachers of Corinth.

Paul now concludes this passage. He began with the contrastive, 'But to us God has revealed [the coming glory] through the Spirit'. Now he ends with, 'but we have the mind of Christ' (v. 16). God alone knows his own mind through the Spirit and he has revealed this, his 'hidden wisdom', his plans for his future kingdom, to Paul through the same Spirit (v. 11). Thus Paul, through the Spirit of God, has 'the mind of Christ'.

---

1   The Greek word psycikos is masculine.

In this Paul, with other apostles, was uniquely blessed by God, as he wrote to the readers of Ephesians.

> Surely you have heard about the administration of God's grace that was given to me for you, that is, the mystery made known to me by revelation...my insight into the mystery of Christ, which was not made known to men in other generations as it has now been revealed by the Spirit to God's holy apostles and prophets (Eph. 3:2-5).

In short, God made his mind known by revelation through the Spirit directly to the apostles and indirectly through them to their readers then and now. We enter into the 'mind of Christ' as we read carefully the text of these apostolic letters and apply their teachings to ourselves.

3. Babes in Christ (3:1-4)

Once again Paul introduces a new section with, 'And I...'(see on 2:1). In that previous reference and in this reference Paul recalls his ministry in Corinth which had begun five years earlier. In the first reference he recalls that his preaching then was 'not in lofty words of wisdom...as he knew nothing among them but Jesus Christ and him crucified'. In the second reference he recalls, with regret, the spiritual immaturity of the Corinthians at that time: 'I was not able to speak to you as spiritual men and women, but...as babes in Christ.' Such was their immaturity then that he was not able to 'feed them with meat...but only with milk'. Despite Paul's one and a half years with them they were not ready for solid teaching about the faith. He must limit their spiritual diet to milk, to simple and basic teaching which they were not ready to leave behind. Like many then and since, they are 'milk Christians', not 'meat Christians'.

Paul uses an interesting word for these 'babyish' Corinthians. He calls them *sarkinoi*, 'men and women of *flesh*'[2] (v. 1). To be sure, they are Christian believers; they are not psycikoi, people who belong to this present age and not the next, who are not at all Christians. But neither are they like him, *pneumatikoi*, 'men and women of the *Spirit*', those whom earlier he called 'the mature' (2:6). Because they are 'fleshly' (immature) and not 'spiritual' (mature) he is 'still' not able to feed them with solid

---

2   Derived from the Greek, *sarx*, 'flesh'.

food (v. 2). At face value, and somewhat to our surprise, this means the present letter (or, perhaps, this section of the letter) is not 'solid' food, but 'milk'.

Why does Paul call them 'babes in Christ' and 'fleshly' people who live according to merely 'human standards'? Here Paul takes them and us back to the beginning of the letter and his primary concern in writing (see on 1:10-17). It is their factiousness, their evident 'jealousy and strife' (v. 4), which demonstrates their immaturity. 'One says, "I am of Paul," and another says, "I am of Apollos."' Factionalism based on personal loyalties to particular ministers is all too 'human', says Paul, and a sure sign that they remain 'babyish' and of having a 'fleshly' nature.

These verses, along with 2:6-16, with their references to *psychikoi*, *sarkinoi* and *pneumatikoi*, have been taken to refer to different grades of Christians. This was anything but Paul's intention. As already noted *psychikoi* are not Christians at all, but *unbelievers* locked into this present age. For their part, *pneumatikoi* are simply Christians who understand apostolic truth but who behave in a spiritually mature way. They are what all believers should reasonably be expected to become and be. The *sarkinoi* are believers who have made little progress in their understanding and who need to 'grow up' in the Lord by submitting to good teaching and by behaving in a godly way. There is not the slightest hint here that *sarkinoi* become *pneumatikoi* by some kind of 'second' experience of the Spirit as advocated by various holiness movements throughout Christian history.

In what follows (vv. 5-23) Paul proceeds to give precisely the teaching about ministers like Apollos, Cephas/Peter and himself that the Corinthians need to understand and implement if they are to progress beyond 'babyish' behaviour to become mature and adult Christians.

4. 'Who are Apollos and Paul?' (3:5-9)
So, to put them on the path of 'wise' understanding and 'mature' behaviour as fitting for 'spiritual' men and women, Paul gives some simple 'milk'-like instruction about himself and Apollos. 'Who are these men?' he asks.

First and of primary importance, these men are 'servants through whom you believed' (v. 5). Both Paul and Apollos had engaged in evangelism in Corinth; the Corinthians came to 'believe' through their ministry. The verb case[3] indicates the moment their 'belief' in Christ became a reality. The preposition 'through' is pointed, given the Corinthians' preoccupation with personalities. They did not become believers 'in' Paul and Apollos but 'in' the Lord Jesus Christ 'through' the preaching of these his servants.

The word 'servant' (*diakonos*) originally meant someone who served at tables. It also carried the sense of serving on behalf of a *master*, in his name and under his authority. Paul often uses the language of the 'servant' to describe his own ministry (see, e.g., 2 Cor. 3:6; 6:4). Being a 'servant' implied an element of autonomy, however, unlike a 'slave' (*doulos*) who was utterly subservient and dependent on his *owner*. Paul also applied the word 'slave' to himself (see e.g., 2 Cor. 4:5). Let the Corinthians understand that Paul and Apollos are the humble 'servants' of their Lord 'through' whose 'service' many in the church became believers. Furthermore, the effectiveness of these men was not due to their innate abilities, which might perhaps have justified a greater recognition of the eloquent Apollos over Paul. On the contrary, it was, literally, 'to each as the Lord gave'. The NIV translates verse 5b, 'as the Lord has assigned to each his task', connecting 'assigned' with Paul's and Apollos' *tasks* of 'planting' and 'watering' as in the verses following. It makes better sense,[4] however, to understand 'the Lord gave' as referring to the *believers* in Corinth whom the Lord 'gave' to either man 'through' his ministry.

Paul now explains the ministries of himself and Apollos by a simple example. The congregation is 'God's paddock' (*geōrgion* v. 9) and Paul and Apollos are farm 'workers', in fact 'co-workers with God' (v. 9). These workers have differing tasks in the paddock. One man plants, another who comes after him waters. But God causes the plants to grow (v. 6).

Paul makes three observations about these 'servants', 'co-workers with God' in 'God's paddock'. First, neither the planter nor the waterer is 'anything'; it is God, not they, who causes the growth (v. 7). To be sure, they do need to plant and water; their

---

3   Called 'aorist', pointing to a moment when something occurred, for example, 'The Corinthians *believed* in Christ.'

4   *Contra* Fee, p. 131.

work is needed. But the energy for the germination, growth and fruition comes from God. It is in this sense that they are 'not anything'.

Secondly, despite having different functions, the planter and the waterer are 'one'. Both are needed and neither can do without the other. The planter must plant or the crop will not begin and the waterer must water or the plants will die. Though they have differing roles it is the 'one' operation in which they share.

Thirdly, each man will receive from God a reward according to his 'labour'. All believers are saved by grace through the death and resurrection of Christ. Here, Paul's focus is not on believers in general but on preachers and teachers of the church. For such, there are differing rewards, depending on his servants' faithfulness and application, what the Bible calls 'stewardship'. But and this is critical for the Corinthians to grasp it is the Lord and not they who rewards the labourer. Paul and Apollos are stewards of the Lord, and accountable to him, not to the Corinthians (see on 4:1-5).

5. But Paul Laid the Foundation (3:10-17)

In the last sentence of the previous section Paul shifts the imagery of the congregation from 'paddock' to 'building'. He does this for two reasons. First, he seeks to establish that he, Paul, was the one who 'laid the foundation' of the congregation in Corinth (v. 10). Let those teachers who add to the structure take great care as to the quality of the materials they use in building on his foundation (vv. 11-15). Secondly, Paul wants to move on to speak about the church as a specific kind of building, that is, a 'holy temple' (vv. 16-17).

As he often does, Paul first gives us a short statement (v. 10), which he then explains in what follows (vv. 11-15). So Paul reminds the Corinthians of the incontrovertible fact that *he* laid the foundation at Corinth. It was not Apollos, nor Cephas, nor some 'wise' teacher who has arisen in the meantime, but Paul who first came and preached the gospel in the Achaian capital. Here he makes two sharply pointed remarks directed at the Corinthians. First, he did so 'by the grace of God which was given to him', God's unique 'gift' to him as an apostle and church-planter. The foundation-laying for the church at

Corinth was no merely human act of *Paul's* that could give rise to a pro-Paul faction in the church. It was God's work done 'through' him by the 'gift' of the Spirit. Secondly, Paul laid this foundation as, literally, 'a *wise* architect' (*architektōn* the word literally meant 'chief builder'). Contrary to recent criticism of him, Paul is 'wise', in particular, because he preaches God's 'wise' message centred on 'Christ crucified' (see on 1:18-25).

Paul now adds, ominously and mysteriously, '*Another* is building on' his foundation. Paul says no more and gives no name. But it must have been abundantly obvious to the congregation who this unnamed 'builder' is. I presume that it was one of the teachers of 'wisdom' with whom Paul has been interacting for the greater part of the letter to this point. So Paul gives this warning, 'Let each one be careful how he builds', something he amplifies in the verses following (vv. 12-15; see on 4:6).

Critical to verse 11 is the little word, 'For', which explains his reasons 'for' what he has just stated. Paul was a 'wise' 'master-builder' *for* he laid the only foundation that could possibly ever be laid for a church, 'Jesus Christ'. Let the one who currently teaches in the church take great care how he builds, *for* no other foundation is able to be laid. This suggests that this person or persons, by teaching something different, is actually laying *another* foundation. But there is only one foundation that is able to be laid for this or any church, 'Jesus Christ', that is, Jesus Christ *crucified*. Whenever Paul mentions that name he means us to connect to it his crucifixion. We must not disconnect Christ from the cross nor the cross from Christ (see on 1:18-25).

Nothing could be clearer than that Paul wanted the teachers in the church to build a superstructure with the same material as the foundation. The foundation was Paul's teaching about 'Jesus Christ and him crucified'. But as the building rises from its foundations it must be built of the same teaching about *who* Jesus is and *what* he has done for us in his death and resurrection.

'For', declares Paul, a 'day is coming, when the fires of judgement will sweep through, leaving only what is incombustible' (v. 13). Only that teaching which is centred in and true to Jesus crucified and risen will stand the test of the fires of God's judgement on the Last Day. This is the point Paul is making by referring to 'gold, silver, precious stones, dry wood, hay and straw' (v. 12). He is not giving an allegory of materials that make for a beautiful church, spiritually understood. Rather, he is saying that inferior or unfaithful teaching will not survive those fires, but that strong and faithful teaching will. The 'work' of each minister will be 'tested' in the flames of the Great Day.

So Paul addresses those whose 'work' remains after that fiery trial. 'They will receive a reward', he assures them (v. 14). That reward will be the warm approval, the 'well done, faithful servant', of the Lord which true ministers of the gospel long to hear.

But those whose 'work' is burnt to ashes will 'suffer loss'. That 'loss' will not be their salvation (v. 15b), which is not dependent on the work of ministry, but on the 'work' of 'Christ crucified' on their behalf. Rather, it will be the 'loss' of warm commendation from Jesus and the 'loss' of a life's work in ministry, because it has been defective in truth. The man will be saved, says Paul, 'but only as one escaping through the flames'. This is a metaphor, probably based on Amos 4:11 ('a firebrand plucked from the burning'). The man will escape the flames of hell, 'by the skin of his teeth' as it were, or 'just in the nick of time'. But he will have all eternity to regret what his ministry *might* have been, had he been faithful to the gospel. Charles Dickens' fictional character, the mean-spirited Scrooge, became a changed man following a series of 'dreams' in which were revealed to him his failures to take opportunities to do good. In the age to come there are no 'second chances'. This life is no dress rehearsal, but the one and only opportunity to do the will of God. Ministers of the gospel, take note!

Ours is an age preoccupied with style and appearance rather than substance, which has affected the life of the church and the ministry. This is the day of creating ambience, of TV style presentation, of management systems, of pop psychology, of outreach 'programmes', of anything but the simple and unadorned truth of God, 'Jesus Christ and him crucified'. It is not so much that we ministers today are heretical or outright unbelievers, but that we so easily fail to teach the plain truth about Jesus. Because we are success-driven and failure-shy we apply all manner of sugar coating to the rich almond that is the true message. In the end it gets down to this, whose approval do we really seek, Christ's or those around us?

Paul's words about the 'fire' of *the* Day also apply to the time beforehand. Other times of severe testing come to our churches, whether through the indifference of affluence, the moist winds of seductive false teaching or the sharp pain of persecution. In reality we do not have to wait for the flames of God in the final hour. Only those who teach truly and well will see their work survive in the meantime.

6. The Temple of God (3:16-17)

Paul introduced the metaphor of 'building' for the Christian congregation (v. 10) in order to lead into a more developed image of the church as 'the temple of God'. The congregation is not the outer part of the temple but the inner sanctum (*naos*), the holiest place of all. The idea that a group of *people* should be thought of as such a 'temple' is striking and to my knowledge unparalleled, historically speaking. People tend to see religious *buildings* as holy places. But this group of people did not even have their own separate building at this point in history. By contrast the Jews had thousands of synagogue buildings scattered around the Mediterranean region.

Naturally we are curious to know which temple Paul has in mind. Was it the great Temple of Yahweh in Jerusalem, arguably the most imposing structure in the world at the time, or was it, for example, the temple of Apollo or one of the other temples in Corinth? Most probably Paul is thinking of the Temple in Jerusalem, which was used for the worship of the God of Israel, rather than the local temples used for pagan idolatry and sexual prostitution.

But how can these *people* be the temple of God? It is because they are indwelt individually (6:19), and therefore corporately, by the Spirit of God. The Holy Spirit of God makes them the holy *people* of God, his saints. In his Second Letter Paul writes:

> What agreement is there between the temple of God and idols?
> For we are the temple of the living God.
> As God has said:
> 'I will live with them and walk among them, and
> I will be their God, and they will be my people'
> (2 Cor. 6:16; cf. Eph. 2:21).

There, in 2 Corinthians, the issue is holiness. Paul is calling for the separation of 'the temple of God' from 'idols', that is, the believers' participation in the worship of idols in one of the numerous pagan temples in Corinth. Holiness would be destroyed by association with unholy religion, with its accompanying sexual practices.

In the First Letter the emphasis is also on holiness, but a holiness that would be destroyed by the *disunity* of the people in the church. This is to be inferred by his words, 'if anyone destroys the temple of God, God will destroy him' (v. 17). Paul is returning to the vexed matter of factionalism in the church associated with personality cults focused on individual ministers, Paul, Apollos or Cephas (see on 1:10-17). God intends his gathered church to be united in Christ. A dire warning is directed to those who wilfully and willingly destroy God's sacred shrine by their divisions.

The verbal artistry of Paul's original word order and word play should be noted.

If anyone God's temple *destroys,*
destroy this person God will.

The teacher who has built badly may barely escape the flames of God's judgement. Not so the divider of the Lord's people in his holy assembly. Paul's words are the severest warning to us, telling how much God's church means to him. Let the factious of Corinth and of all other churches know this, '...the temple of God is holy, which you yourselves are'!

7. Final Warning about Wisdom (3:18-23)
Paul makes an interim conclusion to the problem of 'wisdom' in Corinth which he began back at 1:18-25. The ultimate conclusion of the section begun at 1:10 is not reached until 4:21.

He begins with the advice, 'Let no one deceive himself'. Who is in mind here? Nobody in particular, or, more probably the unnamed 'wisdom' teacher referred to in verse 10? Whoever 'this one' is, let him not, literally, '*thoroughly* deceive himself'. The usual word 'deceive' (*apatō*) is intensified by the prefix *ex* (*exapatō*). There is self-deception but this person is in danger of self-inflicted blindness, metaphorically speaking.

Paul now returns to the contrast between 'wisdom' and 'foolishness' (begun in 1:18-25) as he launches into a full blooded comparison of this present age and God's coming age. 'Let the man who thinks himself "wise" according to this age among you (i.e., in the Corinthian church) become a fool that he might become wise.' In other words, let this man pull his thinking inside out, identifying now with God's scale of 'wisdom' seen in God's 'foolish' message of 'Christ crucified' which is to be taught not with 'lofty words of wisdom... but in demonstration of the Spirit and of power' (see on 2:1,4).

He substantiates this advice to the 'wise' by his own proverb, or 'wise' saying. '*For* the wisdom of this world is foolishness with God.' The values and standards of 'this age' (v. 18) or 'this world' (v. 19) are topsy turvy. The self-deceived 'wise' man of Corinth needs to overturn his own thinking and see truth through the eyes of God. Paul further substantiates his 'wisdom' by an appeal to two texts from the Scriptures:

'He catches the wise in their craftiness' (Job 5:13)

and

'The Lord knows that the thoughts of the wise are futile' (Ps. 94:11).

Both texts are significant in their Old Testament contexts, speaking of God's judgement of the self-styled 'wise'. In the first the 'wise' are high-minded and 'crafty', but God overturns their plans. In the second the 'wise' are arrogant, but the Lord will bring their thoughts to nothing. Let the 'wise' man of Corinth become a 'fool' so that he may become 'wise' by God's standards.

Paul now turns from his advice to this 'wise' man to address the congregation at large, 'So then, no more boasting in men'. There is a rightful pride which is directed to God's saviour, Jesus Christ crucified and risen. But at Corinth there is a wrongful pride in men, Paul included. Let the Corinthians understand that Paul's ministry was empowered by the grace of God (3:10) and that he is merely a servant 'through' whom the Corinthians came to believe 'in' the Lord (3:5). No faith or pride was to be directed to Paul but only 'in' the Lord who had worked 'through' Paul. The same was true of Apollos. How much more true is it, therefore, of a local 'wise' teacher in the church whose message was questionable and whose florid style of presentation was quite unsuited to the preaching of the cross of Christ.

Paul concludes his appeal to the Corinthians with a splendid theological statement.

'Everything belongs to you', he assures them (v. 21). 'Whether the teachers who have come to the city of Corinth Paul, Apollos or

Cephas or the world, or life, or death, or things present, or things to come', all is yours. 'All this Christian ministers and the whole gamut of human experience under the hand of God belongs to you now.'

The world, and this age, fallen and corrupt as it is, remains under the grasp of God's providential, all-powerful hand. Thus Paul is life affirming, world affirming and this age affirming. Notwithstanding God's subversion of this world's 'wisdom' and values in the message of 'Christ crucified', Paul is no world-denying Manichee.

Just as 'all' this 'belongs to you', so too, 'you belong to Christ'. You are safe in his kingdom, kept for the coming age of God. Christ, too, is safe, kept for the coming age of God because he in turn 'belongs to' God. All things are yours, and you are Christ's and Christ is God's. I am reminded of mandarin-style moulded dolls I once saw in a shop window. A small one fitted exactly into a larger one which in turn fitted into a larger one. God ultimately holds all things safe in his mighty hand.

SOME QUESTIONS FOR PERSONAL REFLECTION:

1. Is Paul's verdict on the spiritual blindness of 'the rulers of this age' still true of the political and intellectual rulers at this present time?

2. In my attitude to ministers am I 'mature', a *pneumatikos* / 'spiritual' person or 'babyish', a *sarkinos* / 'fleshly' person?

3. What is the significance to us today of Paul having 'the mind of Christ'?

STUDY QUESTIONS:

1. What is the wisdom of God which Paul is reminding the Corinthians of?

2. Who is the 'psycikos man'? What is his problem?

3. Where does Paul say his wisdom comes from?

4. Why does Paul call them 'babes in Christ' and fleshly people living by 'human standards'?

5. Why does Paul apply the word "slave" to himself? What does he want to display to the Corinthians in doing so?

6. Why does Paul go to great lengths to remind the Corinthians that he 'laid the foundation' for them? What does he caution in the building upon it?

4

Appreciate Your Apostle
(1 Cor. 4:1-21)

In this chapter Paul at last makes crystal clear the concerns which he has been addressing from the beginning of the letter. He began by speaking of the problems of factions associated with Paul, Apollos, Cephas and 'Christ' (1:12). But as this will now be made clear it was, in a sense, a face saving device for those of that culture for whom 'shame' was unbearable. Paul is really targeting a local teacher or teachers of 'wisdom' that is, a false 'wisdom' who are taking over the leadership of the church (3:10, 17). But he does not name them, for that would probably be to 'shame' them out of the church altogether. Rather, he teaches them about his own accountability as an apostle, which is not to the church but to the Lord (4:1-5). He chides the church for its spiritual self-satisfaction, its belief that it had 'arrived', and moreover arrived 'without' its apostle. So he must tell them what being an apostle has meant to him in terms of suffering and sacrifice in order for them to hear the gospel. But this is not to 'shame' them, but to tell them by his example the pattern of discipleship which they are to imitate. He is sending Timothy to remind them about Paul's 'ways in Christ' since they appear to have forgotten! Finally, let not those who have risen up in Corinth delude themselves that Paul will not return. He will indeed return. So let the people put things right beforehand so that he will come as a pastor not as a policeman!

1. What is an Apostle? (4:1-5)

Who are the 'us' that Paul is speaking about in verses 1-5? Is it a general reference to 'ministers through whom you believed' (3:5), people like Paul and Apollos, but not limited to them, or is it to himself as an *apostle*, referring to himself in an 'apostolic plural'? References to Apollos before and after this section (3:4, 5, 6, 22; 4:6) might suggest the former. However, the strong reference to 'us apostles' (4:9) tips the balance in favour of the latter. Nonetheless, there is a sting in Paul's words, for they apply pointedly to the teacher or teachers who are building unhelpfully on his foundations (see on 4:6-7). Beyond that pastors and missionaries in all times and places will find deeply relevant teaching here for their own ministries. Christ crucified is the only foundation and the only superstructure.

Paul's opening words, 'Men ought to regard *us*...' (v. 1) reveals his obvious concern that the Corinthians have a correct grasp of his role as an *apostle*, the inference being that they do not have a right view of him. 'Think of us', he says first, 'as servants of Christ'. Here his word is not *diakonos*, 'minister' (as in 3:5), but *hypēretēs* which originally meant 'under rower', the slave rower in a trireme who occupied the miserable, lowest bank of oars. By New Testament times *hypēretēs* had come to mean an 'assistant' or 'servant', as for example, the 'attendant' in the synagogue of Nazareth who handed Jesus the scroll for him to read (Luke 4:20). John Mark accompanied Barnabas and Paul on the first missionary journey as their 'assistant' (Acts 13:5). But *hypēretēs* is also applied to those who 'from the beginning were *ministers* of the word' (Luke 1:2). Paul's reference to himself as 'a servant of Christ' carried the idea of 'humility' and 'obedient service' to one whom he regarded as his Master.

But 'think of us,' he says, secondly, as 'stewards of the mysteries of God'. As noted earlier 'mystery' is Paul's daring reference to the 'mystery' cults of the time (see on 2:1). In brief, he means us to understand the gospel which he preaches as the 'mystery' of God. This had been the long 'hidden' plan of God, but which was now 'open' to every ear in the preaching of the gospel of Christ crucified and risen.

Paul is a 'steward' or 'trustee' of these 'mysteries'. In that culture a 'steward' (*oikonomos*), often an educated slave, was employed to distribute money and goods within an extended household or farming establishment. Fundamental to his work, apart from competence, was a steward's faithfulness (v. 2). Paul is saying that as a 'steward' he was called, above all, to be faithful in distributing to others what he had received from God.

'Stewards' then were held to account by their masters for their distributions by some kind of audit process. But to whom is the 'steward' of God answerable? Paul raises three possible judges of his 'stewardship': the Corinthians, a human tribunal or himself. Is he judged by the church in Corinth? 'Not at all', says Paul. 'It does not matter in the least to me that I am judged by you' (v. 3). In fact, he continues, 'I am not judged by any human tribunal' nor even 'by myself'.

As it happened Paul says that he did not know anything against his stewardship (v. 4). But that is irrelevant, beside the point. Paul's own positive verdict on his ministry does not amount to an acquittal. It is, he states, 'the Lord who judges me'.

This is an extremely important consideration. Ministers are delivered from being 'people-pleasers' by this great reality. If the Lord, not the church in particular nor people in general, is the judge then I can be courageous and independent in my ministry. On the other hand, we must be cautious about passing judgement on the ministries of others. Many have confessed, with deep sorrow of heart, harsh judgments of ministers which in the fullness of time have proved to be wrong. Leave the judging of ministers, and indeed other Christians, to their Lord (see Rom. 14:4).

So, Paul concludes, 'judge nothing before the appointed time'; wait till the Lord comes (v. 5). Closely connected here are the Lord's 'coming', the resurrection of all, and the Lord's 'judgement' of all (see on 15:23, 52; cf. 2 Cor. 4:14; 5:10). That will be a day of 'revelation'. The Lord will cast light on hidden things of darkness and expose the motives of human hearts. We wait expectantly for many things in life exam results to be announced, photos of holidays to be duly processed and, more soberly, results of medical X-rays to be shown to us disclosing their good or bad news. Above everything else we await the revelations of God about us which he will make known on the Last Day.

Then, says Paul, each 'steward' will receive 'his praise from God' (v. 5b). Failure to be faithful will not attract God's praise on the Last Day. This is the 'loss' the shoddy builder will 'suffer', as referred to earlier (see on 3:15). It must be said again that ministers of the gospel are not finally answerable to their churches but to God. Sadly, however, some ministers take this as a justification to do as they please without any accountability for their use of time. Pastoral and missionary ministry has boundaries within which God's servants must work to the best of their ability in God's strength. Because of sin every minister needs at least one honest person, an interim judge, as it were, who will hold the minister accountable. Nonetheless, the minister's ultimate answerability is to the Lord Jesus, not the mentor, nor the deacons nor the Bishop. Mindful of this one minister felt impelled to say to his rather overbearing deacons, 'Gentlemen, I may be your servant, but you are not my master'.

Paul's words in their original setting were not written in the abstract. Rather, they are quite pointed and intentional. Paul is directing them squarely to the unnamed teacher or teachers of 'wisdom' who have built inappropriately on his 'foundation' in Corinth, the preaching of Jesus Christ crucified (see on 3:10). Implicit in his words is a double warning, first, that they are answerable to the Lord for their 'stewardship', but also, secondly, that they should not pass judgement on him; Christ is their judge and his.

2. Divisions from Pride (4:6-7)

Reading these words is like listening to someone speaking on the phone, but we cannot work out who he is talking to or, for that matter, what exactly is being discussed. To be candid, we are left to guess to whom Paul is speaking and what, really, he is saying. The original readers would have known precisely what and to whom his words were directed, but we don't.

First, Paul is saying that 'I have applied these things to myself and Apollos for your benefit' (v. 6). 'These things' must refer to all he has said about himself and Apollos (as, respectively, a 'planter' and 'waterer' in God's 'paddock' and as a 'foundation layer' and a 'superstructure builder' in the Corinthian church) and to divisions which have arisen around them. But it is clear from the greater context of 1:17–3:23 that there is 'something

else' happening in Corinth and this is connected with a teacher
or teachers of 'wisdom' in the church.

In my view, Paul chooses not to name such persons, perhaps
to 'save their face(s)', or perhaps to avoid over-dignifying their
error by explicit reference to them. Thus as a device appropriate
to that culture and situation Paul 'applies' the problems associated with these teachers instead to himself and Apollos. This
is not to say this is altogether a 'fiction', but that for pastoral
reasons he may have 'blown up' the matters of parties associated with himself, Apollos and Cephas as a means of referring
to those other teachers and the divisions they are causing.

Understood in this way the Corinthians are to learn from
himself and Apollos 'not to go beyond what is written'. Evidently
this was a local proverb, whose origins are lost to us, that Paul
transfers to this situation. We might say something like, 'keep
within your boundaries', or 'stay within bounds'. This applies,
so it appears, to local leaders and teachers who might, as it were,
'become too big for their boots', assuming too great a role within
the congregation. As potential leaders stay within reasonable
limits the members of the church 'will not be inflated in pride,
one man over against another'. Leaders within churches, then,
have a responsibility not to seize the pre-eminence, as Diotrephes
did (see 3 John 9). Otherwise they will surely create a personal
following which will divide congregations.

Paul concludes his exhortation with a series of questions to
humble those who are 'puffed up' with pride, as they favoured
one leader against another or were themselves favoured above
others. *First*, he asks them pointedly, 'Who discriminates you
from others?', that is, 'who singles you out as a leader?' *Secondly*,
he demands, 'What do you have that you did not receive?',
that is, 'from *God*'? Then with relentless logic, *thirdly*, 'And if
you received it why do you boast as if you did not receive it?'

Paul has now exposed the wilful individualism of the Corinthians. In their overweening pride they simply do not grasp
that all that they have done has been by God's 'gift' to them
through the Spirit, including 'gifts' of teaching, knowledge and
leadership. Ambitious individuals have risen up, each with
their body of followers, who have felt 'proud' of their leader.
Later Paul will teach that God's gifts for his people are not at all
for the individuals' ego-tripping, but for the expression of that

'gift' in love for others in the 'body' (14:1). Factionalism arising from pride has two terrible consequences for the congregation: first, the congregation is not 'built up' (cf. 14:12), and secondly, the church is actually shattered and is potentially scattered altogether by this wickedness.

One of the consequences of this jockeying for pre-eminence based on competing teachers is that Paul himself has been marginalised in the church. In the passage following, Paul speaks movingly of them 'going it alone' without him. At last, so it seems, we have come to the real point of the letter, namely, Paul's relationship with the church. We may have thought it was the divisions over Paul, Apollos, Cephas, 'Christ'. But no. It was really the divisions caused by competing local 'wisdom' teachers. What is really going on at Corinth is that the church and their apostle have parted company. That is the real issue in the first four chapters.

3. 'Us Apostles Last of All' (4:8-13)
This passage is powerfully rhetorical, with ironical contrasts made between Paul and the Corinthians.

1. So You think You have 'Arrived'? (4:8)
Paul had come to hear of the spiritual self-satisfaction of the Corinthians, perhaps from Chloe's people (see on 1:11). Paul's words, which probably echo back to them some of their own opinions, are filled with irony.

Already	you are filled?		
Already	you are rich?		
Without us	you have	begun to rule?	
Would that	you had, in fact, begun to rule,		
that			
we also		might rule with you.	

'Already filled', 'already rich', 'begun to rule' expresses the distorted understanding of the Corinthians. Yes, 'the fulfilment of the ages has come' in the preaching of the death and resurrection of Jesus (see on 10:11). God has 'already' taken his great power and begun to rule (Rev. 11:17). In Jesus' resurrection God's future rule has come in *behind* us, fulfilling his promises made through the Old Testament prophets. Paul's word 'already' splendidly captures what has been called 'realized eschatology', the belief that the future has come into the present 'in Christ'. Yet there is a sharp tension. The kingdom has also 'not yet' come because Christ has 'not yet' come back and this is painfully evident in the corruption, sin and suffering which surrounds us, including within the church. The believer must affirm two realities, 'already' and 'not yet', and live with the tension between them.

The Corinthian Christians, however, were strong on the 'already' but weak about the 'not yet'. It appears that having been 'made rich' in Christ in 'all speech' and 'all knowledge' (see on 1:5) including, we suppose, the riches of 'wisdom' the Corinthians have persuaded themselves that the 'kingdom of God' has, somehow, 'already' come.

This over-emphasis on 'already' has been called '*over*realized eschatology', and has reappeared throughout history in various experience-based 'Holy Spirit' movements. Equally, however, there has often been over-emphasis on 'not yet' and an under emphasis on 'already'. This could be called '*under*realized eschatology' and this has been evident where the church's dogma has been dominant.

Paul's savage irony points to the Corinthians' self-delusion. 'You say, "Already we are filled, already we are rich," but you are actually "babyish," "deficient in the Spirit" and "fleshly" ' (see on 2:14–3:4). 'Can I remind you of your crass individualism, your splinter groups and the jostling for power and influence among your leaders and teachers?'

Powerfully ironic, Paul wishes they had, in fact, 'begun to rule,' that is, *ethically* as well as in the excitement of their pneumatic gifts. In that case Paul says that he might 'rule with them'. But the irony is heavy. His joint rule with theirs is not in prospect.

Indeed, the profusion of these gifts of 'knowledge' and 'speech' evident among them, including their teachers, is such that Paul is no longer seen by them within their frame of reference. They are 'already filled...already rich'...have begun to rule *without* Paul. His foundation-laying evangelism of the past and his authority in the present are irrelevant to them. They have moved on and away from their apostle. Later he will ask them, again with irony, 'Did the word of God originate with you? Or are you the only ones to whom it has come' (see on 14:36)?

2. Fools for Christ's Sake, and Theirs (4:9-13).

Apostles, heralds of the cross, themselves re-live the Messiah's cross they preach. Here Paul uses a metaphor from the savagery of the gladiatorial arena, which was a commonplace in Paul's day through the influence of the Romans. The gentler theatre of the Greeks in which plays were performed had given way to a different kind of 'theatre' where people came to watch men fight for their lives with men, and yes, women with women fighting to the death, hand to hand as gladiators.[1] Perhaps Paul had tasted the terrors of being in just such an arena in Ephesus, from which this letter is written. 'I fought with wild beasts in Ephesus' (see on 15:32) may be metaphorical, but equally it may be literal, pointing to some terrifying experience in that horrifying 'theatre'.

The Corinthians thought they were 'filled', 'rich' and 'ruling'. Paul, for his part, uses the arena imagery conscious that God had 'exhibited' the apostles 'last of all' (v. 9). He says that he has been 'sentenced to death' and been made 'a spectacle' (*theatron*) 'to the world, to angels and to men'. This is as graphic as it is gruesome, showing how difficult life was for one who truly preached Christ crucified, with its demands for repentance and 'self-crucifixion', relative to the soft and easy message of the 'wisdom of this world' currently being touted in Corinth.

Paul's words come as the sharpest of rebukes for the kind of religion Christianity was in danger of becoming in the Achaian capital, as he states in three staccato contrasts between himself and them (v. 10):

We are fools,	but you are wise.
We are weak,	but you are strong.
You are honoured,	but we are despised.

He peels off in rapid succession what it has meant for him to be an apostle for the past twenty years, 'until that very hour' (vv. 11-12a).

Hungry,
thirsty,

---

[1]   On display in the British Museum in London is a frieze taken from Halicarnassus to the south of Ephesus depicting the hand to hand struggle between the female gladiators Amazonia and Achillia.

poorly clothed,
beaten,
constantly on the move,
labouring with my own hands night and day.

Impelled by the call of Christ to take the word of God to the Gentiles, Paul has suffered unspeakably in the uncertainty and vulnerability of the itinerant's life (see further 2 Cor. 6:3-10; 11:23-12:10). Tent-making[2] is touched on here, but all romantic notions must be dispelled. Tents were of leather which had to be cut and stitched, as well as mended, along with saddles and shoes and other leather goods. This was exhausting and stinking work, done at night so that Paul and his co-workers could offer the gospel free of charge (see on 9:3-18). It was one of the chief sources of his exhaustion and humiliation in a culture that despised physical labour.

We sense that this catalogue of sufferings is Christ-related, as though Jesus' Golgotha is replicated in the sufferings of the apostle wherever he preaches the message of the crucified. This is confirmed by the non-vindictive behaviour following, so evocative of Jesus' forgiveness of those who shamefully mistreated him (vv. 12b-13a; cf. 1 Pet 2:22-23):

Reviled,   we bless.
Persecuted,   we endure.
Vilified,   we speak gently.

In the centuries to come the non-retaliatory behaviour of the Christian martyrs was a major factor for the victory of the cross in the Roman world. Few words of Jesus have sunk so deeply as his, 'Father forgive them...' (Luke 23:34). There is no power so apparently weak, and yet in reality so strong, as the power shown in forgiving those who have done you wrong.

During World War 2 the Bishop of Singapore was repeatedly beaten by his guards, whom he consciously forgave. Years later the Bishop baptized and confirmed one of his torturers, so moved had he been by the forgiveness shown to him.

Paul concludes his list of privation and humiliation, 'We have become the scum of the earth, the refuse of the world'

---

2   See P. Barnett, 'Tentmaking', *Dictionary of Paul and His Letters* (Downers grove: IVP, 1993) pp. 925-7.

(v. 13 b, c). The two words 'scum' and 'refuse' are almost synonymous and were used for 'rubbish swept up' or 'filth scraped off'. Some commentators have seen here a sacrificial allusion to blood and entrails scraped off an altar after the sacrifice of an animal in a temple, as if Paul were pointing to his sufferings as some kind of 'offering'. But this is rather speculative. Rather, Paul is pointing to the depth of his humiliation and suffering bringing the gospel to the Corinthians, who, by contrast, are not preaching and living the same message as Paul, 'Jesus Christ and him crucified', but rather some kind of 'wisdom' doctrine.

Paul's language in verses 9-13 is extreme, but no exaggeration. His message of the cross was uncompromising but unwelcome wherever he went, whether to Jews or Greeks and Romans. He bore in his own body the very sufferings of his Lord in bringing the message of Jesus to the world. Those sufferings were of a different order, since Christ is the only saviour of sinners. Yet Paul's sufferings and those of all pioneer missionaries since were deep and real. And they were sufferings *for* others, 'that they might live'. In this case those 'others' were the 'wisdom'-intoxicated Corinthians who lived in the relative comfort of Corinth and who thought that they had 'arrived' and were 'already' ruling in God's kingdom and that they had reached these lofty heights *'without'* their apostle!

4. Many Tutors, One Father (4:14-17)

Paul has used very strong language, both about their 'self-satisfaction' (v. 8) and his 'humiliation' as the apostle (vv. 9, 11-13), which were suffered to bring the word of God to them (v. 10). But this was not to 'shame' them but rather to 'warn' them, which he does 'as my much-loved children' (v. 14). Shallow sentiment seldom issues warnings, because it cares more about being well liked than the welfare of the other person, who may be in spiritual danger. True love, as shown by a parent, however, will express concern and, if appropriate, a warning.

Paul uses an exaggerated scenario, 'Even if you had ten thousand tutors (*paidagōgoi*) you do not have many fathers' (v. 15). In fact, he implies, you only have one father, 'for', he continues, 'in Christ I personally begat you through the gospel'. In a great man's household there may have been numbers of 'pedagogues', usually educated slaves who taught the children.

But they did not bring about these children's birth; only the father did that. The Corinthians have been visited by Apollos and Cephas/Peter and they now have a number of local teachers. But these are mere 'pedagogues'. Only Paul is their father since he preached the gospel initially and, as it were, sowed the seed that bore fruit in their conversion to Christ.

Paul often uses the imagery of the father in relation to his 'children' in the Lord. Sometimes he is the father who brought them to birth (2 Cor. 6:13). At other times he is the father who 'betrothed' a daughter to a husband (2 Cor. 11:2) or a father who must provide for his children (2 Cor. 12:14-15). While there are serious problems about ministers being called 'father' (Matt. 23:9), the *role* of the missionary and pastor as 'father' is quite biblical.

On the basis of his role as father, 'therefore', let them 'become imitators of him' (v. 16). Paul frequently urges imitation of various aspects of his life and ministry (see on 11:1; cf. Phil. 3:17). Few statements of Paul have been so open to misunderstanding as these, since Paul easily appears to be boasting of being perfect. In reality, Paul called himself 'the worst of sinners' (1 Tim 1:12-16). No. Paul lived out certain key aspects of Christian behaviour and did so deliberately to use his own example as a teaching medium. Hard work to support himself in a culture of laziness is one example (2 Thess. 3:7,9). This is not arrogance but the true insight that living example is more powerful than mere words. What we *do* always speaks more loudly than what we say.

But what is it here that Paul wants the Corinthians to 'imitate' in him? I think Paul is pointing to his example of preaching Christ and him crucified as both the fundamental foundation as well as the superstructure of the church. That certainly has been his emphasis to this point in the letter as it has unfolded (see on 1:17, 18, 23; 2:2). Closely connected is Paul's teaching on costly discipleship as set out in his own example just given (vv. 11-14). This was not spelled out to 'shame' but to 'warn' and, as in verse 16, to provide an example for the Corinthians to follow.

For their greater understanding of his 'ways', which they appear to have forgotten, Paul is sending his 'much loved child', the 'faithful' Timothy to visit them (v. 17; 16:10-11). He will remind them of Paul's 'ways', that is, of preaching and living

'Christ crucified' for their imitation. For these 'ways' are what Paul teaches everywhere in the network of Gentile churches in Galatia, Macedonia, Achaia and Asia. He is not pressing on them things different from teachings he expects to be followed in 'every church'.

Here is a reminder that 'core' beliefs and practices of Christians are to be the same everywhere. Styles of worship vary from culture to culture and from age to age, but not the things that really matter. This is the notion of the 'church catholic', first mooted by Bishop Ignatius of Antioch early in the second century. The word 'catholic' (*kath' 'holikē*, 'according to the whole') speaks of the need for Christians everywhere to conform their beliefs, values and actions to the scriptural revelation. This is what Paul is doing with the Corinthians.

5. A Coup d'Etat in Corinth? (4:18-21)

We come now to the climax of this section, which is also the climax of the entire letter to this point. The arrogant upstarts who have usurped Paul's position within the church now come into view more clearly than they have previously (see on 3:10, 17). He picks up from verse 6 a reference to those who are 'inflated', literally, 'puffed up'. Here he appears to be hinting at the unnamed teacher or teachers of 'wisdom' against whom, in effect, the whole letter to this moment has been addressed. These have risen up in the church, 'as if Paul were not intending to return to Corinth' (v. 18). Apparently they have said to themselves, 'Paul is not returning to Corinth. The church is ours. Now we can teach what we like'.

In short, it was hoped, by some at least, that the church in Corinth would no longer be a 'Pauline' church, that their church would be taken out of his network of churches. In my view this is '*the* Corinthian error'. I say 'is' rather than 'was' since it is very common today. It is the error of rejecting Paul's authority as an apostle to direct the faith and behaviour of the churches. The Corinthians had a faulty grasp on many things, for example, their compromise with pagan sexuality and idolatry (5, 8-10), their love of law courts (6), their crass individualism (1, 12-14), and their disbelief in the coming resurrection of the dead (15). But these were just symptoms of a deeper illness, a refusal to submit to the authority of the apostle to the Gentiles.

This is also very common today. Many in the churches look to the Gospels, but downgrade Paul, using only passages like the chapter on 'love' in 1 Corinthians chapter 13. The modern problem with Paul was the Corinthians' ancient problem with Paul, that is, his directness of teaching about being a Christian in a pagan environment, which ours in the developed world has become. This is a failure to grasp the differing functions of a Gospel as opposed to a Letter. A Gospel has a narrow goal, to inform readers about Jesus, his life and the teachings he gave in the context of Galilee and Judaea, and to call for repentance and faith. The Letters of the New Testament, however, address a breadth of day-to-day issues in the churches, including the churches of the Gentiles where different problems were encountered from those in the Jewish churches. By their nature the Gospels, as biographies of Jesus set in a Jewish context, simply do not address issues with the specific directness of Paul's Letters which were addressed to readers in a world of rampant idolatry and sexuality. But we must be in no doubt that the writers of the Gospels would have had exactly the same views as Paul on matters where his views are objected to.

But the usurpers in Corinth will have no comfort. Paul is planning to return to Corinth in the near future (v. 19; see on 16:3-7), and for an extended visit. In the meantime Paul is sending Timothy sometime in the near future. These troublemakers are being put on notice that they must curtail their misbehaviour. Timothy will come and Paul himself will come soon.

As it happens, things turned out very differently. Timothy arrived sometime after the letter (16:10) but found a church in crisis. He returned to Ephesus and reported to Paul, who immediately came to Corinth, for what he called his 'painful' visit (2 Cor. 2:1). Even Paul himself could not bring the church to order, provoking their jibe that 'his letters are weighty and strong but his bodily presence is weak and his speech of no account' (2 Cor. 10:10, RSV). Indeed, so serious were the difficulties in the Corinthian church that it would take many months to set things in order. Upon his return to Ephesus he wrote a further letter, the so-called 'letter written in tears' (2 Cor. 2:2-4; 7:8-13), which has not survived. Titus (not Timothy) was the bearer of this letter to the Corinthians. Then, forced from Ephesus by the silversmiths' riot, Paul travelled to Troas, then on to Macedonia where eventually he was reunited with Titus and, based on his latest reports, wrote our Second Corinthians (2 Cor. 1:8-10; 2:12-13; 7:5-7; Acts 19:23-20:1). Paul's final visit to Corinth, lasting several months (Acts 20:2-3), would be needed before problems in this turbulent church were resolved.

When he adds, 'If the Lord wills' (v. 19b), he recognized that 'man proposes but God disposes', to quote an old proverb. Here Paul is acknowledging the sovereignty in and over history of the 'Lord', that is, the Lord Jesus Christ. Paul quite appropriately made plans, as we all need to do, but he understood clearly that such plans are subject to a greater 'plan' and a higher 'will' (cf. James 4:13-17).

Paul did not regard the unfolding of circumstances the Lord's 'will' necessarily as *guidance* and direction for what he *should* do. For example, when he left Ephesus and came to Troas 'for the gospel,' which apparently had longed to preach there, the 'Lord opened a door' for his ministry. Surely this was guidance from the Lord to stay in Troas and go through that 'door'. But instead he left for Macedonia to press on the sooner to Corinth (2 Cor. 2:12-13; 7:5-7). Thus while Paul submitted to the 'will' of the Lord shown in the unfolding circumstances of life, these were subject to the higher 'will' of the Lord revealed to him on the Damascus Road, namely, that he preach the gospel to the Gentiles, *regardless* of the circumstances. Impelled by *this*, Paul must go to Jerusalem because this would be, at last, the final stepping-stone to Rome, capital of the Gentile world. Even the warnings of a prophet about perils in Jerusalem did not deflect him from that journey (Rom. 15:31; Acts 20:22-23; 21:10-14).

At his prospective coming to Corinth he will 'know not the mere word but the power of these "puffed up" men', referring to the arrogant ones who have risen up in the church in recent times (v. 19c). Paul's verb tense (*pephusiōmenōn* perfect tense) indicates that there was a point at which these upstarts arose when they *began* to hold sway within the church, which they *continue* to do. This sounds as if some kind of a *coup d'etat* had recently occurred in the Corinthian church!

Paul gives his own 'wise' saying against these men. Literally it is, 'The kingdom of God is not *word* but *power*' (v. 20). This has been taken to mean wrongly that miracles ('power') is what the 'Kingdom of God' is about, not preaching ('word'). Thus preaching and evangelism is seen to be power-less, but miracles as powerful. But this fails to understand Paul's teaching in the context of the four chapters of which verses 18-21 are the climax. The 'word' that Paul speaks of is the 'wisdom of this world' spoken by these 'puffed up' usurpers in Corinth. What *is* 'powerful' is Paul's preaching of the 'word of the cross' (1:17). The message of 'Christ crucified' is 'the power of God' which 'saves' people (1:18, 22; cf. Rom. 1:16-17). Unlike the 'wisdom' preachers of Corinth, Paul will not preach the 'world's wisdom' precisely because this would empty 'the word of the cross of *its* power' (1:17). Paul is not even thinking about 'miracles' when he refers to 'power' but rather of the 'power' of 'Jesus Christ and him crucified', which is the only message he preached when present in Corinth (2:2). That was the foundation for the church and that, too, must be its superstructure, not something else. The modern fascination with miracles and consequent downgrading of the preaching of the cross is a misunderstanding of the teaching of the apostle Paul in the first four chapters of this letter.

So Paul concludes both the section, the chapter, but also the passage of thought begun at the opening words of the letter. 'What do you prefer?' 'You must choose', he tells them. 'Am I to come to exercise discipline among you ("with a stick", metaphorically speaking), or am I to come more congenially ("in love and a meek spirit")?' Paul may be alluding here to Jesus who was characterised by 'love' and who said 'I am meek...' (Matt. 11:29), but who took a whip to drive the traders from the Temple (John 2:15). Must Paul exchange the preferred manner of Christ for something else which he must do, as Jesus did, in the face of evil?

Few aspects of modern church life are so at odds with the apostles as our failure to exercise godly discipline in the churches, whether in regard to unrepented immorality or unrepented heresy. But that is the subject of the next chapter.

SOME QUESTIONS FOR PERSONAL REFLECTION:

1. Do you think one can be over-loyal to a minister? Are Paul's comments about 'pride' in one's favourite pastor still applicable?

2. What can we learn from Paul's own life about the 'cost of discipleship'?

3. Is there a danger today of downgrading Paul's authority in the churches and in the lives of individual Christians?

STUDY QUESTIONS:

1. Who are the 'us' that Paul is speaking about in verses 1-5?

2. What does Paul mean in his use of the word 'mystery', especially the 'mystery of God'?

3. Why does Paul call himself a 'steward'?

4. Why does Paul contrast his life as an Apostle with theirs, being one of some wisdom doctrine? What does Paul want to show them?

5. What does Paul desire the Corinthians to imitate from him?

6. Why is Paul so passionate about defending his 'birthing' (fathering) of the church at Corinth?

5

Celebrate the Festival!
(1 Cor. 5:1-13)

In his first four chapters Paul has followed an important pastoral strategy. He has attempted to re-connect with a congregation that was breaking free from his authority as its founding apostle. Hopefully having now secured that relationship Paul turns to address the next most urgent problem in Corinth. Broadly speaking, this is the subject of 'holiness' which he touched on in his opening sentences (see on 1:2). Here we may discern a parallel with the 'Holiness Code' for the people of Israel found in the teachings of Moses in Leviticus (especially chapters 18–21). By these 'holiness' teachings the Israelites were to separate themselves from the practices of Egypt which lay behind them and those of Canaan which lay ahead of them (Lev. 18:3-4).

The first aspect of that 'holiness' in the Levitical Code related to sexuality (see Lev. 18:6-30). This finds a close parallel in First Corinthians where, with the exception of his comments on litigation (6:1-8), Paul's teaching on sexual practices (chapters 5–7) forms the first part of his *Christian* 'Holiness Code'.

The first of Paul's *sexual* 'holiness' teachings relates to a man who had a sexual relationship with 'his father's wife'. Remarkably, one of the first matters in the Levitical 'Holiness Code' correspond with this (see Lev. 18:6-8). The people who were chosen and redeemed by God were to demonstrate the 'holiness' of their Lord by strict adherence to the sexual practices he had sanctioned and scrupulous avoidance of those he had condemned. The practices of the Egyptians and Canaanites were also found among the Gentiles of Corinth and other cities to which Paul brought the gospel of the Messiah, Jesus. Paul was to give them a 'Holiness Code' for the people who belonged to Christ by which they would demonstrate themselves to be the New Israel of God.

1. Sin in the Church (5:1-2)
Paul makes no effort to disguise his astonishment in his first words, 'It is *actually* reported', adding that the transgression 'is of *such a kind* that does not *even* occur among the Gentiles' (v. 1a,b). We assume that the 'report' came from Chloe's people (see on 1:11) or from Stephanas' party (see on 16:17).

What, then, was this sin? It was 'sexual immorality' (*porneia*), a word used for all sexual activity outside marriage. God created and creates humans as sexual beings, but as sexual opposites, as male and female. That sexuality is to find expression within the covenant 'boundary' of a lifelong commitment between a man and a woman in marriage. All other expressions of sexuality are called *porneia*, whether pre-marital intercourse, post-marital unfaithfulness, incest, same sex relationships or bestiality. Part of God's 'Holiness Code' sets out various sexual practices in which God's redeemed people must not engage (Lev. 18:6-30).

Paul, however, describes the *porneia* as 'of such a kind that does not even occur among the Gentiles'. This he amplifies as, literally, 'a certain man has his father's wife'. The present tense 'has' indicates an ongoing sexual union between them.

Paul's words which state the matter obliquely strike us as odd. Why not say directly, 'a certain man has his mother'? This would make the *porneia* an outright case of incest between a man and his mother, something condemned in Leviticus 18:7. Rather, he quotes exactly Leviticus 18:8 which prohibits sexual relationships with a 'father's wife'. Thus Paul is speaking of a man's ongoing sexual liaison with his stepmother. Most probably the man's father is still alive.

A father and a son cohabiting with the same woman is not only condemned in the Bible (see also Deut. 27:20) but was also deeply offensive in Graeco-Roman eyes, despite generally lax attitudes to sexual practices. In that culture, however, where 'shame' and 'loss of face' were to be avoided at all costs, a sexual liaison between a younger man and his stepmother would have been a source of humiliation for the father and given rise to scandal and notoriety for the newly established church in Corinth.

But this is not the only problem. Paul's use of the emphatic pronoun 'you' which he places at the beginning of a series of questions serves to express his utter amazement at the Corinthian behaviour (v. 2a): 'And *you* are puffed up?' The perfect tense he uses indicates that, when the Corinthians first heard of this sin they '*became* inflated with pride' and that they '*continue* to be'. There is *porneia* in their midst and this is their response! Their endorsement of this sin is as bad as the sin itself.

There is a further question (v. 2b), by which he indicates what their proper response should have been, mourning for the offender. 'And you did not rather, grieve?' he asks, adding 'that the one who has done this deed should be removed from your midst'.

Easily missed in these verses is the idea of evil '*among* them' (v. 1a) which is not even found '*among* the Gentiles' and which must be removed '*from the midst*' of the congregation. This echoes the language of Deuteronomy where Moses repeatedly calls for the 'purging' of evil 'from the midst' of Israel, God's redeemed people (see Deut. 22:22; cf. 17:7; 19:19; 21:21; 22:21, 24; 24:7). Clearly, the church is the 'new Israel' and like 'Israel according to the flesh' is to be purified by the removal of moral evil from within. As we shall now see (vv. 3-5), however, this would mean the removal of the offender from the church in contrast to Israel where the offender was often to be put to death.

2. Judgement of the Offender (5:3-5)
Though physically absent from them in Ephesus across the Aegean Sea, Paul was spiritually present in their gathering. Paul states what he has 'already' done. He has 'judged' the one who has done this thing (v. 3). Paul's purpose in declaring what he has 'already' done is to indicate to them what they must *immediately* do.

From this passage and also from Second Corinthians we are able to glean some idea of the disciplinary process in the

early church, which was probably based on synagogue practice, though with modifications. First, an assembly must be
held (v. 4a), whether at a regular meeting of the congregation
or one specially convened. Second, charges must be made by
at least two witnesses (2 Cor. 13:1; cf. Deut. 19:15). 'Due process' must be observed; persons are not to be dealt with on the
basis of hearsay or gossip. Third, a judgement must be made
according to the facts (v. 3a), based on the verdict of a 'majority' (2 Cor. 2:6). Fourth, the punishment of exclusion from the
assembly is executed, though not mechanically, as it were, but
'in the power of our Lord Jesus' (v. 4b). By this the offender is
'handed over to Satan', which is a matter of grief and mourning (v. 2b; 2 Cor. 12:21) and like a spiritual funeral for him.
Fifth, this act of consigning the offender to Satan's 'realm' has
a positive intention, 'the destruction of the flesh that his spirit
may be saved in the day of the Lord' (v. 5). This is no mere
act of excommunication. Perhaps by tasting the bitterness of
life outside the congregation the perpetrator will repent and
be saved. Sixth, the restoration of a penitent was the ultimate
purpose of the discipline (2 Cor. 2:7-10; Gal. 6:1-5).

Israel was to purge the evil from their midst (see above)
by putting to death the evil-doers. To my knowledge there
was no provision for forgiveness of the gross sexual or other
sins in question nor for the restoration of the offender at his
repentance. By contrast, discipline under the New Covenant is
redemptive in intent, consistent with the full and final revelation of God's salvation in the death and resurrection of Jesus,
which was only foreshadowed in the redemption of Israel from
Egypt. However, this does not imply any lack of seriousness
for discipline under the New Covenant. If unrepentant, the
wrongdoer must be excluded 'from the midst of' the congregation. Paul now expands on this in his analogy about removing
leaven from homes at the time of the Passover.

3. Christ our Passover has been Sacrificed (5:6-8)

Earlier Paul said they were 'puffed up' over this matter (v. 2).
Now another unsatisfactory facet of their behaviour emerges.
'Your *boasting* is not good', he adds (v. 6). Their misplaced pride
was also expressed in spoken *words*. Sadly, many churches
become 'parochial', and blind even, to wrong attitudes and

behaviour that is painfully obvious to everybody else except the members of those churches! Perhaps the 'wisdom' teachers in Corinth had somehow deluded the members of the church into thinking that 'wrong' was actually 'right'.

In verses 3-5 Paul's concern was for the salvation of the *offender*. Now in verses 6b-8 he turns to consider the welfare of the *church*. This he does by an appeal to a proverb about the potent effects of even a tiny quantity of leaven in a lump of dough (v. 6 b; cf. Gal. 5:9; Mark 8:15). Leaven consisted of yeast which produced ferment in dough, causing it to rise in the oven. Bread was the staple food and was frequently baked at home. The effects of leaven on a batch of dough, that is, its total change of size and texture, would have been quite evident to his readers. Paul's concern was that this evil 'in their midst' (vv. 1, 2) would corrupt the whole, just as one rotten apple, if left, quickly rots the whole barrel.

Paul's proverb on the evil effects of 'a little leaven' leads him to speak about the Feast of Unleavened Bread. Annually, at the time of the Passover, Jewish people would remove all leaven from their homes, eating only unleavened bread for the week following.

Jewish people continue this practice. Before the Passover anything containing leaven is locked away in a special sealed closet along with the utensils usually used for food preparation and consumption; a separate set of dishes is used during the week of Unleavened Bread. On Passover Eve there is a formal candlelight search for leaven using a spoon, a feather and a paper bag to collect any *Chametz* / 'forbidden food.' In the morning any such 'forbidden food' is burnt.

Though predominantly a Gentile church the Corinthians will have known from the Old Testament the origins of Jewish practice (Exod. 12:15). The climax of God's plagues on Pharaoh and the Egyptians was the death of each first-born son in the land, from which the Hebrews were spared on account of the blood of the lambs smeared on their door posts and lintels. For the next seven days the Hebrews were to eat only unleavened bread as an evidence of their readiness to quit Egypt without delay. From that time the Jews annually remembered the Lord's deliverance in the Feast of Unleavened Bread (Exod. 13:6-10).

Paul's words sound like a riddle:

Get rid of the old leaven
that you might become a new lump,
even as you are unleavened.

Why do they need to get rid of the leaven if they are unleavened? God's new day, his 'Day of Salvation', has come as the Corinthians welcomed the good news of Christ crucified and risen (cf. 2 Cor. 6:2). Thus, in God's eyes the congregation *is* unleavened already, deemed to be 'clean', righteous in Christ (see on 1:30) and a 'new creation' in Christ (2 Cor. 5:17). On the basis of God's gracious act towards them they are to 'become what they are', that is, free of the 'old leaven' of the sins of the former times before the gospel came to them. Paul told the Romans that since they had been 'buried' and 'raised' with Christ in their baptism they were not to allow sin to rule in their lives any longer (Rom. 6:4, 12).

And the reason and basis for ridding themselves of this old leaven?

For Christ our Passover *has been* sacrificed (v. 7c).

This is a remarkable statement. 'Christ' is here more a title than a name. God's anointed king, his 'Messiah' or 'Christ', when he was 'crucified' became 'our Passover'. No ordinary death was taking place when Jesus hung dying on the Roman execution pole, to which his accusation 'KING OF THE JEWS' was also nailed. He 'died for our sins' as Paul will say later (see on 15:3). Here, he calls him 'our Passover...sacrificed', an image evocative of the slaughtered lamb whose 'blood' smeared on the door posts sheltered the people inside when the angel of death passed over Egypt killing all firstborn of people and animals.

This understanding of Jesus' role as the Passover Lamb was first discerned by John the Baptist who, though the son of a priest serving in the Temple, saw in Jesus 'the lamb of God' who would 'bear the sin of the world' (John 1:29), and whose sacrifice would supersede the sacrifices for sins in the Temple of God. John Zebedee, a follower of the Baptist before he followed Jesus, most likely was one of the two disciples of the Baptist who heard his testimony to Jesus as the 'lamb of God'

(John 1:35-40). Later, as an exiled prophet on Patmos Island, John 'saw' Jesus as the 'lion of the tribe of Judah', that is, as the Christ, the one who was the 'lamb slain', whose 'blood purchased men for God' (Rev. 5:6, 9).

Peter, too, was deeply aware of the tradition that Jesus was the Passover Lamb. You are 'redeemed', he told his readers, with the 'precious blood of a lamb, without spot, blemish or defect' (1 Pet. 1:19).

Here, then, is a central teaching about Christ's sacrifice, originating with John the Baptist, affirmed by Jesus who died to fulfil its meaning, and repeated by the apostles Paul, John and Peter. It was anticipated in the original historical Passover in Egypt and made a subject of prophecy by Isaiah (Is. 53:7). Believers need to know that their sins have been 'covered' by the 'blood' of Jesus the Christ, the lamb of God, and that as a result they will not be subject to the wrath of God on the Day of his Judgement.

Because the Passover lamb, Christ, has been sacrificed his people are to 'keep the feast', that is, 'of unleavened bread' (v. 8). This is an image for the radical new style of behaviour to be followed by the people of the Messiah, not just for seven days annually, but for every day, permanently, from the time of Christ's sacrifice onwards. The 'leaven' of the 'old' life, that is, of 'malice and evil', must find no place 'in the midst' of the congregation of Christ's people. Rather, the people are always to be 'bread made without leaven', pure wheaten dough, as it were, characterised by 'sincerity and truth'.

This is very pointed in relation to the Corinthians' toleration of, even their pride in, gross evil 'in their midst'. They, and all congregations since, are called to be assemblies free of known and gross sin.

4. The 'Previous Letter' (5:9-10)
This is not the first occasion Paul has written to the Corinthians on the subject of 'sexual immorality'. In an earlier letter, lost to us, Paul had written on the same matter, calling for them not to 'mix with' the sexually immoral (v. 9). Apparently the Corinthians, or some of them, had over-friendly social associations with those who were actively and consistently immoral.

Although we do not know the details, the Corinthians (or a group among them) took Paul to mean some kind of total withdrawal from society, from 'the sexually immoral *of this world*' (v. 10). To that group Paul adds others: 'extortioners, robbers, idolaters'. These four offenders have two things in common. Their behaviour is evil and it is open. Paul is not speaking here of secret sins done in private, nor of wrong attitudes, but of active breaches of the Ten Commandments which are unambiguous and whose occurrence is public and beyond dispute. With perhaps a touch of wry humour Paul observes that not to 'mix' with such people must mean the believer must actually 'leave the world'. There was no shortage of these people in free-wheeling Corinth.

This 'throwaway' comment is extremely important. Paul, though a Jew from Tarsus of Cilicia in the Diaspora, spent his teens and twenties in Jerusalem. Here he belonged to the sect of the Pharisees, who separated themselves from 'the people of the land', whom the Pharisees despised for their ignorance of God's Law (John 7:49). Even stricter were the Essenes who lived in communes on the edge of major towns and cities, including Jerusalem. The Essenes declined to attend the Temple and they followed their own religious calendar which was different from that followed by the High Priest of the Temple. One Essene group, the community at Qumran near the Dead Sea, were celibate and had withdrawn totally from Jewish society.

Paul's comment shows that he no longer thought like a Pharisee and that his attitude towards the wider community, even in the Gentile world, was quite unlike the Essenes. Indeed, we know that Paul numbered among his friends those who were unbelievers, including among the 'Asiarchs', the highest civic officials in the province of Asia. The public duties of these officials included public worship of the gods and the offering of sacrifices in the temples. Yet several of these men were such good friends of Paul that they effectively saved his life in Ephesus (Acts 19:31).

Paul's brief remark and his example speak eloquently against the understandable inclination to remove oneself from the wickedness and corruption of society into some kind of separatist Christian enclave. Paul does not in any way encourage such an attitude *even in Corinth*; in fact his words discourage it. This is the more remarkable in the light of Paul's background as a Pharisee and zealot (Gal. 1:13; Phil. 3: 5-6;

Acts 22:3). Although the Pharisees did not withdraw physically from society as the Essenes did, especially the celibates at Qumran, yet they despised the people in general for their laxity in moral and religious matters (John 7:49). Paul's attitude has undergone a considerable softening towards the 'sinners' in the wider community, though without any lowering of standards for the church.

5. Drive out the Wicked Man (5:11-13)

Paul now clarifies their misunderstanding. He tells them what he did mean then and how they are to act now. Critical here are his words, 'one who is *called a brother* [or sister' the Greek *adelphos* includes both]. It is the erring fellow-Christian, the fellow-member of the family of God in the congregation, with whom the people are 'not to mix' (v. 11). Who is this person from whom other members must separate themselves? He is a *known* brother but one who is *known* to be a 'sexually immoral' person, an 'extortioner', an 'idolater', a 'user of violent language', a 'drunkard', or a 'robber'. To those mentioned in verse 10 Paul has added, by way of example, the 'user of violent language' the 'drunkard' and the 'rapist'.[1] But all such practices are unambiguously evil and unquestionably open.

'With such a one', Paul directs, 'do not eat'. Paul has in mind not only the Remembrance Meal instituted by Jesus within the congregation, but also meals at home. For all acts of 'eating together' are sacred, since the blessing of God in prayer and thanksgiving is invoked. How can believers have fellowship with God in prayer and benediction in the presence of a professed 'brother' when that man or woman is flagrantly living in open sin?

Of course, Paul is still addressing the grievous specific situation which had been reported to him (v. 1) concerning the 'sexually immoral man' who is a *known* 'brother'. That person, and others whose sins are a matter of public knowledge, have no place in the midst of the Lord's assembly. By remaining, the offender is under no moral or spiritual pressure to repent. Furthermore, that evil leaven will, in time, corrupt the whole community.

---

1   Greek: *harpax* could be kidnapper, pirate or rapist.

In the next chapter Paul will again mention those whose behaviour is morally offensive, along with others whose lifestyle is overtly evil (see on 6:9-11). There he will point to the radical conversion of numbers of such persons, who have been 'washed, sanctified and justified in the name of the Lord Jesus and in the Spirit of our God'. Thus Paul's present teaching is not merely 'moralistic' and 'disciplinary'. Rather, he is reflecting pastorally on the power of the 'name of the Lord Jesus' and 'the Spirit of our God' in conversion, and seeking in this practical way to reinforce and strengthen that great reality. What sense would it be for some to have been converted from an evil lifestyle to find others who continued unrepentant in that lifestyle within the congregation and sharing the emblems of Christ's body and blood in the Remembrance Meal?

At an international conference of church leaders the subject of same sex relationships was a major topic for resolution. Many advocated liberty in these practices, including some present who were themselves actively involved in homosexual acts. However, a number of former homosexuals visited the conference and pleaded that the biblical standards be maintained. Their conversion to Christ had delivered them from that lifestyle, but at considerable cost. For those present not to have insisted on the Word of God would have been to fail these brothers and sisters in Christ at a critical point. It must be said, however, that all such matters are deeply sensitive and call for understanding and pastoral love, including to those who remain enmeshed in a lifestyle that is outside the sanctions of the 'Holiness Code' of the Old Covenant, which Paul now adapts and translates for the Gentile world in view of the New Covenant in which he is a minister.

It should also be noted that the kinds of sins referred to by Paul have a tenacious power and are not easily left behind. Often they have become habitual, even a matter of addiction. Patience and skill are usually needed for those involved to break free. It rarely happens dramatically in a moment of time.

So Paul concludes this important teaching passage. It is not Paul's role, but God's, to judge those who are 'outside' in the world, including those whose public lifestyle is blatantly evil. But it is Paul's part and the Corinthians' and ours as believers to judge those who are 'inside', that is, the *known* brother and sister whose evil is explicit, extreme and overt. This is not a matter of being 'judgmental', but of merely being aware of the moral reality within our churches.

In times of tolerance it may take courage to discipline the known offender who professes to be a 'brother'. This holds true also for the person who articulates views which are flagrantly heretical, including those who hold high office in the church. Yet not to do so is actually a failure to truly love that person, since he or she will merely continue in ways that will bring spiritual ruin. Equally, not to do so also fails to love and care for the welfare of the church in its witness to the love and holiness of God, whose church it is.

SOME QUESTIONS FOR PERSONAL REFLECTION:

1. Why was a 'Holiness Code' needed for the people of Israel? Why did Paul teach Gentiles along these lines? Is such teaching still relevant?

2. Are there former members who have been excluded or who have themselves withdrawn whom you could profitably contact?

3. How should congregational discipline be applied today if the need arose in your church, and by whom would it be administered?

STUDY QUESTIONS:

1. What was the sexual immorality which Paul addresses? How shameful was it?

2. How does discipline under the old covenant differ from discipline under the new covenant?

3. What is Paul's concern about the effect of this man not being removed from their midst?

4. How does Paul's use of Christ as the 'Passover' illustrate what the church must do? What is the significance?

5. What are the two things which the 'four offenders' have in common? What does this mean?

6. What does it really mean to not exercise church discipline?

6

The Church, the World and God's Timetable
(1 Cor. 6:1-20)

1. 'Judge Yourselves' (6:1-8)

The media love to sensationalize scandal and quarrelling within the church. If a pastor has committed a serious moral offence, or a Bishop has sacked a vicar, or two church factions are in court squabbling over property, we can be confident this will attract more attention than would otherwise be the case. It is as if the world is saying, 'You people tell us what to believe and how to behave. But you don't practise what you preach'. The thinly veiled inference is that we Christians are hypocrites.

This passage and the previous one are closely connected. Both arise out of concern for the negative impact upon the watching world of inappropriate behaviour within the church. Because the 'sexual immorality' in the previous passage was not found '*even* among the Gentiles' (5:1), it must be a matter of scandal in Corinth and beyond. In this passage Paul is concerned that a believer is taking public legal action against a fellow-believer. This, too, must bring notoriety and ill-odour upon the gospel in the Achaian capital.

In a sense this passage seems to be a digression away from the subject matter of chapters 5–7, namely, 'holiness' in sexual behaviour. Paul had signalled in the opening lines of his epistle (see on 1:2) that 'holiness' is to be a major theme in the letter.

Here, however, we see something of the subtlety of Paul's intellect. Near the end of his teaching on disciplining the 'immoral man' he introduced the idea of 'judging'. We who are in the church do not judge 'those outside'. 'God judges those who are outside' (5:13). Paul uses those words and this idea as a 'bridge' into his present apparent digression on the need for 'those who are within' the church to judge one another and not to go to 'those outside' in the wider community for the adjudication of cases between believers. Just as 'those who are within' are to 'judge' the 'immoral man' (by excluding him from membership 5:13), so, too, 'those who are within' are to judge one another where matters of litigation arise between members.

Paul expresses his indignation about their behaviour by no less than eight staccato-like questions.

1. Judgement by the 'Unrighteous' (6:1-4)

We are not told the reason for the dispute between one man and his fellow-Christian within the congregation at Corinth. No doubt the Corinthians knew exactly what Paul was talking about. Paul explodes, 'One of you even dares to take his neighbour to court' (v. 1). We feel the heat of his outrage in the question, 'And are you to be judged by "the unrighteous" and not by the saints?'

Is Paul denigrating the law-courts of Corinth by calling their judges 'the unrighteous'? Not at all. In fact, Paul owed his freedom to the 'righteous' decision of the Roman proconsul Gallio when accused before him in Corinth three years earlier (Acts 18:12-17). It is important to notice Paul's way of referring to 'those who are outside' as 'unrighteous' and 'unbelievers' (see v. 6) and to believers as 'the saints' (vv. 1,2) and 'brothers' (vv. 5, 6, 8). He is thinking of the coming age when those who do not belong to Christ will be revealed to be 'unrighteous' because their sins are unforgiven. By contrast, believers will be revealed to be 'saints' because, by the grace of God, they are just that God's 'holy ones'. In God's sight they are 'righteous' through belonging to their sacrificed Passover lamb, Christ crucified, 'in' whom they have the forgiveness of sins (see on 1:30; 5:7; 15:3). In the second sentence of the letter Paul pointedly stated that they were 'sanctified in Christ Jesus and called to be saints'. But they are meant to translate their righteous standing 'in Christ' into righteousness in the daily realities of life. Let them live out in practical matters the 'holiness' or 'sanctity' they enjoy in the sight of God, including the resolution of conflicts within their community of faith.

So Paul peppers these 'saints' with a second question, 'Do you not know that the saints will judge the world?' (v. 2a). His words, 'Do you not know?' which occur no less than five times in this chapter are a rebuke. As part of their instruction in the basics of the faith they had been taught from Daniel 7:22[1] that 'judgement was given to the saints of the Most High' (see also Luke 22:30; Rev. 3:21; 20:4). At the end of the present age the people of the Messiah who have proved faithful to him will sit with their King as judges of 'the world' and of 'angels' (vv. 2 and 3). So Paul asks, 'Why do you not "know" this?'

In passing, we must notice Paul's way of speaking of 'the world'. He does not mean the 'physical' world in which we live, as created by God and declared to be *'good...very* good' (Gen. 1:10, 31). Rather, it is a 'people' composed of 'those whom God in company with his 'saints' will judge at the end of the age (5:12, 13). Paul means us to understand that 'those outside' and their beliefs and values are what he means by 'the world'. From the Greek word for 'world' (*kosmos*) we derive our word 'cosmetic'. The 'world' in the New Testament is beautiful, but deceptively so and superficial, masking darkness and evil, even the demonic. John warns us:

> Do not love the world or anything in the world. If anyone loves the world, the love of the Father is not in that person. For everything in the world —the cravings of sin, the lust of eyes and the boasting of possessions and deeds —comes not from the Father but from the world. The world and its desires pass away, but whoever does the will of God lives forever (1 John 2:15-17).

So understood, 'the world' is shallow and transient, but dangerously seductive. It was then and it remains so now.

Paul now re-states his question, but as a premise which is followed by a question that gets to the heart of the current

---

1   The Greek translation of Daniel 7:22. Paul and most NT writers quote from Greek translations of the Hebrew OT, the best known of which was the Septuagint or LXX. According to legend seventy scholars in Alexandria about two hundred years BC were commissioned to make this translation. Since Greek was at that time the universal language the Septuagint became, in effect, the OT for the early church.

pastoral problem (v. 2b). 'If the world is to be judged by you', he says, 'are you not fit to organize the smallest tribunal?' There is a touch of irony here. They will be law-lords in the greatest legal act imaginable, the judgement of the world no less, yet are they not capable of acting as justices of the peace in a tiny backstreet courtroom?

Another question follows, introduced with a rebuke and expressed with incredulity (v. 3). 'Do you not know that we will judge angels, to say nothing of everyday matters?' Once more there is a huge contrast. The saints will not only judge fallen angels like Satan himself but also the smallest act of shoplifting in the market place. What a range of judging the saints will be doing! Perhaps Paul is hinting that putting their minds to adjudicating their small local matter will equip them for the great task that lies ahead at the end of the ages. But this means they must not shirk their present duty.

Now follows a question that clinches the matter (v. 4). 'If you have tribunals for these everyday problems, as indeed you do, why do you appoint as judges those who are of no account in the church?' The grammar (*men oun* 'Indeed, therefore …') is particularly strong and points to the existence of such tribunals in the churches to deal with domestic matters as, for example, the disciplining of the 'immoral man' in the previous chapter. So why do they hand over the decision-making in this present dispute to judges who are 'outside', who belong to 'the world' and who have no standing *inside* the church?

Paul can barely conceal his amazement at their behaviour.

It must not be thought that this problem occurred only in Corinth in those distant times. Far from it! Disputes still occur between Christians. Sadly, these are sometimes taken to the secular courts. This may be necessary as a last resort where a fundamental matter of justice is involved. Paul's words are not to be taken as a mandate to sweep injustice under the carpet, nor do they represent an absolute prohibition against court action by believers against fellow-Christians. But there is much to lose when disputes are taken into the public arena. Apart from the high costs, an intensification of bitter feeling between the parties and the reality that if one will win then the other will lose, there is also the accompanying notoriety the media like to magnify. Far better in every way for the dispute to be settled by some process of mediation beforehand. Thankfully, there are today skilled Christian mediators who serve the Christian community. Their services should be sought before the matter is taken to the courts.

2. Brother Judging Brother (6:5-8)
In those times 'shame' (or being 'dishonoured') was unendurable, as is 'loss of face' in some cultures today. Paul does not lightly impose 'shame'. In only one other place in all his writings, which is in this letter, does he do so (see on 15:34). Yet he writes, 'I say this to shame you' (v. 5a; see also 15:34). Paul's words should not be treated as a blueprint for us to 'shame' others. Paul and the Corinthians lived in a different culture. Nor do we know the context behind these words. Yet what he says must underline the seriousness of their inaction in this matter. An act of injustice has occurred among them. Not only have they failed to bring a just settlement, they have allowed the dispute to go to the public courts.

A further incredulous question follows, 'Has it come to this, that there is not even one wise man among you who is able to arbitrate between one fellow-Christian and another?' (v. 5b). Paul is amazed. But there is also heavy irony in the word 'wise'. 'Wisdom' was their great boast, for which Paul rebukes them throughout the first four chapters. Yet there is not even one among them 'wise' enough for this present task!

Another question follows, which is more an exclamation, 'But brother goes to court with brother, and this before unbelievers (v. 6)?' Here are two evils. One is that between 'brothers', men who trust in the same Lord, who belong to the same Father, who are indwelt by the same Spirit and who are destined for the same eternal kingdom between *these* litigation has erupted! The other is that *this* dreadful thing has occurred in front of those who are 'unbelievers', 'lost' people to whom the gospel is yet to be presented. Paul is saying to these litigants, 'Your very presence in the court is a categorical denial of all that you profess and is unhelpful in the extreme!'

3. Two Communities and Two Ages
Paul's words tell us of two related realities that we easily forget or perhaps have never learned. One is that believers belong at

the same time to two communities, the 'church' and the 'world'. The other is that the 'saints' are to judge themselves *now* and only to judge the world *then*.

The 'church' is an assembly of 'holy ones' drawn together by the gospel of Christ crucified and risen. The 'world' is a 'fallen' community which either does not know the gospel or which has turned its back on it. Paul made it clear that God's 'holy ones' are not to withdraw physically from the 'unrighteous' (see on 5:9-13). Nor are the 'saints' to pass judgement on the people of the world until the Last Day.

Rather, the people of the faith community at this present time are to express and preserve among themselves the moral purity which by grace they enjoy 'in Christ'. To that end they will discern known and gross evil in their midst and, if necessary, 'drive out' the perpetrators (see on 5:13). Furthermore, where there is dispute among them they are to seek resolution of the conflict among themselves without recourse to those outside in the public courts (vv. 1-8).

Thus Paul places great emphasis on the moral and spiritual quality of their life together as the assembly of God's 'holy ones'. By contrast, Paul does not attempt to set right the evils within the secular community of Achaia nor does he exhort the Corinthian Christians to do so. God's standards are quite clear and the means of expressing those standards are straightforward, namely, by pastoral teaching and, where necessary, prudent discipline of notorious evildoers. But believers are not able to create 'holiness' in the 'world', nor are they called upon to do so.

I do not think Christians have always struck the right balance in regard to these communities and this timetable. Sometimes we have appeared to express condemnation of the community, especially in sexual matters, easily giving the impression that our chief vocation is to be arbiters of morality, and a rather narrow morality at that! In reality, our chief calling is to bear witness to the gospel of Christ to the world and God's great power to redeem the lost. In recent times some church leaders have taken it upon themselves to dictate social and economic policy to governments while at the same time showing little concern for known evil within the church, for example, adultery among professed Christians. This is the exact reverse of Paul's view of the two communities and a failure to grasp God's timetable.

God and his saints will judge the 'world' *then*, but his people must not tolerate evil within the 'church' *now*.

Of course, where there is grave injustice or evil in the wider community Christians should speak as, generally throughout history, they have not failed to do. But we should do so in the context of practical and compassionate ministry in the face of such injustice. For example, persuading a woman not to terminate a pregnancy for, let us say, financial reasons needs to be accompanied by the provision of practical support for her. The robust purity of the church, accompanied by prophetic speech against evil and practical and compassionate action, serves as 'salt' and 'light' to the world. Where this has occurred the presence of Christians has historically proved to be God's blessing to those societies.

2. The Kingdom of God and the 'Unrighteous' (6:9-11)

Paul has been speaking about the 'unrighteous' and the 'world' (6:1, 2) in relationship to the present age as part of God's timetable. At the end of history God and his 'holy ones' will judge those who are 'outside' (5:12, 13). But until that moment comes Christians are not to withdraw from the 'unrighteous' of the world, nor be their judges (5:10). On the other hand, believers are not to 'eat with' the professed 'brother' or 'sister' who engages in 'unrighteous' behaviour (5:9-11), but to expel the offender from the community of faith.

When the moment of divine judgement comes, what will be the destiny of the 'unrighteous'? Paul now turns to address this question and in so doing brings his readers back to the issue of the unrepentant 'immoral man' from the 'church' who must be sent back into the 'world' outside.

The 'shape' of this short passage is of particular interest. Verses 9 and 10 are what is called an 'inclusio'[22] because they begin and end with identical words, 'will not inherit the kingdom of God'. Within this 'inclusio' is a list of people who 'will not inherit the kingdom of God'. Then by way of sharp contrast in verse 11 Paul says, 'and such *were* some of you, *but...but...but...*'

---

2   An 'inclusio' is created by using words at the beginning and end which 'encircle' a passage. Paul often uses this so-called 'ring' composition (see e.g. 2 Cor. 2:14-17 and 4:1-6). In a very clear way it marks off a passage as a unit.

His threefold 'but' (*alla*[3]) could not be more emphatic. In short, in verses 9-11 Paul is starkly contrasting the 'unrighteous'/ the 'world' with the 'assembly of God's holy ones', on one hand, and the present and the coming ages, on the other.

This brief passage prompts a number of questions.

The first is, what is the 'kingdom of God'? Jesus' own preaching in summary form was his announcement of the coming of the 'kingdom of God' (see e.g., Mark 1:14-15). What Jesus meant by this was God's active and righteous rule overturning Satan's evil domination in the world. God's 'kingdom' became a reality when Jesus died for our sins and was raised bodily within three days. God brings his 'kingdom' to people by his 'word', the gospel about his Son, Jesus the Christ. The 'kingdom of God' is invisible in this present age, yet it is able to be glimpsed when people are brought by the 'word' of God from the dark dominion of Satan in the 'world' into the bright assembly of God's 'holy ones'. The 'kingdom of God' will be visible permanently and perfectly in the coming age in the 'lost' who have been redeemed and gathered by the 'word' of God proclaimed among the nations throughout history. Twice Paul uses the word 'inherit', reminding us that the 'kingdom' is God's gift to be humbly received; it cannot be earned or achieved by human merit.

Secondly, what are these activities which exclude people from the 'kingdom of God'? Significantly, the list is similar to that given earlier (5:10-11), but with a few additions. Common to both lists are the 'sexually immoral', the 'extortioners', the 'robbers', the 'idolaters', the 'users of violent language', the 'drunkards' and the 'rapists'. As noted earlier, these activities are both public and unquestionably evil by the standards revealed in the Scriptures.

To that list, however, Paul now adds three other groups of people, each of which belongs to the broad category of 'sexual immorality' (*porneia*). First, there are 'adulterers', those men or women who break the sacred bonds of marriage by sexual intercourse with another person. Second, Paul mentions those who engage in homosexual activities as 'receptors' or ones 'sodomized'. The Greek word *malakos* means 'soft' and may

---

3   *Alla* is the strongest Greek word available to convey the idea of contrast.

refer to boys or youths who assumed a passive or 'feminine' sexual role in the homosexual act. These are closely connected with the third category, the *arsenokoitoi*, a word that combines 'sexual intercourse' (*koitē*) and 'man' (*arsēn*) meaning, literally, 'men who have sexual intercourse with men'. The bracketing of *malakoi* with *arsenokoitoi* is deliberate and shows emphatically the apostle's negative attitude towards the homosexual act.

Homosexual acts were quite common in Graeco-Roman culture,[4] as well as in the world of Egypt from which the Hebrews had been rescued and in Canaan for which they were headed. The 'Holiness Code' God gave to Israel at Mt Sinai made clear his views on such activities:

> Do not lie with a man as one lies with a woman;
> that is detestable (Lev. 18:22).

In the fullness of time God made open a way for Gentiles to be included in his covenant people through his Messiah crucified and risen. But just as God had a 'Holiness Code' for Israel, so too through the Apostle Paul God has a 'Holiness Code' for his 'New Israel'. This emerges from this passage, as well as from others written by Paul. Thus in this passage homosexual acts are a barrier to inheriting 'the kingdom of God' (v. 9); elsewhere Paul says they are a perversion of 'nature' (Rom. 1:26-27) and an example of lawbreaking (1 Tim. 1:10). But it must be emphasised that Paul is speaking about homosexual *acts* for which those involved can and must take responsibility and not a homosexual *inclination* which may be due to upbringing or circumstances.

The biblical norm for sexual expression is clear. It is *either* abstinent singleness *or* heterosexual marriage. This is precisely the teaching of Jesus the Christ (see Matt. 19:3-12) which the apostle to the Gentiles followed closely (see 7:1-40). Anything else is *porneia* / 'fornication', and is not sanctioned by God. Yet, as we will notice, sexual practices easily become addictive, not least if reinforced by one's involvement in a powerful sexual sub-culture, whether heterosexual or homosexual. Those who

---

4   Philo, a Jew from Alexandria, and a contemporary of Paul, writes of 'these hybrids of man and woman continually strutting through the thick of the market, heading the procession of the feasts ...' (*Special Laws* 3:42).

seek to break free face significant problems. There will be false starts and lapses. Pastors and helpers need skill, compassion and patience. But the Bible teaches, and experience confirms, that God's power is greater than our problems.

Paul's list is explicit and detailed. He warns, 'Don't be led astray' (v. 9), suggesting that among them were those who saw no problem with these activities. They have counterparts today, including some church leaders who sanction behaviour condemned by the Bible. Yet the 'Holiness Code' as echoed here by Paul remains as a permanent standard for the 'New Israel'. Those who practise these things will find no place in the kingdom of God.

This raises a third question. Not every person 'out there' in the 'world' was (or is) sexually immoral, or an extortioner, or a thief. So we ask: Is Paul implying that unbelievers, citizens of the 'world', who do not engage in the activities as listed will be found in the kingdom of God? Will good people who are unbelievers be found in heaven? Paul and other New Testament writers are quite clear that only those who are 'in Christ' will inherit the kingdom of God (see on 1:30). Only in those people is God's kingdom active through their submission to Jesus Christ as Lord and their trust in him as saviour. A moral lifestyle, though admirable, in itself is no evidence of membership of the kingdom of God.

Furthermore, the salutary impact of Christians over many centuries brought many 'kingdom' qualities to Britain, to take one example. Under the impulse of Christian agitation slavery was abolished, child labour banned, and workers' rights secured through trade unions. However, as the tide of Christian faith began to recede, many of the evils of the 'world' have reappeared in the past few decades. The wicked activities in Greece and Rome listed by Paul are now commonplace in nations which until recently were markedly Christian, along with the new problems like spreading drug abuse.

Tourists who visit the remains of classical civilizations may have the impression of ancient societies marked by order and beauty. However, the moral and spiritual darkness of white marbled Corinth is easily missed. The city had 'many gods and many lords' (see on 8:5), with numerous temples and shrines to a bewildering array of 'gods' and 'lords' in the public square for Artemis, Dionysius, Fortune, Apollo, Poseidon, Aphrodite, Hermes, Zeus, Athena and Octavia the sister of Augustus.[5] The province of Achaia was one of a network of provinces belonging to the world super-power, Rome, dominated by the Emperor of the day. The system of government was operated by patronage and was riddled with corruption from top to bottom. In this city Paul would have addressed people who regularly visited the temples, worshipped the gods and had sexual intercourse with temple prostitutes, both male and female. Corinth belonged to a culture which sanctioned bloody combats in the arena, exposed unwanted children to the elements, and bought and sold men, women and children as slaves. In short, that culture was fallen and corrupt and was characterized by sexual immorality, idolatry, adultery, homosexuality and theft, even though not every member joined in these activities. It may be asked if modern cultures are any different in principle?

A fourth question is prompted by Paul's words, 'And such *were* some of you' (v. 11). The question is: How were these Corinthian evil-doers redeemed from such behaviour? Some present members of the 'assembly of holy ones' had previously been sexually immoral, idolaters, adulterers, homosexuals, thieves, extortioners, drunkards, 'louts' and rapists. The word 'were' is the imperfect tense of the verb 'to be', indicating their past, continuing pattern of behaviour. Presumably these people were Gentiles; Jews would not have practised these things.

By contrast, Paul now uses three verbs in a verb tense (aorist) which indicates a single event, each introduced by the very strong word 'but'. '*But* you were wash*ed*. *But* you were sanctif*ied*. *But* you were justif*ied*'. These words are a window through which we glimpse Paul's mission work in Corinth. First, he came and preached Christ crucified and risen (see on 15:1-4; cf. 2:1-5). Then, as various people accepted the 'word of God' they were given the assurance that they were now 'in Christ' (see on 1:30), that is, they 'belonged to Christ' (see on 15:23) and on *his* account had been 'washed' (forgiven), 'sanctified' (set apart for God), and 'justified' (declared righteous by God). These assurances were probably given or repeated at

---

5   Pausanias, *Description of Greece* 2.6-7. Pausanias was a travel writer who visited
     Corinth some time after Paul.

their baptism when they were brought into the 'assembly of the holy ones' (see on 12:12).

Critical to Paul's words in verse 11 is the small word 'in', which signifies the means or instrument by which believers are 'washed', 'sanctified', 'justified'. Paul is reflecting on their public confession that 'Jesus is Lord' (see on 12:3), probably at the time of baptism, a confession made possible only 'in (by means of) the Holy Spirit' (12:3). At that confession and baptism the convert was pronounced 'washed', 'sanctified', 'justified', each a great act of deliverance by God, made possible only by 'the name of the Lord Jesus Christ' and 'the Spirit of our God'. 'In' also appears when Paul reminds them, '*In* one Spirit we were all baptized into one body...' (see on 12:13). This was not only the point of entry to the assembly of 'holy ones' but also into the coming age, by anticipation, as it were.

Fifthly, if such is the power of Christian conversion, how did the adulterer of 5:1 'fall' into his sin? Possibly his conversion was not genuine. In any case, however, conversion brings liberty 'not to sin', not absolute 'freedom from sin'. The painful reality is that even those with the Spirit of God are able to fall back into sin. The 'flesh' remains a potent force within the believer's life (see Gal. 5:16-26). For this reason this and other letters of the New Testament repeatedly address converts, now teaching, now reminding, now rebuking, now encouraging. Christians today, no less than the Corinthians then, need to listen to the voice of God through the Spirit-borne words of his apostle, Paul. Yet, though temptations from the 'world' around us are strong, our faithful God promises a way of escape from them when they come (see on 10:13).

The processes of inquiry, discipline and expulsion evident from the case of the 'sexually immoral' man of chapter 5 were in place to preserve the purity of the congregation, but also to reinforce in converts the reality of the great moment when they had been 'rescued from the dominion of darkness and brought into the kingdom of the Son he loves' (Col. 1:13). To those ends Paul and the apostles upheld the highest standards of holiness. This is clear from Paul's 'Holiness Code' found in chapters 5–7. It is equally clear that various people in these churches 'fell' prey to moral temptation (cf. Gal. 6:1-5). Paul, however, did not weaken the demands of holiness expected of the covenant people. Rather, those who succumbed to temptation were subject to discipline, but with a view to the merciful rehabilitation of the offender and his restoration to the assembly (Gal. 6:1-5; 2 Cor. 2:5-11). Today, given modern knowledge, this may also mean extensive pastoral and even clinical counselling of those who have fallen into sin. But the pressure to lower moral and spiritual standards evident in the passage following was resisted by the apostle Paul, as it is to be resisted today.

3. Pressure to Lower Moral Standards (6:12-20)

The subject of 'sexual immorality' and the purity of the 'assembly of holy ones' begun in chapter 5 continues. There the issue related to a member who was living adulterously with his stepmother, which other members wrongly believed the man was at liberty to do.

In the verses following Paul is addressing another difficult situation, where a member or members of the assembly were visiting prostitutes (v. 16). Almost certainly these were not prostitutes in brothels as in modern societies, but prostitutes in the various pagan temples in Corinth. Temple cults and sacred prostitution went together in the Graeco-Roman world. This immorality, too, appears to have been supported and encouraged within the sacred assembly of believers in Corinth by expressions of false wisdom (vv. 12-13). But, says Paul, the body of the Christian is to be joined to the risen Lord, not to a prostitute (vv. 14-17). That body is a sacred temple for God's Spirit and it has been 'purchased' by God at the highest price imaginable, the death of the Son of God (vv. 18-20).

1. The Voice of False-Wisdom (6:12-13)

On what basis were members of the church in Corinth encouraging sexual activities with (temple) prostitutes? They were doing so by teachings (which Paul quotes back to them):

'All things are lawful'

and

'Food for the stomach
and the stomach for food.'

Perhaps these are examples of 'words of wisdom' from the teacher or teachers of wisdom against whom Paul spoke earlier (see on 3:10,17). Other possible examples of such 'words' are found later (see on 8:4; 10:23).

In my opinion these sayings were teachings of Jesus which somehow had found their way to Corinth where they had been twisted to sanction immoral behaviour. The word 'lawful' often arose in the Pharisees' debates with Jesus. For example, Jesus taught that it was 'lawful' to heal on the Sabbath (Mark 3:4). Another debate was over their demand for ritual washing of hands before eating. Jesus taught that such washing was unnecessary since impurity flowed from the human heart not from food that might have been touched by sinful hands. Thus Jesus declared all foods 'clean' and fit for 'the stomach' (Mark 7:19). Did (some of) the Corinthians twist Jesus' teaching that Sabbath healing and unwashed eating was 'lawful' into '*all things* are lawful'? Further, did they extend Jesus' permission to eat all things as permission for sexual freedom as well as table freedom?

Paul must correct these words of false wisdom (v. 12). First, he echoes their words 'All things are lawful' which he qualifies by, 'But all things are not helpful'. And the reason? Some 'things' have the power to bring us under their control, for example, sexual promiscuity. Next, he repeats their, 'Food for the stomach, etc'. adding, 'God will destroy both', that is, at the dawning of the coming age.

Now the apostle gives a word of true wisdom, 'The body is not for sexual immorality, but for the Lord and the Lord for the body' (v. 13). Here Paul takes the present tawdry situation in Corinth as an opportunity to lay down a principle of the gospel which is to guide us in all aspects of our existence. In all things the Christian is not to live in and for this age and its appetites as if this is all there will be. Rather, the believer is to be totally dedicated to the Lord and the age which is yet to come.

2. The Risen Lord and the Body (6:14-17)

Why is this so? It is because the Lord is the *risen* Lord and because we, his people, will also be raised (v. 14). The resurrection of Jesus is a fact of history as also is the resurrection of all, though it lies in the future. Indeed, his resurrection and ours are integrally connected, as Paul will say later (see on

15:23). God's resurrection harvest has begun with the raising of Christ, the 'first fruits'. At his coming the harvest will be completed with the resurrection of all his people. Thus the believer's body is destined for resurrection and, therefore, as it will be 'for the Lord' in the coming age, so it is also 'for the Lord' in the present age.

Paul's mention of the resurrection of Jesus is made in passing, as a matter of his own conviction, but also of theirs. Clearly he assumes the Corinthians are not in any doubt about the resurrection of Jesus as historically true (see on 15:12). This is a central plank in the raft of biblical faith. Detach it from other planks the incarnation, the atonement and the second advent and the whole raft sinks. No part of our faith is under greater threat at this time than the bodily resurrection of Jesus from the dead.

But the risen body of the Lord is spiritually connected on earth with the 'assembly of holy ones', which Paul actually calls 'Christ' (see on 12:12) or elsewhere, 'the body of Christ' (see on 12:27). The church is not only like a body, it *is* a body, Christ's body, and those who are part of it are 'his members'. Appealing to a known Christian teaching Paul asks (v. 15), 'Do you not know that your bodies are members of Christ?' 'Therefore', he asks further, 'shall I take the members of Christ and join them to a prostitute?' He replies in the strongest terms, 'Never!'

Again he asks a question, prefaced by 'Do you not know?' Clearly they should know that the man who is sexually joined to a prostitute is 'one flesh with her', as he illustrates from the text of Genesis 2:24 in relation to the sexual union of Adam and Eve. But such a 'one flesh' union with a prostitute is impossible to contemplate for the Christian since, 'He who is joined to the Lord is *one Spirit* with him'. The Father bestowed the Spirit on the Son at his baptism in the Jordan and at his ascension (Luke 3:22; Acts 2:33). The risen Lord now gives the same Spirit to his people, joining them to him as 'one Spirit'. In brief, whoever is 'one Spirit' with the risen Lord must not be 'one flesh' with a harlot.

3. Flee From Fornication (6:18-20)
So Paul immediately urges (v. 18), 'Flee from fornication', which in this context means sexual intercourse with prostitutes, most likely *temple* prostitutes. But in the broader passage begun at chapter 5 the word *porneia* means other kinds of

unlawful sexual expression mentioned, whether adultery or homosexuality, to which we may justly add pre-marital sex. There is a special quality in sexual sin. 'Every other sin', Paul observes, is 'outside the body'. The Corinthians are quite wrong. That 'the stomach is for food and food for the stomach' does not mean that 'genitals are for sex and sex is for genitals'. Having a stomach indeed points to the need to eat. But having sexual organs does not of itself imply the necessity for sexual gratification. Further, eating food does not establish a special bond with the eater. But it is otherwise between two people coupled in a sexual relationship. They are 'one flesh'. A bond is created in sexual intercourse.

As well, Paul teaches that the man or woman who fornicates 'sins against his or her own body' or person. This he establishes by another question introduced by, 'Do you not know?' What they do not know, but should know, in that one's 'body' is a 'temple of the Holy Spirit'. The 'body' is not merely flesh, organs and bones, but the total person including mind, memory, conscience and emotions. The 'body' of the Christian believer, so understood, is a sacred shrine indwelt by the Spirit of God. That 'body' is meant for union with the Lord, with whom each Christian is 'one Spirit'. To break that spiritual union with the risen Lord by fornicating is to sin against oneself, one's own 'body'. Furthermore, as he declared earlier, such fornicating barred one from 'inheriting the kingdom of God' (6:10-11).

In fact, Paul teaches that the 'body' is not actually theirs at all (v. 20). 'You are not your own', he says to our surprise. No. 'You have your body *from God.*' You don't own yourself. 'For', he writes, 'you were *bought* for a price' (also 7:23). You now belong to your purchaser. Slaves were sometimes set free after having saved enough money to purchase their liberty. Alternatively a benefactor could set them free. Sometimes this 'act of redemption' occurred in a pagan temple where the liberated slave took the name of the god. Those who through the gospel are 'in Christ' and who are 'one Spirit' with him have been 'washed' from the filth of moral stain, 'sanctified' or set apart as God's 'holy' person, and 'justified' or acquitted by God. Furthermore, they find that God 'breaks the power of cancelled sin' and that he 'sets the prisoner free' (cf. Rom. 6:17-18). The 'price' paid for their freedom from the penalty and the power of sin was unimaginably high, the sacrifice of the Messiah for their sins (see on 5:7; 1 Cor. 15:3).

Fornication joins two persons as 'one flesh', which means rupturing the 'one Spirit' relationship with the risen Lord. It means sinning against one's own body which has been purchased by God at the immeasurably high price, the sacrificial death of Jesus. Therefore, the believer is to 'glorify God' in the body by living in sexual purity.

The Corinthians are well warned, as are we, by the apostle's words, 'Flee from fornication'. Few forces in life prove to be as overwhelming as sexual arousal. This powerful fire is easily lit and very difficult to extinguish. Lack of self-discipline quickly leads to addiction so that sexual gratification becomes a 'prison'. Its destructive danger needs to be recognised ahead of times of temptations. We should take care not to expose our vulnerability by reading inappropriate literature, watching unsuitable videos or visiting the seductive sites on the world-wide net. Not only is our relationship with the Lord broken by fornication, but marriages are ruined and families destroyed. Paul had ample opportunity to observe the devastating effect of fornication. In urging, 'Flee from fornication', he is regarding it as a fierce forest fire. 'Turn from it and *run*', he says.

Some questions for personal reflection:

1. Paul is saying that we are responsible for 'holiness' and 'justice' within the churches, but not for the 'world'. Do you think we do or should follow his teachings in this?

2. Is tolerating low moral standards in the church a problem today?

3. What does it mean in practice that 'we do not own our bodies' but that God does?

Study questions:

1. Is Paul denigrating the law-courts of Corinth by calling their judges 'the unrighteous'?

2. What does Paul mean by his use of the word 'world'? Who are 'those outside'?

3. Why does Paul not want matters between believers taken to a public court?

4. What are the activities which exclude people from the kingdom of God?

5. Paul warns the church to not be 'led astray'. How were they being led astray?

6. How were the Corinthian believers 'pressured' into lowering their standards? How was this the current 'wisdom' which Paul takes issue with?

7
Marriage and Singleness
(1 Cor. 7:1-40)

This chapter, which is devoted to marriage and singleness, completes Paul's 'Holiness Code' begun in chapter 5. More immediately it follows directly from the preceding passage about 'fornication'. The 'body' of the Christian was made 'one Spirit' with the risen Lord at the moment of public confession and baptism. That 'body' is not to become 'one flesh' by fornication, by sexual intercourse outside marriage. The coming age began for the believer at the time of conversion. Although the present age drags on until the return of Christ, uppermost for Christians is that we live for the Lord and the coming age.

Clearly sexual holiness is important. As the apostle of the Messiah to the Nations Paul was deeply concerned that the Gentiles who were brought into the covenant people should understand and practise the will of God in this significant part of life. The people of the Nations, those who lived outside the covenant of God, were renowned for their sexual promiscuity and for frequent divorce.

Thus Paul begins by affirming the teaching of Genesis 1–3 and of Jesus that the sexual union of a man and a woman in marriage (vv. 1-5) is to be an exclusive, lifelong commitment (vv. 10-16). To be sure, Paul expresses personal preference for singleness, though he recognizes that not all share that 'gift' with him (vv. 6-9). This prompts him to emphasise that Christians should remain in the circumstances in which they were at the time of their conversion (vv. 17-24). But since the coming age is now close our priority should be to 'please the

Lord' which the single person finds easier than those who are married (vv. 29-35). During this chapter Paul also responds to questions from fathers who have arranged marriages for their daughters (vv. 25-28, 36-38). Finally, he gives advice to widows about remarriage (vv. 39-40).

In this chapter Paul begins to answer questions from a letter sent by the Corinthians (see vv. 1 and 25). Yet he has so arranged his letter that his replies fall within the block of teaching on sexual holiness which he began at 5:1. This chapter, in which Paul gives his positive teaching on sexuality, forms a fitting conclusion to the longer preceding passage in which Paul admonished the adulterer (5:1-8) and those fornicating with prostitutes (6:12-20). Those sections form the immediate context for his teaching on marriage in this chapter.

Although Paul's preference was for singleness, his teachings here and in other letters recognised that a majority of believers would be married. Throughout this chapter, however, Paul appears to be answering a group who held quite extreme and negative views about sexual relationships. Some of them were urging sexual abstinence within marriage (see on vv. 1, 3-5), others that they should withdraw altogether from their marriages with unbelievers (see on vv. 10-14). Who were these ascetically minded members of the Corinthian church? Here we face a problem. They are unlikely to have been Gentiles, who were noted for easy going attitudes to sexuality. Equally, identifying them with Jews creates problems since that race was noted for their hearty affirmation of sexual intercourse and for large families. One possibility is that they knew of and were influenced by the teachings of the Essene community of celibates at Qumran near the Dead Sea.

One of the skills in reading this letter is to recognise that Paul is responding to a real-life situation at that time, one moreover that is not clear to us at every point. We need to enter into his dialogue with the Corinthians as best we can and seek to discern the principles underlying Paul's words which we will then apply to our circumstances. The point is that Paul's words as they stand are not an exact blueprint nor a cut and dried legal code which we can neatly and unthinkingly follow. This is not in any way to diminish the authority of these words of Paul as bearing the will of God for us. But it does call for a careful and sympathetic reading of this text.

1. Let Each Have his Own Wife/Husband (7:1-5)

Paul's words, 'Now concerning the matters about which you wrote' (v. 1), signal that he now begins to answer the questions sent to him by members of the Corinthian church. His replies indicate two things about the questions. First, the interrogators were not simply seeking information but attempting to establish their point of view. As well, they were probably not at all representing the interests of the whole church, but their own sectional interests. In chapters 5 and 6 Paul has been responding to those Corinthians who saw no problems with *porneia*, 'sexual immorality'. Presumably these were Gentiles, well attuned to the free-wheeling sexual practices of a Graeco-Roman city like Corinth. By contrast, Paul's responses in this passage suggest that the questioners held ascetical opinions about sexual intercourse. Who were they? The context suggests that these were married women perhaps Jewish women who felt that the onset of the new age of the Messiah meant that the time had now passed for conceiving children or for sexual relationships altogether.

At once Paul concedes that '*it is good* for a man not to touch a woman', a reference to sexual intercourse. Rather, as he picks up the same words a few verses later, '*it is good* for the [unmarried and widows] to remain like [Paul]'; (for the identification of the 'unmarried', see on v. 8). The single person is not encumbered with complex marriage and family responsibilities but is free to 'please the Lord', a theme Paul will develop later in the chapter (vv. 32-35). Paul's sense is that ultimate 'good' relates to the Lord and the coming age of the Kingdom of God.

Ever the realist, however, he immediately adds, 'But ...' And it is a big 'but', namely, 'on account of porneia 'sexual immorality'. This *porneia* includes the current problems in the church in Corinth, a man's adultery with his stepmother (5:1) and men from the church resorting to prostitutes female and male in the local temples (6:15-16). Sexual appetite is powerful and sexual practices habit-forming. He speaks soon of people 'burning' with sexual passion (see on v. 9) and of not all having the 'gift' of singleness (see on v. 7).

Implicit is Paul's contrast between the coming age of the Kingdom of God and the present age in a fallen world. While the Kingdom of God and fellowship with the risen Lord is the ultimate reality for the Christian, the immediate and pressing reality in this age is God's call to sexual holiness in the face of sexual drive and sexual temptation in a culture which glorifies sexual 'freedom'. Thus Paul urges, 'Let each man have his own wife and each woman her own husband'. Remarkably for that male-dominated society Paul addresses equally the needs of the man and the woman.

In saying, 'Let each...have his own wife, let each have her own husband', he sees that relationship as *monogamous* and, as he declares later, *lifelong* (see on v. 39). Paul's teaching, which de-rived from Jesus, was in sharp contrast with the serial divorce/ remarriage cycle in the Graeco-Roman world or with Islam later where one man could have up to four wives at one time, any of whom he could divorce at will. Marriage is to be a sexually exclusive relationship between one man and one woman for the whole of their life together. The Lord's teaching on marriage has made an incomparable contribution to the welfare of women and children and the stability of families and therefore of those societies in which Christianity has taken root. We see the force of this when we consider the plight of women and children in non-Christian societies, but also of societies which used to be Christian. Formerly Christian societies are now like cut flow-ers whose beauty is fading fast because they are severed from their source of life, the teaching of Jesus and the Spirit of God.

It follows that a husband must 'render' to his wife 'what he owes her' and likewise the wife 'what she owes her' husband (v. 3). Paul uses the same word as in Jesus' direction to '*render* to Caesar the things that are Caesar's' (Mark 12:17). Paul is not speaking here of conjugal 'rights', from the viewpoint of de-mands of the recipient. Rather, he places the emphasis on the *giver's* responsibility to meet the sexual needs of the marriage partner. Sexual activity for the Christian is not to be centred in oneself but in the other. Paradoxically, though, the more this is for the pleasure of the other the greater the pleasure to the giver. Nonetheless, each partner needs to be sensitive to those seasons of life when having one's own needs met is not easy for the other. Where partners find difficulties in their sexual expression it should be a matter of loving discussion and tender understanding between them, perhaps with medical help sought.

This rests on a principle which Paul gives in very stark terms. 'The wife does not have authority over her body but the husband' and, 'Likewise, the husband does not have authority over his own body but the wife' (v. 4). Here is a statement which must be given in its entirety; one half or the other would miss the point. But by saying that 'each has authority over the body of the other' he is emphasizing the teaching of the previous verse, that sexuality is primarily not for oneself but for the other. A man and a woman approaching their marriage with a 'What's in it for me?' attitude may be likened to 'two ticks on a dog, but there's no dog!' In such a marriage each is attempting to consume the other. From this passage the attitude would rather be, 'How can I serve my partner sexually, as well as in all things?'

Paul now reaches his punch line where the original context may be discerned. 'Don't deprive one another', he says (v. 5). This is precisely what may have been happening among some couples in Corinth, based on a mistaken eschatology which said, 'If the ends of the age have come to us, we must abstain' (see on 10:11). His verb 'deprive' could be understood as 'defraud' or 'cheat', highlighting once more the emphasis on the responsibility to meet the needs of the other person rather than demanding one's own rights.

Paul does allow the possibility of a period of sexual abstinence, but it is to be only by mutual agreement and for a brief period for the couple to be occupied in prayer, whether singly or together. In passing, we note Paul's expectation that Christians should pray at home, as well as at the public meeting of believers. But then let the couple 'be together again', sexually that is. And the reason? 'That Satan not test you through your lack of self-control.'

The adulterer with his father's wife and the temple fornicators from the church in Corinth are probably in Paul's mind as he writes, aware of the power and addictiveness of uncontrolled sexuality. It is safe to say that few forces are so destructive of oneself or of others as rampant sex, whether heterosexual or homosexual. Not least, it is fed by the hopeless lie that the meaning of life is to be found in sexual gratification. Driven by this illusion many crash on through life, bringing misery to themselves and to all others in their path. Such an illusion is, indeed, 'Satanic'. Sexuality which is expressed in loving care of the partner, in contrast, is magnificently creative. Its energies are directed towards work and homemaking and care of children and carry benefits which are felt far and wide in neighbourhoods and society itself. The world owes more than it knows to the teaching of Jesus, as echoed here by his apostle.

2. The 'Gifts' of Sexuality (7:6-9)

Paul now adds some qualifications to his positive teaching on the need for marriage in the face of *porneia*, 'sexual immorality', that he gave in the previous verses.

First, let the Corinthians understand that his words about marrying are a matter of his 'advice' not a 'command' (v. 6). For Paul to preach the gospel was the 'command' of the Lord (Rom. 15:28; 1 Tim. 1:1; Titus 1:3), yet for many areas of the believers' life and witness he merely gave his 'advice', the response to which was indeed a matter of obedience to God, but worked out at the prayerful discretion of the individual (see on 7:25; 2 Cor. 8:10; Phlm. 14).

This is because, secondly, 'Each has his own gift from God, one for this, the other for that' (v. 7). One's need to be married or one's capacity not to be is called a *charisma*, a Holy Spirit infused 'donation' from God.[1] In Paul's mind this is not merely a matter of natural temperament, passively to be borne. Rather it is to be seized gratefully, as God's gift to oneself.

Yet, thirdly, in view of the lateness of the eschatological hour, Paul has a distinct preference for singleness, as he will expand upon shortly (see on vv. 32-35). To the unmarried and the widows he recommends, 'It is good to remain as I am', that is, single (v. 8). 'Remain' is a keyword in this chapter. Evidently, some of the Corinthians were agitated at a time of 'crisis' (see on v. 26) and were seeking to make significant lifestyle changes. Some wives sought to stop having sexual relationships with

---

1   The Greek *charisma*, 'gift' is closely related to *charis*, 'grace'.

their husbands (vv. 1-5). Some members felt they should be separated from spouses who were not Christians (vv. 10-14). Some Gentiles thought they should be Jews and some Jews thought they should be Gentiles (vv. 18-19). Slaves understandably wanted to be free (vv. 21-23). Younger unmarried men and women were seeking release from betrothal obligations (vv. 25-26). Paul cautions against 'change for change's sake' by his use of the verb 'remain' throughout the chapter (vv. 11,20, 24, 40) and quite specifically in one passage (vv. 17-24).

Paul is single and intends to 'remain' single. Paul is not an ascetic on account of the sexual temptations around him like, for example, the early church father Origen who had himself castrated to overcome sexual temptation. Rather, Paul is future-oriented, looking onwards towards the risen Lord and the Kingdom of God. Singleness was not a negative for Paul, a means of escaping from sin, but a positive attitude, based on a desire to please the Lord by obedient service. No doubt some will be unconvinced, placing instead dark Freudian interpretations upon Paul's words. Yet these are his only words on the subject and it is better to take them at face value than to attempt to read other motives into his mind, especially from this distance.

Having stated that personal preference, however, Paul is quick to return to the reality of human nature and sexual temptations. 'If they cannot control themselves' if that is not their 'gift' then 'let them marry' (v. 9). He explains, 'For it is better to marry than to burn.' In mind here is the 'heat' of sexual passion which is absorbed, softened and cooled within the intimacy of the marriage commitment. Otherwise it would 'burn' out of control, bringing destruction to all parties. But there may be at the same time a deeper meaning. Paul is thinking of 'burning' as an image for hell fire. Who can forget the final scene in Mozart's great opera when the fires of hell swallow up the womanizer Don Giovanni, whose 'catalogue' of sexual conquests ran into thousands.[2] It is easy to mock medieval images of hell. Yet the reality of eternal separation from God, which the image of fire portrays, is truly awesome. Paul teaches that the sexually promiscuous will not inherit the Kingdom of God (6:9-11).

---

2   Cf. Leporello's famous 'Catalogue' aria about the Don's sexual appetite.

3. The Marriage Bond (7:10-14)

Having addressed the 'unmarried and widows' (v. 8) Paul turns to those 'already married'. He is quick to add, however, that he is now quoting the 'command' of the Lord. He is not replicating an extensive version of Jesus' teaching about marriage as a lifelong commitment. I assume the Corinthians would have 'received' this tradition from Paul when he established the church. Rather he appeals to the teaching of Jesus, crafting its wording to the current pastoral situation in Corinth:

> A wife must not separate herself from her husband
>   but if she does let her   remain unmarried
>   or be reconciled to her husband.
> And a husband is not to divorce his wife (vv. 10-11).

What is happening in Corinth that leads Paul to bring these words to the church? Verse 10, buttressed by verses 12-14, suggests that some Corinthian wives were 'separating from their husbands' and for no other reason than that these men were not believers. Apparently these wives felt they were 'unholy', perhaps through sexual union with unbelieving husbands. The teaching of the Lord as appealed to by Paul is this: if a Christian woman withdraws from a husband for *this reason*, let her remain unmarried or else be reconciled to the husband. Likewise a Christian man is not to divorce his wife because she is a non-Christian (vv. 10, 12).

Presumably Paul only had to make the briefest allusion to Jesus' teaching for them to know what he was talking about. Doubtless they knew a fuller version of Jesus' words, like that found in the Gospel of Mark:

> '... at the beginning of creation God "made them male and female."
> "For this reason a man will leave his father and mother
> and be united to his wife, and the two will become one flesh."
> So they are no longer two, but one.
> Therefore what God has joined together, let man not separate.'
> When they were in the house again, the disciples asked Jesus about this.
> He answered, 'Anyone who divorces his wife and marries another woman commits adultery against her.
> And if she divorces her husband and marries another man, she commits adultery' (Mark 10:6-12).

According to Jesus, in marriage God so unites a man and a woman that remarriage following divorce amounts to adultery. Paul repeats that teaching in verse 11 and in Romans 7:2-3. The one exception Jesus made was where a spouse had engaged in *porneia*, 'sexual immorality' (Matt. 19:9), that is, in sexual intercourse with another person. Paul appears to make a further exception where the unbelieving spouse withdraws from the marriage (v. 15), the so-called 'Pauline Privilege'. In that case the wife is 'not bound', that is, to remain unmarried; presumably she is free to remarry in those circumstances.[3]

Does this exhaust the exceptions to remarrying? Personally, I do not think so. But Jesus' 'sexual immorality' and Paul's 'desertion' exceptions, which are both serious and weighty matters, give us some idea that remarriage after divorce should only occur where the misbehaviour of the other party is onerous and substantial. It is dangerous to give examples so I will not do so. Suffice to say that remarriage after divorce is only justified in most extreme circumstances. Even then justifiable grounds do not necessarily mean that the 'innocent party' *must* dissolve the marriage. Many a wife or husband has persevered because he or she has believed under God that it was right to do so or because there was no alternative to do otherwise.

In contrast with weighty matters like adultery or desertion, inter-personal relational difficulties can be found in most marriages, sometimes for protracted periods. Though grievous they are often able to be mollified through patience, prayer and skilled counselling. Indeed, all marriages need the investment of loving thoughtfulness and unselfish effort. The teaching of the Lord and his apostle reflected in this passage show how seriously believers should approach marriage. No decision for this life is so important or far-reaching. What is clear in this passage is that a believer must not separate from an unbeliever nor contemplate remarriage for no other reason than that the spouse is an unbeliever.

In writing, 'The rest I say, not the Lord', Paul makes clear that he is no longer quoting the Lord but is now giving his own teaching (v. 12). It is evident that in Paul's mind his teaching was

---

3   For the contrary view, that the spouse was 'not bound' to keep the marriage intact at all costs, see Fee pp. 302-3.

to be kept separate from the teachings of Jesus. The apostle did not invent words to put into the mouth of Jesus, which he might easily have done to resolve difficult issues in the churches. His careful distinction encourages us to feel that the words of the Lord here and in the Gospels are recorded accurately.

Although the precise problem involved wives in particular who sought to separate from unbelieving husbands (v. 10), Paul now addresses both men and women in the church.

> If any brother has a wife who is an unbeliever,
> and she is content to live with him
> let him not divorce her.
>
> And if any wife has a husband who is an unbeliever,
> and he is content to live with her,
> let her not divorce the husband   (vv. 12-13).

We note a symmetry here, a moral even-handedness. Exactly the same advice is given to the 'wife' as to the 'brother', indicating that both the men and the women were subject to the same limitations (see on v. 15).[4] If the unbeliever is content to stay married the Christian partner is not at liberty to divorce that spouse.

Paul now gives his reason for this teaching, as signalled by the small word 'for'. Believers, especially the wives, may have felt that being yoked to an unbeliever meant that they were somehow 'unholy' or 'unclean' in that union (through its sexual expression?). But in fact, says Paul, the opposite is true. It is not that the believer is made 'unholy' in the unbeliever but that the unbeliever is made 'holy' in the believer! 'For', he explains, 'the unbelieving husband is *sanctified* in the wife and the unbelieving wife is *sanctified* in the brother' (v. 14).

But what does he mean by 'sanctified'? 'Sanctify' belongs to a family of words which feature significantly in this letter, including 'holy', 'holy ones' and 'holiness'. Indeed, it is not too much to say that these words reach the heart of the letter, namely, the imputed as well as practical 'holiness' of the people of God in Christ (see on 1:30; cf. 1:2). The root idea of 'holiness' is two-sided. It is to be like God in his purity and love and unlike fellow humans in their wilfulness and sin.

---

4   In contemporary Jewish culture there was no provision for a wife to divorce her husband.

Paul's words, 'the unbelieving husband is sanctified in the wife' and vice versa probably do not mean that the unbeliever somehow 'becomes holy', as if by some kind of spiritual progress based on the principle of osmosis. Rather, Paul probably means that God treats their marriage union as 'holy' on account of the *partner* who is one of God's 'holy' ones. This does not mean that the unbeliever is 'saved' automatically by being married to a Christian as, indeed, verse 16 makes clear. Yet the unbeliever's marriage with a believer places him or her in a place of greater opportunity to find salvation than would otherwise be the case.

Paul clinches this point with an appeal to something they already knew. 'Otherwise your children are not unclean, but now they are holy', he assures them (v. 14c). As descendants of Adam the sinner, all children are likewise predisposed to rebellion against God (Rom. 5:12) and therefore are morally 'unclean'. Earlier Paul wrote that believers were 'washed, sanctified, justified in the name of the Lord Jesus and in the Spirit of our God' (see on 6:11). Covenantal commitment to God in Christ by repentance and faith in Christ crucified and risen, as sealed by the outward sign of baptism, brought the assurance that the new believer was 'washed, sanctified and justified'. Paul's confidence that the children were 'not unclean but now were holy' suggests that they somehow entered into the same blessings as their now-believing parents.

On that account, many argue that children were baptized along with their parents at the time of their conversion and baptism.[5] This view finds support in Paul's baptism of 'the *household* of Stephanas' (see on 1:16) which probably included children as well as slaves and retainers.[6] Certainly, the book of Acts gives examples of whole households being baptized.[7] It appears that God's covenant of 'holiness' extends to the children of believers as it did under the Old Testament in the sign of circumcision for baby sons of the covenant (Gen. 17:9-14). The

---

5   It is likely that from this developed the practice of baptizing the children of church members and then the practice of baptizing children indiscriminately. There are many Christians who reject altogether the practice of baptizing children.

6   See 1 Cor. 16:15-18.

7   Acts 16:34; 18:8.

sign of baptism, however, does not automatically convey the blessings of the covenant. These must be appropriated by each person in turn. Yet the child of a believing parent or parents will be much prayed over. Furthermore, they are in touch with the covenantal faith in a way that other children are not.

The addition of church members from constituent families is sometimes called 'biological growth' as if it were an inferior form of church growth. On the contrary, it should be called 'covenant growth' since it is entirely in line with God's covenantal purposes for the children of his people.

4. Don't Stop Them Leaving (7:15-16)

To this point Paul has been admonishing the Corinthians the wife in particular not to withdraw from an unbelieving partner. Paul assures her that she is not unholy through such a union, but that her husband is 'sanctified' by his union with her.

However, the words 'But if...' (v. 15) signify a completely new twist to the pastoral situation in Corinth. Here it seems that the unbelieving spouses were seeking to leave and the believing partners were attempting to stop them going. How does the apostle respond? 'If the unbeliever departs, let him or her depart' (v. 15). He adds, 'The brother or sister is not "bound" (literally, "enslaved") in such circumstances. But God has called you in peace'.

If, after all your efforts, an unbelieving spouse is determined to leave, then so be it, let him or her leave. In other words, while the Lord taught that believers were not to leave a marriage because the spouse is an unbeliever, there is no binding obligation to stop the unbeliever leaving. How could there be? God calls on us to take responsibility for our own actions not for the actions of others, in this case, spouses who were determined to leave.

Spiritual heartache is evident in Paul's questions, 'Wife, how do you know that you will save your husband? Husband, how do you know that you will save your wife?' (v. 16). These words mirror the anxiety of the Christian to keep the unbelieving partner tethered in the marriage, in order to 'save' that person. True, the believer's highest responsibility to others is to seek their salvation (see on 10:23-11:1). 'But', says Paul, 'you don't know if this will happen, so don't fret about your "lost" wife or husband who is determined to leave and do not attempt to prevent him or her from going'.

But what is the situation of the believer who has been 'left' by the unbeliever? Is the believer now free to remarry? The strictures upon the believers not to leave unbelievers were reinforced by his admonition *in that case* to remain unmarried or else be reconciled to the spouse (v. 10). But these strictures do not apply here. In this reversed situation the *other* party withdrew from the marriage, leaving the one who remains 'not bound' to stop them and to be 'in peace'. While Paul does not address the question it appears that the one left behind is free to remarry in these circumstances. Pastorally, strong efforts should be made to seek reconciliation, but if these fail, the partner left behind should not be held hostage to the actions of the departing spouse.

5. 'Remain as You Are' (7:17-24)

Reading a little 'between the lines', as it were, it appears that a kind of 'eschatological madness' was agitating the Corinthians at the time Paul is writing. Of course, Paul had preached that in the death and resurrection of Jesus and the coming of the Spirit 'the end of the ages' had actually come in, so that Christians are *already* saved, *already* living in the last times (see on 10:11). Nonetheless, the Kingdom of God is *not yet* finally revealed. We stand at the brink of the New Age, but the End has yet to arrive.[8]

But again and again in this chapter Paul must urge the Corinthians to 'remain' as they were at the time of their 'call' in the gospel. Some were seeking to change their outward circumstances wives ceasing sexual intercourse, wives leaving unbelieving husbands, Jews and Gentiles seeking to reverse their race, and slaves agitating for liberty. What was happening in Corinth that Paul has to settle things down in the way he does throughout the chapter? There is evidence of chronic famine and food shortage at that time. It is also possible that an outbreak of disease had occurred in Corinth which had touched the lives of the congregation. Perhaps, too, there had

---

8   Scholars call this 'already ... not yet' tension 'realized eschatology'. But the Corinthians appear to have been embracing what has been called an over-realized eschatology.

been accompanying manifestations of tongues-speaking and prophesying (see on v. 26). Whatever the case, some of the members are convinced that the usual arrangements of life should be laid aside.

Paul immediately gives a principle to guide the people at this time (v. 17) which he expands by several specific cases. What is this principle? It is that the circumstances of life marriage, race, slavery are as the Lord has 'assigned' and as the Lord has 'called'. Let each person continue to live in those circumstances which applied at the time of his or her conversion in Christ. This is what Paul teaches in 'all the churches', that is, in the churches of the Gentiles established by him in Galatia, Macedonia, Achaia and Asia. In other words, being caught up into the kingdom of God through the gospel brings many changes, including liberation from the forces of evil and a sure hope of resurrection into the Kingdom of God. The Spirit has brought a revolution in heart and mind which has found expression in every aspect of life here and now. But such a revolution does not change every outward circumstance, nor is it to do so.

Now Paul turns to the specific cases where people may have been attempting to change their 'calling'. 'Let the circumcised man not attempt to remove his circumcision' (v. 18a). In the era before Christ, when Israel had come under the influence of the Greeks following Alexander's conquests, many wealthy and younger Jewish men attempted surgically to mask their circumcision. Jewish men living in the powerful culture of a Graeco-Roman city like Corinth doubtless often felt tempted to abandon the faith of their fathers and its sign in their bodies. On the other hand, Paul urges Gentiles, 'Let the uncircumcised man not be circumcised'. For many years large numbers of Gentiles had been attending the synagogues as 'God-fearers', only some of whom took the radical further step to become proselytes to Judaism by circumcision. Likewise Paul advises against that. In both cases serious surgical process was involved, whether to remove circumcision or to submit to circumcision. Each action signified a dramatic change, either disowning Jewishness or embracing it.

Yet Paul urges against such changes (v. 19). And the reason? 'Circumcision is nothing and uncircumcision is nothing. All that matters is keeping the commandments of God.' As a former Pharisee and 'zealot' Paul had 'preached circumcision' (Gal. 5:11) to 'fence off' the covenant of God from Gentiles and God-fearers who wanted an easy access to salvation. But in the light of Christ crucified and risen Paul saw that circumcision was now irrelevant. He told the Galatians that 'neither circumcision nor uncircumcision means anything; what counts is a new creation' (Gal. 6:15). Now he declares that 'keeping the commandments' is the bedrock issue. But how can this be since Paul teaches elsewhere that the descendants of Adam are unable to keep the commandments of God given under the Mosaic covenant (see Rom. 5–7)? How then can we 'keep' them? Here we need to anticipate his explanation of Romans 8:1-4 where he teaches that we are deemed to have 'kept' the commandments 'in' the sin-free Messiah, whose death was a 'sin offering' for us. Furthermore, by the power of the indwelling Spirit we begin to keep 'the just requirements of the law'. Clearly, then, the integrity of the righteous Law of God as explained in its true meaning by Jesus in the Sermon on the Mount is upheld by the death of Christ and the Spirit-empowered living of the people of the New Covenant.

Paul concludes his directions to both the 'circumcised' and the 'uncircumcised' with an exhortation that picks up the words with which he began, 'Let each person remain in the calling in which he was called' (v. 20). The word 'called', echoing 'called' a few verses earlier, rounds off the section of verses 17-21. In turn 'called' will be re-echoed in verse 24.

He now addresses a further group who were seeking change, the slaves in the congregation. Here, however, he is not so categorically opposed to change. He begins by encouraging the slaves, 'Were you called when a slave? Don't let it trouble you' (v. 21a). Later Paul wrote to his friend Philemon in Colosse encouraging him to receive back the runaway slave Onesimus who had become a Christian through Paul's ministry. But Philemon is not asked to liberate Onesimus, but to treat him now as a much loved brother in Christ. Whatever Paul thought of slavery, the idea of its abolition was not destined to come for many centuries. Ever the realist, then, he encouraged the slaves, 'Don't let it trouble you'. To have said otherwise would have doomed slaves to crucifixion. Romans were ruthless in their suppression of slave uprisings. A century earlier Spartacus and his fellow-slaves rose up to gain their freedom but were crucified by the thousands along the Appian Way leading into Rome. On the other hand, not all masters were bad. Some slaves were well treated and enjoyed shelter and regular food that many free people did not have.

Nonetheless, there was much about being a slave that was very troubling the demeaned status, being owned body and soul by another person, exposure to cruelty and neglect without redress. Slavery was a pernicious evil that continued from the dawn of history and has to this day not been eradicated. George Washington, the first president of the new United States, and an enlightened man, kept slaves; only in the nineteenth century was slavery abolished in the USA.[9] In the twentieth century the Communists and Nazis kept millions enslaved in the gulags of Siberia and the concentration camps of Germany and Poland. It is fervently to be hoped that slavery will be driven from the world by the early years of the twenty-first century.

We are glad, therefore, to hear Paul's response to the Christian slaves in Corinth. His opening words, 'But if in fact', are in deep contrast with his attempted consolation of the previous sentence, 'Don't let it trouble you'. '*But if in fact* you are able to gain freedom, do it!' Clearly Paul saw no good in slavery and gave his strongest and unqualified support for slaves to gain their freedom. A household slave might find freedom in several ways, whether by saving the price of freedom or by a benefactor paying that price. The farm slave, by contrast, had no opportunity to earn money and probably had no friends who might secure his manumission.

Paul takes the opportunity to give the Corinthians a theological proverb, a wise oracle, based on his practical advice to slaves (v. 22):

For who was a slave   when called in the Lord is the Lord's freedman.

Likewise the   free man when called   is the   slave of Christ.

---

9   George Washington's home at Mt. Vernon was a model farm at that time where the slaves enjoyed a secure and good life and in which many chose to remain when offered their freedom.

Paul is thinking of the more profound slavery to the 'lord' sin, with its bondage to Satan, guilt, fear, strong evil forces and death. Such a person when 'called in the Lord' by the gospel into the community of faith becomes the Lord's 'freedman'. A 'freedman' was a slave who had been set free as opposed to a free man or woman who had not been a slave.[10] Paul is doubtless thinking by name of those from Corinth who had been enslaved to the vices mentioned earlier, but who had been liberated by 'the name of the Lord Jesus and the Spirit of our God' (see on 6:9-11).

But whether a 'freedman' spiritually speaking or a 'free man' socially speaking, both are to be 'the slaves of Christ'. We must not confuse categories here. There is a large difference between a 'slave' and a 'servant'. A 'servant' 'serves' a 'master' whether for payment or voluntarily. But here he speaks of a 'slave' and a 'Lord', that is, of a mere *chattel* and an *owner*. It is true that we are to be the servants of our Master, Christ, to whom we have a stewardship of accountability. But from this text we discover that we are to be *slaves, owned* by the Lord Christ and having no rights, doing his bidding whatever the cost to us. This was so awesome an idea that the King James Version of the Bible tended to soften references to 'slavery' to 'service'.

Accordingly Paul reminds the 'slaves' of the means of their 'redemption' (see on 1:30):

You were bought at a price.
Do not become the slaves of men (v. 23).

This is the second occasion Paul has spoken of the purchase price for freedom having been paid (see on 6:20). We ask, 'To *whom* has the price been paid?' This is probably the wrong question. Paul's words here are metaphorical and should not be pushed too far. In early Christian centuries it was held that God paid the Devil the price of the death of Christ as a ransom for the liberation of his slaves. It is safe to say that this is entirely conjectural and probably unhelpful. Paul is probably only thinking of our liberation from the lordship of sin, on the one hand, and that our deliverance from that slavery came at an immeasurably high price, the death of Christ.

10　Or who had not long been set free from slavery. On manumission the liberated former slave was called a 'freedman' for a period of time, often remaining in the service of the former owner.

Since the 'price has been paid' and the former slaves are now free, it is inconceivable that they would bring themselves once more under bondage. By his encouragement, 'Do not become the slaves of men', Paul has in mind the real possibility of the redeemed returning to their old vices. Few things are so tragic as those set free from evil returning to it. For them it appears Christ paid the price in vain. All believers do well to recognise the lure of temptation and the power of unhelpful company. It is sensible to reflect on our moral and spiritual 'Achilles' heels' and to be steeled beforehand to our besetting temptations. Nor should God's provision in the security and strength of Christian fellowship be overlooked. We need strong teaching and supportive friends who will caringly hold us accountable for all that we do. For his part Paul made his 'body his slave', so determined was he that having preached to others he would not be a moral and spiritual castaway (see on 9:27).

So Paul brings this section to a close. Once more he invokes the word 'called' which appeared at the beginning (v. 17), and which reappeared in verse 20 to provide an interim end to the sub-section (vv. 17-20). Now 'called' reappears to end the whole passage begun at verse 17. Thinking of the wives, the Jews, the Gentiles and the slaves he has been addressing, he directs them, 'Let each man or woman *remain* in that circumstance in which they were called'. But there are two critical words which appear at the very end, *para theou* ('before God'). Many of life's circumstancesthe things to which we are 'called' by God are onerous, oppressive and seemingly unendurable. Yet, one day at a time, we are to submit to our 'calling' *before God*. We place ourselves humbly beneath his mighty fatherly hand, casting our cares on him in the knowledge that he cares for us and gives us his strength for our 'thorn', whatever it might be (1 Pet. 5:6-7; 2 Cor. 12:7-9).

6. The Time is Short (7:25-35)[11]

Paul's opening words, 'Now about' are a shorter form of 'Now about *the matters about which you wrote*' (see on 7:1). These signal

---

11   This passage and the next (7:36-40) are the most difficult in the epistle, as witnessed by the divergent opinions of commentaters and translators. The comments that follow are hesitatingly offered!

that Paul is now moving to the next item in their letter seeking answers from him. The question came from fathers about their as-yet unmarried daughters, whose marriages it fell to them to arrange. 'Paul, should we or should we not betroth our daughters?'

Paul has no 'command' from the Lord on this matter (v. 25). However, in giving his 'judgement' (NIV) no lack of authority over the Corinthians is thereby conceded. He claims directly to be an apostle at other points in the letter (1:1; 9:1; 15:9). This claim is also implied by his words 'as one who has received mercy from the Lord to be trustworthy', a reference to Christ's 'call' to be an apostle which Paul received near Damascus (cf. 2 Cor. 4:1). Furthermore, he does have the Spirit of God (see on 7:40). Paul has the status and authority as an apostle of Christ, though he is prudent not to 'pull rank' too often. Rather, he makes his apostolic office visible in the background, but seeks to win the hearts and minds of his readers by persuasion along Christian lines, as throughout this great letter. Sadly, church leaders have not always followed Paul's example.

In passing, we note once more that Paul could easily have invented a 'command of the Lord' and imposed it on the Corinthians (see on v. 12). His care in distinguishing the words of Jesus from his own words fill us with encouragement about the integrity of the words of Jesus we find in this Letter and in the Gospels.

Paul now gives his 'judgment' as follows: 'I therefore think it is good for a person to remain as he or she was, on account of the present crisis' (v. 26). Once more Paul is urging his readers not to change their 'calling', specifically those who are as yet unmarried. But what is the 'present crisis'? Clearly the Corinthians knew what he meant, but because he doesn't say more we are driven to conjecture. Several matters of a general kind are known to have been critical at that time. One was the shortage of food in the eastern Mediterranean due to the protracted famine which began in the late forties and whose effects were felt for many years. This was exacerbated by a coincidental series of heavy floodings of the Nile, preventing harvests for some years from the 'food bowl' of the Roman world. Food prices were inflated for many years due to these natural disasters. Local rioting due to food shortage and overpricing was common. It is known that the Emperor Claudius distributed food relief throughout Greece in the early fifties. Another problem, local to Corinth, was Claudius' creation of an Imperial Cult in Corinth in AD 54 which must have placed considerable pressure on Christians to offer public worship to the gods.

Evidence from the present letter suggests that the 'present crisis' was related to a spate of recent illnesses and *not a few* deaths within the congregation (see on 11:30). Outbreaks of plagues were common in the unhygienic settlements of that time, whose stench could be smelled some distance away. Disease wiped out whole populations of cities. Food shortage, social unrest and disease possibly combined to create a 'crisis' that had struck Corinth at the time Paul wrote this letter. Perhaps, too, the outburst of Spirit-inspired prophesying and tongues-speaking in Corinth was in some way connected with this.

Whatever the 'present crisis' actually was, Paul interpreted it as evidence that 'the time is shortened' (v. 29) until the end. This prompts Paul to observe that 'the form of this world is passing away' (v. 31). When this finally occurs everything will then change. In the coming age all circumstances will be overturned (vv. 29-31), but not beforehand. In line with all that he has been urging throughout the chapter Paul admonishes the Corinthians to 'remain' in whatever calling they were 'in' at the time they were overtaken by the coming age. 'Do not make a change for change's sake', he pleads.

None of this means, however, that Paul thought that Christ would return in the next few minutes, as some scholars claim. On the contrary, the apostles understood from Jesus that his 'coming' was to be preceded by a number of pre-determined events (see e.g., 2 Thess. 2:1-12). However, once Christ had been raised from the dead 'the time is shortened' and the End is now plainly 'in sight'.

Thus he addresses those who are not yet married but could be married in the near future (v. 27).[12] Here he is referring to the practice of betrothal where two fathers 'arranged' the marriage between a son and a daughter. To those men already committed

---

12   NIV takes this verse as applying to marriage and divorce. But Paul has moved
     on to a new topic now Fee (pp. 331-2) argues for a reference here to betrothal
     obligations and discharge from them.

through betrothal to a 'wife' he says, 'You are "tied" to a wife? Do not seek to be released from it.' To those not yet betrothed he says, 'You are not "tied" to a wife? Do not seek to ["be tied to"] a wife.' In other words, Paul is encouraging a 'stay as you are' attitude, whether to the already betrothed or to the not yet betrothed.

Ever the pastor, Paul wishes to relieve a potential burden of guilt from those who were as yet unmarried (v. 28a,b). 'If you marry you have not sinned', he says to a man who is soon to marry the woman betrothed to him. 'If a virgin marries she has not sinned', he says most probably to the girl's father.[13] So there is no question of sin either in marrying or not marrying for the man or the woman.

Thus Paul is not an ascetic, as the members of the Qumran community near Jericho were and as Christian monastics became. Rather, as he now proceeds to say, all believers are to be people of the *future*, that is, God's future. At this present time we only see that future 'through a glass darkly' (see on 13:12). Our future is not here, in this present age, but in our inheritance in the Kingdom of God (see on 6:9-10). So his attitudes to this world are informed by his hope for a glory-laden future and are not negative *per se* about life here and now. Rather, he longs for what 'eye has not seen nor ear heard' in the Kingdom, to see the Lord 'face to face' (see on 2:8-10; 13:12). He sees this age through the glorious lenses of God's future.

So far as this present fallen age is concerned he knows that it is characterised by 'pressures[14] in the flesh', 'anxieties' (see on v. 33) and 'distractions' (v. 35), many of which arise from difficult or broken relationships. There is no pain in human experience comparable with bonds torn apart between spouses or between parents and children or between brothers and sisters. Paul was no doubt aware of such suffering among the members of the churches. Addressing those who face marriage Paul says, 'I want to spare you from these' (v. 28c). He will expand upon his concern for them in verses 32-35.

But until he returns to the specific pastoral needs of the unmarried he offers a set of contrasts between this age and the

---

13 Women were mostly married in the early teen years.

14 Thus NIV but the Greek thlipsis more literally means 'a tightening', 'a pinching' or 'pressure'.

coming age (vv. 29-31). The onset of the New Age will herald the Great Reversal. He introduces his 'mini' apocalypse authoritatively, 'But this I say...'

> The time is shortened,
> henceforth
>> those who have wives [will be[15]] as those who do not [have wives]
>> those who weep as those who do not weep
>> those who rejoice as those who do not rejoice
>> those who buy as those who have nothing
>> those who use this world as those who do not.
> For the outward form of this world is passing away.

Paul's words are rather compressed, so that various interpret-ations have been offered. I have taken them to be prophetic of the reversal of circumstances when the Kingdom of God appears. Behind Paul's poetic words is his realistic and straightforward reminder that our 'calling' in this life will be radically different in the Kingdom. Marriage will be no more; those who weep will rejoice; those who rejoice will weep; those who own possessions will be bereft; those who use the world will be at a loss. Jesus taught that marriage was for this age only and that weeping would be replaced by laughter. Paul's contrasts given above probably echo the words of Jesus, some of which are also repeated by James.[16]

The 'present crisis', whatever it was and the detail is not finally important prompts Paul to reflect to his readers, us included, that 'the outward form of this world is passing away'. Every crisis, whether 'front page news' or a private domestic tragedy, tells us that this old world is 'passing away', dying as we watch it. Such 'crises' are signs to the eye of faith telling us what is to come. Our future is not here but in the kingdom, where God will wipe away every tear (Rev. 21:4). Elsewhere Paul calls such things 'birth pangs' as of a woman in labour which, however, tell us that the birth of the new age is near.[17]

Having 'shown up' this world in comparison to the next Paul now contrasts the circumstances of the unmarried man

---

15 NIV takes Paul's grammar to mean a set of implied imperatives (also Fee, p. 338). Based on the context, however, I have taken him to be contrasting what is *now* with what *will be then*.

16 See e.g. Mark 12:25; Luke 6:21; James 4:9.

17 Rom. 8:21-22.

with the married man (vv. 32-34 a). He begins and ends by expressing concern for them.

> I would like you to be anxiety-free.
> The unmarried man is anxious for the things of the Lord, how to please the Lord.
> The married man is anxious for the things of the world, how to please his wife
> and he is divided.

This is Paul in practical mode. A husband is, indeed, 'divided' within himself as he bears the onerous task of providing for his wife and children while also seeking to serve the Lord. An aspect of his responsibility is to 'please his wife'. That is, he is called on to love, encourage and nurture her.[18] This is the priority for the married man, but the unmarried man is relieved of these responsibilities. He is free to be fully absorbed in 'the things of the Lord, how to please the Lord'.

Naturally, Paul cannot but compare his relative freedom in ministry as an apostle with the responsibilities borne by married men in the churches whom he sees as 'divided'. But again we must point out that Paul is no 'world denying' monastic or ascetic. He is being quite objective. His practical priorities are for the Kingdom and not for the here and now, as they must be for married men. Throughout history there have been men whose calling was to be an itinerant missionary or preacher like Paul. If men like John Wesley, C.T. Studd or David Livingstone had read Paul's words as I think he intended them to be understood, they may have chosen a life of singleness like Paul in the discharge of their calling.

Paul now completes the picture. He contrasts the concerns of unmarried women as against married women (v. 34). Since the presenting question related to younger unmarried women who might be betrothed, Paul's discussion is rather more extended than for unmarried men.

> The unmarried woman and the virgin is anxious for the things of the Lord that she might be holy in body and spirit.
> But the married woman is anxious for the things of the world, how to please her husband.

---

18   See Eph. 5:25-32; Col. 3:19; 1 Pet. 3:7.

Is Paul hinting that, in his opinion, women have a distinctive concern for 'holiness in body and spirit'? Possibly he thinks in this way. Either way, though, he does not differentiate between married men and women. Inevitably both are occupied with the needs of the partner, physical, spiritual and emotional. It cannot be helped.

Paul brings his 'judgement' about the unmarried to a conclusion (v. 35). His preference for the unmarried, clearly, is for them to remain in that 'calling'.

> This I say for your own advantage
> not to throw a noose around you
> but for that which is seemly
> and that you might be devoted to the Lord without distraction.

This verse is one of those transitional sentences much loved by Paul.[19] On the one hand, it is a summary of the whole passage (vv. 25-35) and on the other, as the introduction of the word 'seemly' indicates, it is a 'bridge' into the section following (vv. 36-40). Paul will not place a 'snare' trapping people in *porneia*, 'sexual immorality', by his expressed preference for singleness (see on vv. 2, 7, 9). Singleness is a 'gift' which not all have received (see on v. 7). Yet though Paul does have that 'gift', and therefore that preference, it is not based on an ascetical denial of this world, but rather on his longing for the Kingdom of God and his passionate desire to 'please the Lord' and to be 'devoted to him without distraction'.

7. Advice to a Father (7:36-38)

At last Paul may now be dealing with the particular case to which he began to reply back in verse 25. From verses 26-35 he has been encouraging the single to stay as they are, in order to so live in this present age as to 'please the Lord'. Now, in verses 36-38, he answers the question put to him in the Corinthians' letter.

Apparently a father from the congregation has expressed concern that in barring the way for the marriage of a daughter who is somewhat older than the norm (v. 36; see on v. 25) he may have acted in an 'unseemly' way. Apparently the man feels 'obligated' by undertakings already made to the other father. His anxieties are intensified by the age of his daughter, though

---

19 See e.g., 2 Cor. 2:12-13; 7:2-4; 12:13.

she is unlikely to have been older than late teens. Perhaps, though, she is now beyond marrying age in that culture.

Paul's attitude is clear and compassionate. 'Whatever he decides to do, let him do it. He has not sinned. Let them marry.' References to 'sin' associated with marriage (see also v. 28) probably are attributable to the wives who wished to abstain from sexual relationships with their husbands and to those wives who wished to withdraw from their marriage partners (see on vv. 1,11-14). Was this aversion to sexual intercourse[20] coming from the Jewish ascetics in the Qumran community?

On the other hand, if the man has decided not to proceed with the betrothal through to a marriage, that also is a valid course of action (v. 37). In this case the father has thought carefully, come to a firm conviction and was not subject merely to outside pressure. Let him keep his daughter. Were some people hinting that such a man was withholding his daughter for ulterior motives, perhaps for her to render ongoing help in the home? Paul encourages the man to resist such external pressure, if that were the case.

Paul draws his judgement on this question, begun at verse 25, to a close (v. 38). He encourages the father that either course is acceptable, though one is preferable in his view. 'So then', he begins, 'he who gives his daughter in marriage does well, but he who does not give her in marriage does better!' In the end Paul leaves the decision to the man.

The apostle has set out his preferences and given his reasons. He could easily have fallen in with the wives in Corinth who were ascetically minded and strongly discouraged the marriage of these young women. But he does not do that, though it would have been the line of least resistance. Paul the apostle was a man who upheld the highest principles and who, above all, taught people to think through issues, even to take decisions that would be different from his own. This is why he writes at such length about sexual matters in this chapter, drawing people into the spiritual and intellectual issues. He could easily have dealt with the questions raised by the Corinthians in

---

20   Jews generally had a robust and positive attitude to marriage, sexual relation-
     ships and family life. The same is true of the Essene sect. But members of the
     Qumran community from the Dead Sea region, the strictest of the Essenes, did
     not marry.

a few terse commands. But he does not. One of the glories of this Letter is that by sitting at Paul's feet and thinking things through with him we learn how to make decisions for ourselves based on the principles of the gospel. It is a mark of a guru, but not of a true pastor, to demand that people follow his policies in matters which belong to the realm of personal choice.

8. Advice to Widows (vv. 39-40)

Although Paul mentioned widows in passing earlier (v. 8) his concern up to this point has been wives and young unmarried women. So now, briefly, it is the turn of the widows to hear from the apostle (v. 39). What will he say to them?

> A woman is bound to her husband as long as he lives,[21]
> but if the husband falls asleep
> she is free to marry whom she will.[22]

But now he adds this terse rider of only three words in the original,

> only in [the] Lord.

Clearly she was formerly married to a believer; only believers are said to 'fall asleep'. The widow may remarry, but 'only' within the circle of membership of the community of faith.

These words reach beyond widows in their application. Where a man or a woman was already married at the time of conversion in Christ he or she is not to leave or divorce a spouse because that person is an unbeliever (see on vv. 10-14). But if one is already a Christian he or she is 'not free' to marry 'outside' the Lord.

Opinions differ whether this is 'good advice' or a 'command' which if broken would be sin. But this seems to be more than just 'good advice'.[23] Paul gives 'advice' in this chapter (vv. 25,

---

21   So, too, Rom. 7:2. The words 'as long as he lives' are new, but they reiterate his teaching on divorce and remarriage from verses 10-16 which in turn are based on Jesus' instruction that in marriage a man and a woman are made 'one flesh' by God and that remarriage breaks the commandment forbidding adultery (Mark 10:6-12).

22   Paul does not canvass here the exception of adultery, given by Jesus nor his own of desertion which might free a man or a woman to remarry (see on vv. 10, 11, 16). His general statement about a wife's life-long obligation prepares the way for what he will say about *widows*.

23   Fee, p. 356 calls it 'good sense'.

40), but he does not use that word here. In my view, Paul's words *at that time* amounted to a 'command', even though he does not use that word as he does earlier (see on vv. 10, 25). Because the unbelieving husband was most likely an idolater or devotee of a pagan religion, Paul's ban on being unequally yoked with an unbeliever would apply here (see 2 Cor. 6:14).

What, then, if the prospective unbelieving husband or wife is not an idolater or pagan but a worthy person at a human level? Perhaps here Paul's words do not altogether amount to a command which if disobeyed would be sin leading to eternal punishment. However, the experience of many pastors is that to be married to an unbeliever means a painfully lopsided life. Prayer together, a precious thing, will not be part of their domestic life (see on v. 5). The moral standards of the unbeliever may be at odds with the wife's conscience. Furthermore, complications may arise in regard to the nurture of children in Christ where only one partner is involved. Many men and women have acted against Paul's words, and while many have struggled successfully against the odds, others have stumbled and fallen. Whether to go against Paul is sin or folly; experience shows that much pain will accompany such a decision.

But now Paul will have the last word on this matter in terms of his own preference for singleness. 'According to my judgment', he writes, 'she is more blessed to remain as she is'. Like the as-yet unmarried younger woman, the widow will be free from the 'pressure', 'anxiety' and 'distraction' associated with marriage and she will be able to devote herself to holiness in body and mind and to pleasing the Lord. Paul adds, 'I think that I also have the Spirit of God' in giving this advice. Here he is appealing to his apostolic insight into the mind of the Lord, to which he referred earlier (see on 2:11-16).

Many would say, 'Indeed, Paul, you are an apostle of Christ and you do have the Spirit of God. But your gift for singleness has not been given to me by the Lord. As you said, not all have this gift. You are right. I am one who does not have that gift. Many "pressures", "anxieties" and "distractions" accompany marriage and then family life with children and then, when they marry, with in-laws. I politely thank you for your well-meant advice which I regret I cannot take. I intend to get married!'

Others would discern that they do have the gift of singleness and a calling to serve God in some special way. It may be a spectacular ministry like Paul's or it may be something that few know about but is, nonetheless, special in its own way. But it will be important to recognise that giving the Lord and the Kingdom this priority does not amount to world-denying asceticism. Nothing was further from Paul's mind.

SOME QUESTIONS FOR PERSONAL REFLECTION:

1. Reflect on the benefit of reading this chapter in terms of the arguments Paul uses, in particular the priority in this life to 'please the Lord'.

2. Think yourself into the minds of the wives who wanted to leave unbelieving husbands. How would they have received Paul's words to them?

3. Are Paul's words about remarrying 'only in the Lord' applicable also to those as yet unmarried? Is going against those words 'sin' or 'folly'?

STUDY QUESTIONS:

1. Why does Paul equally address the needs of both men and women? How does this go against the culture of the day?

2. What was the confusion concerning sexual abstinence? For what reason does Paul allow it?

3. Why does Paul use 'singleness' as being a positive?

4. What was the cause of apparent divorce among those in Corinthian? What was the command of Jesus?

5. How does Paul comfort those believers who are slaves?

6. Do you think that Paul's words to "not be unequally yoked together" is a command or just good sense?

8

Caring for the Weak Brother
(1 Cor. 8:1-13)

Just as chapters 5–7 formed a block of teaching,[1] so too Paul has arranged his material in chapters 8–10 to address a current burning issue, namely, idolatry. Readers in some cultures will know what Paul means when he writes about temples, idols and sacrifices, but to many others, such things are beyond their immediate experience.

Corinth was typical of major cities that ringed the Mediterranean at that time. There were numerous temples and shrines to gods, heroes and emperors in Corinth. The crumbling remains of some of these can still be seen, for example, the temple to Apollo. Pausanias, an ardent traveller of that era, lists more than a dozen temples or shrines devoted to the worship of the gods that formed part of the public square[2] of the city.

The language of 'temple culture' is found throughout these chapters. Paul refers to *eidōlon*, 'an idol' (8:4,7; 10:19), to *eidōlothutos*, 'idol-sacrificed meat' (8:1,4,7,10; 10:19) and to an apparent synonym *hierothutos*, 'temple-sacrificed' meat (10:28). He admonishes them not to attend the *eidōleion*, the 'idol house' (8:10) and to 'flee from' *eidōlolatreia*, 'the worship of idols' (10:14).

---

1   On sexual holiness.

2   Greek: *agora*, 'market-place' but the heart of a city where public affairs were transacted.

In chapters 8–10 Paul touches on three aspects of this 'culture' that affected the Corinthians. One related to being present when the priest sacrificed the animal on the altar for the god (cf. 10:14, 20). This usually occurred in an open space outside the temple. Second, the worshippers ate the food that had been sacrificed to the god. This might occur in the main part of the temple (cf. 10:20-22) or, alternatively, in the small dining rooms attached to the temple where people assembled for a dinner at which the sacrificed food was eaten. However, thirdly, sacrificed meat was also sold in the shops, taken home and eaten (cf. 10:25, 28).

Each of these aspects of 'temple culture' presented acute pastoral problems for the new Christians in Corinth which Paul addresses in these chapters. This was a very important issue since that society was surrounded by 'gods many and lords many' (v. 5). Apart from the Jews *all* the people of this city would have attended the festivals, rubbed shoulders with fellow citizens, discussed local issues, found employment and transacted business. The 'culture' of the temple, its worship and sacrifices permeated the whole of life at that time. Not to participate, in effect, meant to separate oneself from the civic life of the city.

In addressing these matters Paul begins with a body of teaching about which he and the Corinthians were in agreement, their affirmation of the reality of God and their denial of the existence of the gods (vv. 4-6). This merged into a discussion of a related issue, the 'authority' Christians have to eat whatever they like, without religious scruple (vv. 8-13). Without rejecting either of these truths, however, Paul significantly qualifies them with a further consideration, one that the Corinthians had neglected. Love of brother and sister Christians, especially those 'weak' in faith, was something the Corinthians had forgotten and about which Paul must remind them.

1. 'Now Concerning Food Sacrificed to Idols' (8:1-3)

Once more Paul draws attention to a question in their letter to him (see on 7:1). The subject is 'food sacrificed to idols'[3] (v. 1a), that is, the meat of animals which had been offered as sacrifice to the gods in the temples and which was now to be eaten. Most

---

3   Greek: *eidolothutos*, which also appears in verses 4, 7, 10. See also Acts 15:20; 21:25; Rev. 2:14, 20.

likely Paul taught about temples, gods and sacrifices when he established the church five years earlier. Their question was probably not seeking information about a new subject. Rather, they may have been expressing through it some disagreement with Paul's known attitude to these matters. This is to be inferred from his negative tone throughout the chapter. Perhaps the Corinthians, or some of them, were saying that because they 'knew' that there was no real god behind its image this meant they were free to go to the temples, attend the sacrifices and eat the sacrificed meat.

Having introduced the issue Paul takes the opportunity to digress momentarily on the related matter of 'knowing God' (vv. 1b-3). He will return to their question about eating idol sacrificed meat in a temple in verse 4. This short digression is a splendid statement that forms the foundation for his advice to the Corinthians (vv. 4-13), but which stands for all time for a believer's relationship with God. Paul wants his readers then and now to recognise that 'knowing *about* God' does not mean that they 'know God'.

Paul immediately concedes to the Corinthians, 'We know that we all have knowledge' (v. 1b). We ask, what is this 'knowledge'? It is not the so-called 'knowledge' through mystical experience as in gnosticism.[4] Rather it is what Christians 'know' through the 'word of the gospel' and instruction in the faith prior to baptism. This is apparent in Paul's frequent appeals to his readers saying, 'we know', 'knowing that', or 'do you not know?' This is straightforward 'knowledge' *about* God, *about* Christ, *about* salvation, *about* the future hope, *about* the church and *about* Christian behaviour. It is what we might call 'theological knowledge'.

---

4   Gnosticism arose within Judaism based on the separation of God in the absolute purity of heaven above and man in his impurity on earth below. By mystical exercises and spiritual discipline men and women of 'flesh' could eventually merge with 'Spirit' above. Jewish gnosticism began to penetrate Christianity quite early and may be in evidence in Corinth as 'incipient gnosticism'. Its influence appears to have increased and is probably being addressed in Paul's Pastoral Letters and also in 2 Peter and Jude. The so-called *Gospel of Thomas* is a second century gnostic work from Egypt. Gnosticism became a powerful influence in the second century and is repeatedly addressed by such writers as Ignatius and Irenaeus. Gnosticism was uncomfortable with the historical reality of Jesus' Incarnation and Bodily Resurrection. An early version of the Apostles' Creed was formulated to counteract Gnosticism.

But there is always a potential problem with such 'knowledge', which Paul now contrasts with 'love'. 'Knowledge' *about* God can 'inflate' individuals with a sense of pride, spiritual or intellectual. If education in general tends to induce pride, how much more might knowledge about God inflame such conceit. None too subtly Paul tells the 'wisdom'-besotted Corinthians that 'knowing' *about* God brings arrogance. But if 'knowledge puffs up' the *individual who knows*, then by contrast, 'love builds up' *others in their understanding* of the faith.

Now this is precisely where the Corinthians, or some of them, were failing so badly. Shortly Paul will indicate how people like them who have a good knowledge of theology are actually spiritually *destroying* fellow-believers who happen to be less well grounded in the faith (see on vv. 7-13).

Having admonished these knowledgeable ones (in advance) for their unloving behaviour he points, secondly, to their lack of humility (v. 2). 'If any one thinks he knows something, he no longer knows what he should know.' In this riddle Paul is saying that even those who think they know a lot about God, in fact know next to nothing. How could it be otherwise? The subject under discussion is *God* who is eternal, infinite and hidden from sight and sense. God hides himself from those who are wise in their own eyes but reveals himself to the humble and contrite.[5] Genuinely devout humility is a prerequisite for even to begin to 'know' God. Paul does not find this among the Corinthians.

Furthermore, we only know God as he has made himself known to us. This he has done in the 'word of the cross' (see on 1:18, 21). It is as we reach out to God in humble dependence on the One crucified and risen, expressing our love to him for his love to us, that we are 'known by God'. We only know God in his knowing of us. Fundamental to God's knowing of us is that we love him. Paul has moved on from 'knowing facts about God', critical as they are, to actually knowing God and being known by him.

It is not possible to know God unless we know true things about him, as revealed in the word of God. This is not in dispute.

---

5   Cf. Matt. 11:25; Job 37:23-24; Isa. 57:15; Ps. 34:18.

But the reverse is not true. It is possible to know *about* God, but because of lack of love for others, or lack of humility, or lack of love for God, not to actually know him, that is, *relationally*. This was the problem in Corinth, which lay exposed in their question and his answer.

In these few verses Paul has anticipated his great hymn to 'love' in chapter 13. There he points to the futility of having received various 'gifts' of ministry from God which are not used, motivated by love, to 'build up' others in the church. Here in chapter 8 the contrast is between 'knowledge' which is equally God's 'gift' to us and 'love'. The Corinthians were failing to use either their 'knowledge' or their 'gifts' for others and so they stood condemned for their lovelessness.

2. What we know about God and the gods (8:4-6)

Having paused to lay his foundation for a true 'knowing of God' Paul returns to their question about 'food sacrificed to idols' (v. 4). Immediately Paul agrees with the Corinthians about what he and they 'know'.

> We know that an idol is nothing in the world
> and that there is no God but one.

The Corinthians 'know' that no reality exists behind man-made gods. Positively they 'know' there is 'no God but one'. The latter teaching is adapted from the *Shema*, 'Hear O Israel, the Lord our God is *one*' and is also found in various other statements in the New Testament.[6] Yahweh had revealed himself in word and saving act as the *only* 'one' who was to be worshipped and served. His 'oneness' did relate to his indivisibility, arithmetically as it were, but also to his absolute *uniqueness*. He alone *was*, and *is* and *will be*.

Paul's credo also echoes Yahweh's own self-revelation of his uniqueness. The Lord declared, 'I am the Lord and there is no other'.[7] Here the affirmation ('I am the Lord') is clinched by the denial ('and there is no other'). Likewise Paul locks out idolatry by his cleverly reversed statement, 'there is *no* God but *one*'.

---

6   'There is *one* God and Father of us all' (Eph. 4:5) and 'There is *one* God and *one* mediator between God and men, the man Christ Jesus' (1 Tim 2:5).

7   Isa. 45:5.

Such clear teaching was abundantly necessary in Corinth (v. 5). His words 'there are... gods in heaven and on earth' mean that such deities 'in heaven' were currently being worshipped 'on earth' in the temples of Corinth. Such temples and shrines were, indeed, numerous for, 'there are ... gods many and lords many'. As noted above in Pausanias' remarks there were temples in Corinth in whichever direction one looked.

But we must note his twice repeated words, 'said to be' in verse 5. There are *'said to be* "gods in heaven"' as there are *'said to be* "gods many...lords many."'' But these exist only in the minds and words of the people of Corinth. They are merely *'said to be* gods' and *'said to be* Lords'. The reality is: 'There is no God but one' (v. 4). The only and true reality is what we know about the one true God through the gospel and baptismal instruction.

Thus he writes in the strongest terms grammatically[8] available to him, *'But* for us...' (v. 6).

> But for us
> there is
> > one God,
> > the Father
> > > from whom are all things
> > > for whom we exist
>
> and
> > one Lord,
> > Jesus Christ
> > > through whom are all things
> > > through whom we exist.

The Corinthians said, 'There are gods many and lords many' but they are merely 'said-to-be gods'. But the word of God, as echoed in this credo, said, 'There is *one* God, *one* Lord'. At least five interlocking truths must be noted in Paul's solemn words.

First, Yahweh the God of Israel has now revealed himself through Christ as 'God, the *Father*'. While the 'fatherhood' of Yahweh to his people was hinted at in the Old Testament it took Jesus' teaching and especially his address to God in prayer to reveal the astonishing reality that God was *'Abba,* dear Father'. Without Jesus' teaching the true and inner nature of God as 'Father' must have remained hidden, shrouded in mystery. In

---

8   Greek: *alla*, 'But'.

no other religious system is God like the forgiving Father who welcomes home and forgives the wayward prodigal and who seeks to reconcile the elder to the younger brother. But it follows from Jesus' prayers to God as *Abba* and from Paul's words quoted here that Jesus must be the *Son of God*, uniquely so (see also on 1:9).

Second, Paul states that both 'Father' and 'Lord' are 'One', that is, *unique*. The 'Lord' who is the 'Son' is also 'One' that is *co-unique* with the Father. This must mean that the 'One' who is 'Lord' and 'Son' shares in the unique deity of 'God, the Father'.

Third, there is a dynamic relationship between the Father and the Lord in relationship to 'all things'. By 'all things' Paul means the creation and sustenance of the universe but also its redemption for the Kingdom of God. The prepositions 'from' and 'through' give us a glimpse of the workings of the Father and the Son in time, space and history. 'All things' are 'from' the Father and they are 'through' the Son. The Father is the source but the Son is the agent of 'all things'.

Fourth, alongside 'all things' Paul speaks of 'we' believers. 'We' are Christian believers 'through him', that is, the Son who is the Lord. He is the agent both of creation but also of the 'new creation' (2 Cor. 5:17). Believers will be in the Kingdom of God, the new creation, because of their union with Christ crucified and risen.

Fifth, the Father is both the 'source' of 'all things' creation, providence, redemption and the One *'unto'* whom 'all things' *are*. Specially is this true of believers who have been picked up along the way by the gospel. Our whole existence is 'towards' and 'unto' the Father and his Kingdom. We are headed 'towards' the Father and we are 'for' and 'unto' him. Here is our hope.

> Praise God from whom all blessings flow.
> Praise him all creatures here below.
> Praise him above ye heavenly host.
> Praise Father, Son and Holy Ghost.

All these things many of the Corinthians 'know'. But not all know.

3. To Eat or Not to Eat? (8:7-13)
Paul now introduces a situation that most likely came to his attention from a report rather than from the Corinthians' letter.

They are unlikely to have asked him about the specific situation which they must have sensed put them in a bad light.

He begins this new section with very strong words which contrast with the true 'knowledge' about the Father and the Lord (vv. 4, 6). '*But* not all have this knowledge', he interjects (v. 7).

> There are some who accustomed until now to idols
> eat food as if it were sacrificed to an idol.

In other words, 'some' of the members of the church have by long custom eaten idol-sacrificed food believing that the god was actually 'present'. Paul says these Christians are 'weak in their conscience'. By 'conscience' we think of 'a guilty conscience' or a 'clear conscience', an inner voice of right and wrong. But the New Testament means something different. Quite simply, by 'conscience' Paul means our understanding of the gospel as it impacts on behaviour. Because of their lifelong worship of idols these Corinthians, whom we presume are new converts, have not yet come to believe in their hearts as well as their heads that 'an idol has no real existence'. Their return to the temples would mean eating the idol-sacrificed food with a 'defiled conscience'. Once more they would be joined to the unholy deity and be 'unclean' in their understanding of themselves. Their relationship with the Lord Christ would be destroyed.

Paul is quick to anticipate misunderstanding of these words (v. 8). Because 'a god has no real existence and there is no God but one', indeed, the food itself is irrelevant. 'Nothing is unclean of itself', he was to tell the Romans in words echoing the teaching of Jesus (Rom. 14:14; cf. Mark 7:18-19).

> Food does not commend us to God.
> If we do not eat we are not worse off.
> If we do eat we are not better.

Paul does not wish to bring Gentiles back under Jewish food laws, from which Jesus has set humanity free.

Nonetheless, Paul warns (v. 9), 'Take care lest this *authority*[9] of yours to be free of rules about food becomes a stumbling

---

9   Greek *exousia*, delegated authority. In this case the teaching of Jesus that 'all
     foods are clean' (Mark 7:18-19) is the mandate for freedom from the food laws
     under the Old Testament.

stone over which the weak brother or sister will fall'. Earlier Paul had echoed their slogans in tandem: 'Everything is lawful' and 'Food for the stomach and the stomach for food'. In the abstract those slogans are true enough. Indeed, they both appear to derive from Jesus (see on 6:12-13). We remember that Jesus liberated people from the attitudes that some foods were unclean and not to be eaten. The consequence of Jesus' words is that 'all foods are clean' (see Mark 7:14-19). But in the 'real world' of temple culture in Corinth those words could be twisted to suggest that eating idol-sacrificed meat was open to fellow-Christians who still believed that the god was present in the food.

With these words it is clear that Paul has added a further dimension to his discussion about the non-existence of idols (vv. 4-6). He is also concerned to challenge the proposition that they were authorized to eat whatever they chose. It is quite likely that the Corinthians held tenaciously to their supposed freedom. But freedom must be qualified; it is seldom absolute.

Paul's introduction of the word 'authority' is quite striking. Its appearance here anticipates his use of what will be the keyword in the next chapter where it occurs five times. That whole chapter is devoted to examples where 'authority' and therefore 'freedom' is laid aside to fulfil greater and higher considerations. Paul is calling on the Corinthians to put to one side their 'authority' to eat whatever they choose for the sake of the spiritual welfare of other Christians.

Now at last Paul comes to the actual pastoral situation which he describes vividly (v. 10). Here Paul addresses individually the Corinthians about the impact of his or her behaviour on the believer of weak conscience:

> For if someone sees you a man or woman of knowledge
> reclining at a meal in an idol's temple[10]
> will not his weak conscience, being emboldened,
> lead him to eat the idol-sacrificed food?

Archaeology has provided two pieces of information which illuminate verse 10. First, a number of invitations on papyrus have been found, like the one following:

---

10   Greek: *eidoleion.*

> Herais asks you to dine at the dining room of the Sarapeion
> at a banquet of the Lord Serapis tomorrow,
> namely, the 11th from the 9th hour.[11]

Here a man named Herais is inviting friends or family to join him for a meal in the temple in the mid-afternoon. It is evident that meals for small groups were held in the presence of the god Serapis in his temple, the Sarapeion.

Second, excavations at Corinth have unearthed a temple to the goddess Demeter-Kore with forty dining rooms, each about 5 metres x 5 metres, each accommodating nine or ten people, but without cooking facilities. Most likely these facilities were reasonably typical for other temples in Corinth and other cities. The food sacrificed and cooked elsewhere in the precincts of this temple was brought to these small rooms which probably also had a statue of the god. The meal was eaten in fellowship with the god who was thought to be present with his worshippers.

Paul envisages a situation where the believer of 'weak conscience' caught a glimpse of well-instructed Christians attending such a meal in the presence of the god. In an arresting wordplay,[12] Paul says that the 'weak' brother will be, literally, 'built up' to go and eat too! Love 'builds up' sound understanding in others (v. 1), but lovelessness 'builds up' an understanding in them that 'destroys', as he now explains.

Earlier Paul had claimed that the exercise of their 'authority' to eat food might cause a weak believer to fall (v. 9). His initial word, 'For' now substantiates that claim. 'For the weak man is destroyed by your knowledge' (v. 11). These are powerful words since 'destroy'[13] means 'cause to perish', 'to be lost' from the Kingdom of God. In other words, the exercise of 'knowledge' by the well-informed Christian without a caring awareness of the impact of his actions on a fellow-believer has the effect of pushing him back into the spiritual darkness and to eternal desolation. Paul adds, poignantly, 'the brother on whose account Christ died'. Christ died to save him, but by

---

11   Although this papyrus was found in Egypt it is clearly typical of other invitations, including at Corinth.

12   On the Greek word, *oikodomeō*, 'I build up'.

13   Greek: *apollumi*, 'I destroy'.

your 'knowledge' you will destroy him. This is an arresting statement given that the 'knowledge' in question is entirely correct in itself, that 'there is no God but one', that 'all things' exist only on account of the 'one God' and the 'one Lord' and that 'all foods are clean'.

By his action the man of knowledge has sinned against fellow brothers in Christ and wounded their already weak consciences (v. 12). But these are members of the congregation, that body of people for whom Christ died, which Paul here equates with Christ himself. Earlier Paul taught that 'your bodies are members of Christ' (see on 6:15; 12:12). But the members who will be destroyed are 'weak' brothers, a group for whom Paul feels a special responsibility (see 2 Cor. 11:29; Rom. 14:21). Paul's tender pastoral concern for the 'weak' follows Jesus' burden for the 'sinners', the 'lost' and for the 'little ones' in Israel (Luke 15:4; 19:10; Matt. 18:10-14; Mark 9:42).

So Paul concludes this passage with a solemn promise. If eating food would cause a brother Christian to fall Paul will not eat meat ever again (v. 13). We note Paul's shift from 'food', which he has used to this point, to 'meat'. Meat was a luxury beyond the reach of most people and doubtless a special treat for rare occasions of celebration. But not even for this will Paul break his commitment if such eating caused the spiritual downfall of a brother or sister for whom Christ died.

Two issues converge in this passage, one relating to the gods, the other to food. Paul agreed with the Corinthians that no idol but only God has real existence, but out of concern for the 'weak' believers' grasp of the faith, he urged that people of knowledge should not attend the idol's temple and eat food dedicated to the god. As the passage unfolds, however, it becomes apparent that Paul is also reflecting on the 'authority' the Corinthians felt to eat any food whatsoever. This attitude most likely derived from Jesus' liberation of his people from the Levitical food laws. Theologically true though their view was on God and idols, on the one hand, and their liberty to eat food, on the other, Paul qualified both truths with an overriding principle, the care of the 'weak' brother/sister. But this calls for the Corinthians to forgo their 'rights', as they saw them. Paul will devote the chapter following to this great principle.

SOME QUESTIONS FOR PERSONAL REFLECTION:

1. What is involved as a prerequisite to 'knowing' God?

2. Can you think of examples where we care for the 'weak' consciences of fellow Christians?

STUDY QUESTIONS:

1. How can knowledge 'about' God bring arrogance? How can it actually destroy fellow believers?

2. What are the five interlocking truths which Paul states?

3. What was the problem of some of the Corinthian believers in eating food sacrificed to idols?

4. How does the 'man of knowledge' sin against their fellow brothers? How severe is it?

5. Who is the weaker brother? What demonstrates his weakness?

6. What is the solemn promise that Paul makes?

9

Freedom Forsaken
(1 Cor. 9:1-27)

This entire chapter is devoted to Paul's 'freedom' which he enjoyed as a consequence of 'authority' (or 'rights') he had received from the Lord. This picks up his reference from the previous chapter to the Corinthians' 'authority' which, however, they were using to the destruction of weaker members of the congregation. For this reason the present chapter is all about Paul relinquishing his 'rights', forsaking his freedom. This he does because of an overriding principle, his Christ-inspired passion for the lost.

To many modern readers Paul comes across as rather self-important. It is true that he devotes chapter 9 to himself! But there is something we must understand about Paul's use of his own example as a teaching method. He knew that people learn much from a minister's life, perhaps even more than from his words. So Paul set out deliberately to 'model' some critical aspects of the Christian life for these new converts. One example is his determination to work to support himself rather than depend upon others.[1] Work was despised in Graeco-Roman society, something fit only for slaves. So Paul set out to introduce the values of the Kingdom by embodying those values in his own life, often at considerable personal cost since tentmaking

---

1   1 Thess 2:9; 4:11-12; 2 Thess. 3:8-10; Acts 18:3; 20:34-35; 1 Cor. 4:12; 2 Cor. 6:5; 11:23, 27.

(using leather!) was heavy, tiring and unhygienic work.[2] Paul discusses this at some length in verses 13-23. Another example is found in this present chapter where Paul points to 'rights relinquished' so that the Corinthians will do likewise for the 'weak' brothers (8:7-13), but also for unbelievers (10:23–11:1).

But there is more to this chapter than meets the eye. To be sure, Paul is offering his own example of laying aside his 'rights' for the Corinthians. But why is he so defensive, about his apostleship on the one hand (vv. 1-6), and about his refusal to accept payment on the other hand (vv. 13-23)? It is abundantly clear that 'others', as he calls them, who are outside the Corinthian church, do not regard him as an apostle (v. 2a) and 'stand in judgement' over him (v. 3). To be sure, Paul reminds them that he has laid aside his rights. But first he has to remind them that he has those 'rights', that he is an apostle.

What is these outsiders' problem with Paul? Reading a little between the lines there appear to be three points at which he failed to meet their criteria for apostleship. First, he was not a member of the original band of disciples nor a witness to the resurrected Jesus nor commissioned by him, but he had been a persecutor of the church in Jerusalem (v. 1c). Second, they seized upon his decision not to accept payment as proof that he was not an apostle; apparently other apostles, with wives, were financially supported (vv. 4-5; cf. 2 Cor. 11:7-12). Third, they regarded his openness to eating with Gentiles as evidence of having abandoned his Jewishness and therefore any qualification to be an apostle of the (Jewish) Messiah Jesus (vv. 19-23). From Paul's perspective freedom to eat with Gentiles was logical, given that he sought to include the Gentiles in the people of God without circumcision, without the keeping of the Law.

Who might these 'others' have been who rejected Paul's apostleship? Because he fails to tell us we are left to make an educated guess. My guess is that they were the Judaisers from Jerusalem who had followed Paul to Galatia and Syria and who have now spread these negative words about Paul in Achaia. From Paul's self-defence in the first two chapters of the Galatians we get a reasonable idea of the misinformation being spread about him. If this conjecture is correct I further

---

2   See P. W. Barnett, 'Tentmaking' *DPL*, pp. 925-7.

suggest that these persons probably used the networks of the synagogues to sow the seeds of doubt in the minds of Jewish members of the churches, including at Corinth. It does not appear that these opponents of Paul have yet arrived in Corinth. He speaks about them as if they had not yet penetrated that church. That day would not be long in coming. A year later, when he writes Second Corinthians, the Judaisers have arrived and are wreaking havoc in Corinth.[3]

1. Paul an Apostle (9:1-6)

This highly rhetorical section falls into two parts. In the first (vv. 1-2) Paul addresses questions and statements to the Corinthians. In the second (vv. 3-6), however, he turns to speak to people elsewhere who dispute his apostleship. The language is of an imaginary court room and Paul is 'in the dock' facing accusation and making his defence, which he does, in part, by a series of questions back to his accusers.

Paul's opening words, 'Am I not free?' (v. 1a) tell us that Paul is continuing his ministry to the Corinthians about their stubborn insistence to continue eating in the temple of the gods. They based this 'authority' (see on 8:9) on their 'knowledge' that 'there is no God but one' (see on 8:4) and, most likely, on Jesus' abolition of the distinction between 'clean' and 'unclean' food. Paul's dramatic question focuses attention on himself as one who through the 'knowledge' of the gospel was, indeed, 'free'. Throughout the chapter following he will explain that his freedom was not an absolute, but that concern for the salvation of others was a higher concern that qualified his 'rights'.

His second question, 'Am I not an apostle?' (v. 1b) comes as a complete surprise. Why raise this question now? The next two verses, however, make it clear that there were those outside the congregation in Corinth who challenged Paul's apostleship and who stood in judgement over him. But Paul's rhetorical question is phrased grammatically to demand the affirmative, 'Yes, Paul is an apostle'.

Paul answers his question by means of two facts, both of which are posed as questions expecting the answer, 'Yes'. First, 'Have I not seen Jesus our Lord?' Every word here is important.

---

3   See 2 Corinthians 2:17–3:2; 5:11-13; 10:12–11:6, 16-23; 12:11-13.

The perfect tense of the verb indicates not only the *moment* Paul 'saw' but also that Paul *continued* to 'see' Jesus his Lord. The glory Paul 'saw' with his eyes on Damascus Road he still 'sees' inwardly, in his heart. Whom did Paul 'see'? It was, he says, 'Jesus our Lord'. Paul saw the historical Jesus, Jesus of Nazareth, whom the disciples had accompanied for three years. However, whereas those disciples saw Jesus alive on the third day and on various other occasions for 'forty days' prior to his exaltation (Acts 1:3), Paul 'saw' him as the now ascended and glorified 'Lord' in heaven. Paul will make this distinction between himself and the other apostles quite clear later (see on 15:8).

But there were some, apparently, who felt that, because he was not an original disciple of Jesus, nor a witness to his bodily resurrection within the 'forty days', he was not, on those counts, a true apostle, 'sent' forth to preach (cf. vv. 2a, 3). Paul insists, however, that the Lord truly 'sent' him, placing him with the other apostles. For Jesus the Lord not only 'appeared' to Paul but also 'spoke' to him, commissioning him to 'preach him to the Gentiles'.[4] This was no mere 'vision and revelation of the Lord' like that fourteen years prior to the writing of Second Corinthians (2 Cor. 12:1). Rather, Paul the persecutor 'saw' and 'heard' Jesus the Lord on the Road to Damascus who then and there called him to be his apostle. This encounter radically changed the direction of Paul's life.

There is a second reason Paul advances in support of his claim to be an apostle (v. 1d). 'Are you not the result of my work in the Lord?' he asks them.[5] Let the Corinthians look around their assembly. How did they come to be confessing believers in Jesus the Lord except by the ministry of Paul as preacher and pastor? Was it not he who had gathered them as a community of Christian believers? However, it was not by his raw labours, as it were, but work exercised 'in the Lord'. It was due to Paul's spiritual union with the Lord that these people knew the Lord and by which they were a genuinely Christian body. Apart from 'the Lord' blessing and owning Paul's work they would not have been a community of confessing believers.

---

4   Galatians 1:15-16.

5   Paul makes similar appeals to their conversion as evidence of his own genuineness as an apostle in 2 Corinthians 3:2-3; 10:7, 18; 13:5-7.

The reason for Paul's assertion of his apostolicity in the previous verse now emerges (v. 2a) in the words, 'If to others I am not an apostle I am indeed to you'. Whatever problems existed between Paul and the Corinthians *they* were not yet rejecting his apostolic authority. This was to change within a year, however, as his intense defence in the Second Letter reveals (see 2 Cor. 11:1–12:13). As noted above in the introduction to this passage, the opposition to Paul's apostleship was probably from the conservatively Jewish elements within the Jerusalem church. Based on his self-defence in Galatians 1–2 it appears that they attacked his claim to apostleship because (1) he had not been an original disciple, nor (2) a witness of the bodily resurrected Jesus (but only of the ascended Jesus), and (3) that he had included Gentiles in the covenant on a Law-free, circumcision-free basis.

But the Corinthians, who were we suspect mostly Gentiles, would not have been persuaded by these arguments from the Judaising quarter. Indeed, Paul calls the Corinthians 'the seal of my apostleship in the Lord' (v. 2b). A sender made his special imprint on hot wax on a document as a mark of his ownership and therefore of its genuine origin. The church in Corinth was the Lord's seal on Paul, which said 'This man is *my* apostle'. But why should the Corinthians, in particular, be the Lord's 'seal' on Paul's office as apostle? Corinth was, by far, the largest city in which Paul had established a church since he had begun his westwards and Rome-wards mission from Antioch eight years earlier. I think Paul saw his entire mission to the Gentiles dependent on the survival and growth of the gospel in the Achaian capital. This would explain, for example, why Paul sent no less than four letters to this church and paid them no fewer than three visits. Not least, Corinth was chosen to be the launching pad for his ultimate journey to the world centre of the Gentiles, Rome.

Paul now turns from addressing the Corinthians (vv. 1-2) to face these judges from other places (Jerusalem?) who dispute his apostleship. Like a man in court, he says to his accusers, 'This is my defence to you' (v. 3). He then proceeds to fire three questions back at them, each of which contains the word 'authority' (*exousia* vv. 4,5,6). This important word was exactly appropriate for the 'delegated authority' possessed by an apostle, one 'sent' by Christ.

He asks, first, 'Don't we have the *authority* to our food and drink?' (v. 4). In short, don't I have the right to be supported financially in my ministry as an apostle?

Secondly, he asks more specifically (v. 5), 'Don't we have the *authority* to lead about a wife who is a believer, like the rest of the apostles, and the brothers of the Lord and Cephas?' As honoured leaders the 'apostles' and the 'brothers of the Lord' were to be given hospitality and provisions wherever they went among the churches. Jesus' brothers James and Jude are well known from the New Testament as leaders in the early church.[6] Paul insists that he enjoyed the same 'rights' to shelter and food as these 'others' he mentions. Paul's appeal to the Corinthians' experience suggests that they were familiar with the other 'apostles', 'brothers [and sisters?] of the Lord' and with 'Cephas and his wife'. Most likely these leaders had visited Corinth in the three years between Paul's departure from the city and the writing of this letter.

But thirdly (v. 6) he asks, 'Is it only me and Barnabas who do not have the *authority not* to work?' Again, he appears to be appealing to something they knew, namely that Barnabas, too, chose not to exercise his right not to work for his sustenance. Evidently Barnabas[7] was known to the people of Corinth.[8] Otherwise why would Paul refer to him?

---

6   The four brothers of Jesus James, Joseph, Jude and Simon are named in Mark 6:3. James, the eldest, is often referred to in the NT but the third, Jude ('the brother of James' Jude 1) only once. See further, R. J. Bauckham, 'Relatives of Jesus' DLNT pages 1004-1006.

7   Joseph Bar Nabas ('Son of a Prophet') was a Levite from Cyprus, a man of means and the uncle of John Mark (Acts 4:36-37; Col. 4:10). When Paul first returned to Jerusalem to the suspicion of the apostles Barnabas believed in Paul's genuineness and advocated his cause (Acts 9:27). At the time the church in Antioch began to flourish the Jerusalem apostles sent this trusted leader to the Syrian capital (Acts 11:22). Barnabas travelled to Tarsus to bring Paul back to Antioch where the two ministered side by side for some time. Later Barnabas and Paul set out on the first westwards missionary journey, to Cyprus and Galatia (Acts 13–14 *passim*). After the Jerusalem Council in *c.* A.D. 49 their association ended in a dispute and Barnabas went with John Mark to Cyprus (Acts 15:39).

8   Reference to Barnabas and a possible visit by him to Corinth in the early fifties raises interesting possibilities about the authorship of the Letter to the Hebrews, an anonymous work. Hebrews 13:23-24 refers to Timothy's 'release' (from prison?) and sends greetings to the readers from 'those from Italy'. We do not know of Timothy being imprisoned, though he was in Corinth at that time (1 Cor. 16:10-11). So, too, were Priscilla and Aquila who had recently come from Italy (Acts 18:1-3). Barnabas was one of the few leaders in the early church who enjoyed the reputation to write such a letter as Hebrews.

2. The Rights of an Apostle Relinquished (9:7-12)

By a series of homely examples in the form of rhetorical questions Paul now shows the rightness of a congregation providing for the apostle (v. 7). The serving soldier is provided with rations; the vinegrower eats from his crop; the herdsman drinks the milk of his sheep and goats. In short, there is the same connection between the work of an apostle and his nourishment from the congregation as there is between the work of the legionary, viniculturist and shepherd and their sustenance. All ideas of opulent lifestyle, however, must be dismissed. In each case the provision was minimal, the 'bare necessities', as it were.

But Paul is not merely employing examples from life. Again using a rhetorical question he asks (v. 8), 'Doesn't the Law say the same thing?' First he quotes from the 'Law of Moses'[9] (v. 9b) and then follows with a short exposition of that text (vv. 9c-10):

Do not muzzle an ox while it threshes out the grain (Deut. 25:4).[10]

Paul observes that by this provision God cares about the working farm animal. God's justice and mercy dictated that the ox must be sustained from its own labour and allowed to eat as it worked from the grain threshed from the husks. In short, Paul finds the same principle in the 'Law of Moses' as in his own examples given in verse 7. It is a matter of God's 'care' that people and animals derive their sustenance from the work they do.

However, in asking, 'Is it about oxen God is concerned?' Paul gets to the point he wishes to make. He is saying that the 'Law' is to be understood as to its *end-time* meaning, that is, the preaching of the gospel in the light of the resurrection of Jesus. He is not saying that God doesn't now care about oxen! That would be to miss the prophetic point, as he sees it to be in the text of Deuteronomy 25:4.

Accordingly he asks rhetorically (v. 10), 'Surely God says this *for us*, doesn't he?' He adds, '*It* the text cited from Deuteronomy was written *for us*'. In other words, because Paul sees the goal and end-point of the Law as Christ (see Rom. 10:4), he takes it that what is written in the Law about oxen threshing grain is

---

9   That is, the Pentateuch. The first *five* books of the Old Testament, were traditionally attributed to Moses and called the 'Law' (in Hebrew, *torah* and in Greek, *nomos*).

10   Paul also cites this text in 1 Timothy 5:18, adding, 'The labourer is worthy of his hire'. The latter words are used by Jesus (Luke 10:7) for the Mission of the 72.

now to be understood from the vantage point of the ministry of the new covenant of Christ and the Spirit.

So Paul picks up that text about oxen eating the grain that is trodden out and applies it to Christian ministry. 'Because', he continues, 'the ploughman ought to plough in hope and the thresher ought to thresh in hope of sharing in the harvest'. Ministry, like cropping, begins with turning the soil and ends with the grain that is harvested. Ploughmen plough and threshers thresh expecting and anticipating a harvest of grain. Likewise Christian ministers till the soil and sow the seed expecting to reap a harvest of souls for the Kingdom, while deriving their physical sustenance from those labours.

He concludes his brief end-time exposition of Deuteronomy 25:4 with the clinching question (v. 11), 'If we have sowed spiritual things among you, are we expecting too much in reaping a material harvest from you?' That text was written ultimately *for us.* As we have sowed the word of God in Corinth it is our 'right' to expect material sustenance from you. But this 'right' is not merely based on the observable realities that soldiers, vine dressers and shepherds derive their living from their work. Much more Paul secures that 'right' from a passage in the Law of God understood in the light of the 'ends of the age' (see on 10:11) which have been 'fulfilled' among them in the preaching of the gospel in Corinth. This is a 'right' ordained by God in the Sacred Scriptures.

Having established this fundamental 'right' for ministers of the gospel, Paul now returns to the presenting issue (v. 12). He has 'relinquished this right', 'forsaken this freedom'. 'If others have shared in this right', he says thinking of 'other apostles, brothers of the Lord and Peter' (v. 5) who have brought their wives with them and been provided for 'how much more do we have that right?' Paul and his companions Silvanus and Timothy did the initial ploughing, sowing and reaping in Corinth. Paul and his group established the assembly of Christ in that city. It is abundantly clear that he and they enjoyed the God-ordained 'right' and 'authority' to be sustained in Corinth.

Paul interrupts this lengthy argument for his defence (see on v. 3) with a very emphatic 'But ...' followed immediately by a further 'But...' Greek has no stronger way of expressing an opposite view than the word Paul uses.[11]

11　Greek: *alla*, 'but'.

But we have not made use of this 'authority.'
But we have endured all things,
lest we place any obstacle in front of the gospel of Christ.

We should leave aside any romantic notion about 'tentmaking' ministry in Paul's case. Tents were made of leather which was heavy to handle, foul smelling and very unclean to the handlers. Most likely Paul's hand and arms were permanently stained. Paul's trade included the repair of all manner of leather goods like saddles and boots. Furthermore, he plied his trade at night. Because of tentmaking Paul 'endured all things'. For him tentmaking was a source of physical suffering since it was so arduous and exhausting. But in a society that despised work especially manual work as fit only for slaves, it was a source of his social rejection, including from the Christians in Corinth.

Paul hints at three reasons for working to support himself and his colleagues so as not to be a 'burden' on the churches. First, Paul sought to remove the teacher of the gospel from associations of the many travelling teachers and philosophers, many of whom were charlatans who bled those whom they instructed.[12] Those 'others' like 'brothers of the Lord' and 'Cephas' who came after Paul were supported in existing congregations. But Paul as a pioneer missionary would not accept sustenance. This principle still applies in 'trail blazing' missionary situations lest the preacher be thought of as just another guru with his hand out for money. Second, Paul deliberately set the example of work to support himself in a culture where idleness was endemic.[13] Third, Paul regarded God's call to him as giving no alternative but to obey. His payment was to receive no payment (see on vv. 16-18), to preach the gospel 'free of charge'.[14]

3. Paul's gospel 'Free of Charge' (9:13-18)
Again Paul affirms that those who preach the gospel should have their living from the gospel, for two reasons. One is that he does not wish to undermine the rightful claims of those who minister and pastor to be supported. But equally Paul insists on this principle so firmly since it provides the foil against which

---

12   See 1 Thessalonians 1:5; 2:3-6.

13   1 Thessalonians 5:14; 2 Thessalonians 3:6-13.

14   See 2 Corinthians 11:7.

he states his counter principle not to receive such payment.

Why should those who minister be supported financially? Earlier he pointed to the soldier, the vine grower and the shepherd as examples of those who derive their living from their work (see on v. 7). Now he finds in the priests in the Temple in Jerusalem a similar principle (v. 13). Nonetheless, this is not just another example, but one sanctioned in the Sacred Scriptures. His introductory, 'Do you not know...?' routinely appeals to an aspect of catechesis about which they had been instructed. This makes it likely that the case in point is the Jerusalem Temple and not pagan temples.[15] In any case, Paul is unlikely to use as a teaching example such temples, especially in a passage (chapters 8–10) in which he is attacking 'temple culture'. Paul's simple observation is that the priests and those who work in the temple, and in particular those who serve at the altar, have a share of what is sacrificed. 'The priest who offers it shall eat it', declared the Lord to Moses (Lev. 6:26).

Paul buttresses this Old Testament provision for priests with the greater requirement of the Lord Jesus Christ for new covenant ministers, as indicated by his opening words, 'Thus also the Lord ordered...' (v. 14). Here 'ordered' (*dietaxen*) carries the double meaning 'commanded' and 'arranged'. By Jesus' 'command' he provided for an 'ordering' whereby 'those who announce the gospel should live from the gospel'.

We do not have an exact version of these words from Jesus in the Gospels. Rather, Jesus' instructions for the Mission of the Twelve and the Mission of the Seventy-two carried over to the Post-Easter ministry of apostles and others, first in Judaea, Samaria and Galilee and then among the Gentiles. Amongst these instructions was Jesus' proverb, 'The worker is worthy of his pay' (Luke 10:7; Matt. 10:10), which Paul later joins to the word about not muzzling the ox when it threshes the grain (1 Tim. 5:18). In Galatians, Paul's earliest extant letter written about fifteen years after Jesus' ministry, the apostle directs, 'Let the one who is taught the word share all good things with the one who catechizes him' (Gal. 6:6). By that time Jesus' 'ordering' of financial provision for his missionaries and pastors was well established.

---

15 *Contra* Fee, page 412, who thinks it could be either the Jerusalem Temple or a pagan temple.

Having secured the 'rights' for other 'workers', Paul immediately declares his own 'right' not to 'use any of these things'
(v. 15; see on vv. 6, 12b). And lest the Corinthians think he has
changed his mind he is quick to add that he is not writing at
this present time to ask for such provisions. Indeed, he declares
this to be a life and death issue for him, something he will not
go back on. 'It is good for me rather to die than...', he writes
without completing his sentence. But we have no difficulty
working out what he means since he now says, 'No one will
nullify my boast'. This is most unusual. What can he mean?

To our ears 'boast' carries the idea of arrogant and conceited
claims which one makes about oneself. The heavyweight Mu-
hammed Ali used to crow, 'I am the greatest'. Is Paul speaking
like this? Decidedly not. We need to understand that by 'boast'
Paul means his own private thoughts, which he now discloses
to others. By 'boast' Paul means 'my rightful pride before God'.
He is thinking of the Last Day and the verdict of the Lord on
his ministry as an apostle. What will he point to as he stands
before the Judge seated on his throne? 'Not that I preach the
gospel', he will say. 'That cannot be my boast.' This is because,
as he declares, 'Necessity is laid on me. Woe is me if I do *not*
preach the gospel'.

Paul is casting his mind back to the Lord's intervention as the
persecutor journeyed to Damascus. Struck down by the blinding
light the awesome voice directed him to preach to the Gentiles.
There was no negotiation, no discussion, no option, no delay. Just
do it and do it forthwith! So how can he 'boast in', 'take pride in'
anything the heavenly Lord had commanded him to do?

He explains further (v. 17). 'If I do this by *my own choice*,
I have a reward. But if I had no choice, I am simply being obedient to my responsibility.' Because he 'had no choice' then it
was just a matter of doing what he was told by the Lord. The
Lord had imposed on Paul a 'responsibility' (*oikonomia*, 'stewardship') and like an obedient slave he must fulfil his owner's
will. Not that Paul feels coerced or resentful. Paul, like no other,
expresses a passionate love for his Lord in the knowledge of
the immeasurable love of the Lord in dying for him (see e.g.,
2 Cor. 5:14; Gal. 2:20).

But this is not the point he is making now. Rather, he is
responding to those who see in his failure to take his pay an

implicit admission that he was not, after all, an apostle. Apostles were paid, they reasoned. Everybody knew that. Therefore the man who was unpaid must not, *ipso facto*, be an apostle. But, as Paul is now explaining, he could not accept pay since that would remove his only 'boast' to the Lord on the Great Day.

So there is no financial recompense for his labours. Therefore he asks (v. 18a), 'What then is my reward?' This is no rhetorical question for he proceeds immediately to answer, 'That in preaching the gospel I offer it free of charge' (v. 18b). Paul goes on say that his 'reward' to offer the gospel *gratis* is so that he 'might *not make full use of* his rights in the gospel to be paid' (v. 18c).

This latter remark merely completes the circle of thought begun earlier, 'I have *not made use of* any of this' (v. 15; cf. v. 6). So what is Paul's ultimate reason for relinquishing his rights, forsaking his freedom? It is this:

> ...in preaching the gospel I offer it free of charge... (v. 18b)

In a parallel passage Paul says he preaches the gospel 'as a gift' (2 Cor. 11:7). The gospel comes from Paul with 'no strings' attached, no price tag. It is Paul's 'gift' to those who will receive it. As such, Paul's labour in tentmaking, which makes it possible for the gospel to be a 'gift' to its recipients, is itself a potent sign that the salvation he preaches also comes as a 'gift' from God. Elsewhere Paul wrote that we are 'justified as a *gift*, by grace' (Rom. 3:24). Paul's *words* about the grace of God were totally embodied in a *life* of practical sacrifice that gave people the gospel as a 'gift', 'free of charge'. Paul's controversial decision that 'his pay is to receive no pay' was a dramatic demonstration of the controversial, law-free character of the gospel. The gospel is 'free of charge' and Paul offers it 'free of charge'. The stained hands of Paul the tentmaker who preached Christ crucified were a 'sacrament' of the generosity of God giving his righteousness by grace, but not cheaply.

If a conjecture may be permitted, may I propose that Paul's decision to 'relinquish his rights' was his enacted sign that his was a unique apostolicity. He had 'seen the Lord' (v. 1) and had been entrusted with a 'commission' by him (v. 17). He is an apostle. But he is a different apostle, uniquely so. He was confronted not by the resurrected Lord as the other apostles were, but by the resurrected *and exalted* Lord from heaven, outside the forty day time frame of resurrection appearances. Furthermore, Paul alone was charged with preaching Christ to the Gentiles to include them in the covenant people. It was one thing for Paul to insist on 'no pay' when he had the 'authority' of an apostle to be paid, but it was another that he insisted in working to support himself while preaching the gospel 'free of charge'. The twin facts of having rights but forsaking them by working made Paul a unique apostle.

This is his answer to those who stand in judgement over him (see on v. 3). But it is also the living example of 'relinquishing rights'. In view of the Corinthians' insistence on demanding their 'rights' to go to the temples for meals this was a 'message' they needed to hear. He now develops this theme further.

4. 'All Things to All People' (9:19-23)
Paul now speaks in a paradoxical proverb (v. 19).

> For being free from all I have become the slave of all.

Because he has stood aside from his 'rights' Paul is beholden to no one. He is free from obligation to fit in with the expectation that apostles will be paid. He is free from the cultural conventions of Corinth where wealthy people expected to pay visiting lecturers and those lecturers expected to be paid. Because he is Christ's 'slave' and given no choice about serving his owner (v. 17), he is, paradoxically, free from 'all people'.

Yet it is not a selfish freedom, such as was the mark of 'autonomous' men of Greece and Rome who stood aloof from obligations and anxieties. Rather, Paul was 'free' to be the 'slave' of others, whether Jews or Pagans. But he 'freely' embraced that 'slavery' for one reason, to 'gain' the greatest number of people for their allegiance to Jesus the Christ.

Having stated the principle of voluntary slavery Paul now gives examples as to how this has worked out in the years he has been a missionary apostle:

> To Jews   I became as a Jew to gain Jews.
> To those under Law   as under Law,
>   not being myself under Law,
>   to gain those under Law
>   (v. 20).

Being a Jew was a matter of ancestry, of being able to trace one's descent from Abraham (Rom. 11:1; 2 Cor. 11:22). As well, a Jew was defined as being 'under Law',[16] that is, one who was subject to the whole dispensation of Moses as set out in the Pentateuch. While the Ten Commandments were at the heart of being 'under Law', in practice it meant submission to the totality of Jewish ritual and ceremonial culture, including the strict observance of the Calendar and food laws. Paul was 'a Hebrew born of Hebrews; as to the Law a Pharisee' (Phil. 3:5); a younger leader in strict Judaism and a zealous persecutor of those who deviated from it (Gal 1:13-14). He was, however, blinded to the 'hope' of the Old Testament scriptures (2 Cor. 3:12-15). Only when Christ inter-cepted him approaching Damascus did he begin to 'see' the One to whom the promises of the Old Testament pointed (2 Cor. 3:16).

At the moment of slavery to the Lord Christ, however, did Paul become free from the shackles of Judaism? As a man 'in Christ' he was no longer 'under Law'. Nonetheless, to 'gain' those still 'under Law' Paul placed himself 'under Law' when present with Jews in order to 'gain' them. When in the company of Jews Paul kept their feasts and ate their foods. With Jews he was Paul, a Jew.

But he was to a greater degree involved in his God-given mission to the uncircumcised.

To those		without Law
	I became as	without Law
	not	without Law to God
	but	under Law to Christ
	to gain those	without Law

When in the company of Gentiles Paul adapted to their cultural behaviour, but with the qualification that he did not live a Law-less or wicked life. As 'Law-less' persons Gentiles were, for example, given to both idolatry and fornication. Paul is quick to distance himself from those kinds of behaviour for even when present with Gentiles he remained subject to God's rule in all things. This, however, was not through a life lived 'under [Jewish] Law' but as one who was now 'under Law to

---

16   Jesus was 'born of a woman, born under Law' (Gal. 4:4); Jesus was a Jew.

Christ'. This terse statement is meant to sum up the totality of what it meant for Paul to be a man 'in Christ'. For us, this means accepting that we are, with others, 'justified' in Christ crucified and raised, that we are 'slaves' to Jesus as our 'Lord' and subject to his teaching in all things, that we are made strong by his indwelling Spirit. In short, it means all that Paul has been teaching throughout this Letter.

Very pointedly Paul now adds a comment that takes the readers back to the previous chapter where the issue of behaviour towards the 'weak' was raised (see 8:13-9:1).

To the weak I became weak, to gain the weak.

Paul is reminding the Corinthians that he did not go to dining rooms in the local temples and eat the idol-sacrificed meat in the presence of the god. He was 'free' to do so because he knew that there was no deity corresponding to its statue and that he was 'free' to eat all meats. Yet, as he taught in that chapter, those 'weak' in understanding through a lifetime's involvement in the 'temple culture' would surely interpret Paul's presence there as an endorsement to continue in an unholy servitude to the spiritual forces surrounding the worship of the gods (see on 8:7). As a 'slave' of Christ he was 'free' from any need to visit those temples and he exercised that 'freedom' to 'gain' the 'weak'.

The Corinthians had their theology right in regard to idols and meat, but they left out the critical element, 'love'. This meant that their otherwise right doctrines actually became a means of 'destroying' brothers and sisters for whom Christ died. Missing from the Corinthians was a sensitive and loving awareness of the limited understanding of their fellow Christians and the Christ-like unselfishness to forgo their cherished 'authority' and 'freedom' to do what they pleased. Paul was right. 'All things are permissible', as they said (echoing Jesus, perhaps). But his qualifier, which they neglected, was absolutely fundamental. He must remind them that 'not everything builds up' (see on 6:12; 10:23) and that the totality of the Christian life is to 'build up' others in mature understanding, motivated by love.

Paul clinches this entire section going back into the previous chapter with this grand statement, which is intended to be a blueprint for his readers to follow.

To	all men and women
I have become	all things,
that by	all means I will save some.
I do	all things for the gospel,

that I might share in it[s blessings].[17]

Paul has laid before them his status as an apostle and explained why he worked to support himself rather than be paid. Apparently it was necessary for Paul to offer an *apologia* ('defence') for 'relinquishing these rights' which he does for the greater part of the chapter (vv. 3-18). But with a Spirit-inspired ingenuity Paul also used this 'defence' against his detractors to drive home his teaching from chapter 8 to give the needs of the immature Christian a higher priority than oneself and one's own cherished 'rights'. At the heart of this lay personal awareness and sensitivity to others and a desire above all to see them 'gained' for Christ, 'saved' and not 'lost'. In classic style, then, Paul finished this section by directing the Corinthians to his own lifestyle and his carefully crafted policies towards Jews and Gentiles. Above all, they are like him, 'slaves' of the 'Lord' Christ, yet 'set free' by his love-inspired death. They, like him, are to exercise their 'freedom' in love for those whose needs are great, namely, for their salvation (see on 10:23-11:1).

5. Saving Myself (9:24-27)

Paul has been saying that every part of his ministry is directed to 'gaining' people for their allegiance to Christ, whether Jews, Gentiles or the 'weak' (see on vv. 20-23). But Paul does not forget his own salvation, as the verses following illustrate. And yet not merely his own salvation, but theirs also. Those who preach the gospel are spiritually vulnerable to Satan and are, indeed, his special targets. Our Enemy seeks to silence or at least muffle the voice of effective witnesses, evangelists and pastors. Paul knew, as we also should, that our struggles in life are not ultimately with 'flesh and blood' but with 'the spiritual forces of evil in the heavenly realms' (Eph. 6:12). Paul's sober warning prepares us for the solemn admonitions that follow (see on 10:1-13).

Paul lays before the readers the need for spiritual self-discipline by a number of stunning images drawn from the

---

17 Paul simply said, 'that I might share in it'. Most translations reasonably add 'its blessings'.

athletic games. Greece was the home of many such festivals, but none more famous than the contests held every four years at Olympia to the south of Corinth. The games were the opportunity for the ever quarrelling Greek city states to put aside their disputes, at least for a short time! The second most important venue was Isthmia near Corinth where the games were held every two years under the patronage of the Achaian capital. Paul must have had first-hand experience of the Isthmian Games since they were held in the Spring of AD 51 when he was preaching in Corinth. The main contests were chariot races, foot races, wrestling, jumping, boxing, javelin and discus hurling. These were spectacular festivals attracting thousands of athletes and spectators. Paul the tentmaker may have been indirectly involved, since the multitudes of visitors were accommodated in tents.

His introductory, 'Surely you know that...' directs their attention to his first example, foot racing (v. 24). 'In the stadium', as they understood, only one of the runners wins the prize. There is no point in being one who 'also ran' in these fiercely competitive contests. So Paul says, 'So run as to win', because the one who is first across the line 'receives the prize'. What is the prize? Context, that is, the previous verse, tells us that Paul is thinking of 'the blessings of the gospel'. However, Paul's image should not be pushed too far. He is not saying that only one Christian wins the 'prize' of salvation so that all other competitors are 'lost'. Rather, his point is that every one should run as if to win, with complete determination. Paul is speaking about thorough self-discipline and single-eyed focus on the finishing line. The winning athlete overcomes the pain barrier of limbs and lungs because he 'must' win that race.

A second image is wrestling (v. 25). 'Those who wrestle, exercise self-control in all things', he observes. Many months of self-disciplined training precede the event, without which even the best athlete could not hope to win. Early morning training, giving up the 'party life' and careful attention to diet are part of the self-discipline of the athlete. Hand to hand combat requires a cool head as well as strong limbs and muscles, as each wrestler struggles to gain the upper hand. 'But', he notes, 'they do it for a corruptible crown, we an uncorruptible'. The 'crown' itself was indeed 'corruptible', made out of celery! But winning was the thing; the wreath was a mere symbol of success. But the 'wreath' of the believer will not wither and shrivel, but last for ever on the heads of those who struggled against the odds to remain Christian. But it takes spiritual self-control. That is Paul's challenge.

Having stated the need for positive determination in running and wrestling (vv. 24-25), Paul now states what he does not do, relating this to running and boxing. Here the key word is 'aimlessly'. Because focused determination and self-discipline is needed in such fierce competition, Paul notes that he 'does not run aimlessly'. Like the two hundred metre sprinter, Paul fixes his eye on the finishing line and runs for it, striving with every muscle to get there. Likewise, now thinking of himself as a boxer, he does not merely 'beat the air'. Every punch must find its mark if the boxer is to win.

So Paul concludes (v. 27). Whether in the months of training or the actual contest itself Paul speaks of 'buffeting' his body and subjecting it to his control. Once more the vigorous images from the stadium speak vividly of the means by which Paul and other Christians must exercise complete self-control and self-discipline. The temples stood there as symbols of idolatry and sexual self-indulgence. Paul is asking the Corinthians and all his readers to reckon on the reality of temptation and to anticipate its power. Just as the athlete must say 'no' to himself or herself so, too, the Christian must be prepared to say 'no' to the seductive allure of wickedness in all its forms.

Paul gives a reason for this drastic self-discipline. It is, 'so that, having preached to others, I myself might not be a reject'. This appears to change the metaphor from running, wrestling and boxing to building construction. In the world of the New Testament an object like a piece of stone would be examined by the mason and either 'approved' for incorporation in the building or 'rejected' because of a hair line crack or some other flaw. Yet, despite the appearance that Paul is introducing a new idea, it is more likely that he uses the word 'reject' in the sense of a runner's *disqualification* from the race. A breech in the rules of a tournament would result in just that, exclusion from the contest. In other words, Paul is saying that if he failed to discipline himself and became an idolater or a fornicator, he would be 'disqualified' in the eyes of God. Moral failure must render him ineligible for the prize.

Paul is deeply aware of the irony of such a situation. Others find salvation in Christ through Paul's preaching but he, the preacher, is rejected! Shamed by his wilfulness and sent to the sidelines, he sees others win their prizes, which they did through *his* ministry. But he can only watch. Paul is determined never to allow this to happen.

This text is subject to theological debate between Calvinists and Arminians, those who hold that the elect cannot be lost and those who argue that everything depends on the will of the individual Christian. In my view, Paul does uphold the sovereign will of God for the 'perseverance of the saints'.[18] Yet his words here are meant to be a severe challenge to his Christian readers, past and present, to take spiritual self-discipline with utmost seriousness. We should believe that God's strong hand holds his children in their salvation, but that he does so by warnings like this. As Peter teaches we have the responsibility to 'make our calling and election sure' by godly behaviour (2 Peter 1:10) and by rigorous self-discipline.

But this is not the end of Paul's warnings. Here he is pointing to himself as a means of cautioning the Corinthians. But in the next passage he addresses them directly (see on 10:1-13).

Some questions for personal reflection:

1. What would it mean for us if Paul were not, in fact, an apostle?

2. How can we tell what things are secondary and not to be insisted on with unbelievers as opposed to those which are primary and non-negotiable?

3. Are there matters for which we need to exercise particular self-discipline?

Study questions:

1. Why is Paul willing to relinquish his rights in receiving anything from them?

2. What is these 'outsiders' problem with Paul?

---

18 See e.g. John 6:37; 10:27-30; 17:12; 1 Pet. 1:4.

3. What are the reasons which Paul gives to defend his apostleship?

4. Why does Paul relinquish his right to receive financial help? Why does he preach 'free of charge'?

5. How is Paul's apostleship different than the other apostles?

6. Why is Paul willing be 'all things to all people'?

10

Flee From Idolatry
(1 Cor. 10:1–11:1)

Paul continues his caution to them about the danger of disqualification (vv. 1-13). Here he cites the experience of the
Israelites journeying through the wilderness. They had (by anticipation) been 'baptized' in the Red Sea as well as 'eaten' and
'drunk' the signs of their salvation. Yet the greater majority did
not make it to Canaan, the Land of Promise. Thus Paul warns the
Corinthians of the sins which overthrew their 'fathers' idolatry,
sexual immorality, putting Christ to the test and grumbling. Paul
warns them of complacency while assuring them that God will
not allow them to be tested beyond their capacity to endure.

Having warned them of God's likely judgement if they persist
in the same sins as the Israelites, in rather more tender tones he
invites them to think with him why they must 'flee from idolatry'
(vv. 13-22). Not least, let them grasp that sacrifices in temples
are offered to demons, bringing great danger to the worshipper.

Finally, Paul addresses the issue of eating 'temple-sacrificed'
meat at home (vv. 23–11:1). He uses this as an opportunity to
reflect with them about their own 'freedom' and the need to
'seek not their own good' but the 'good' of others.

1. Warnings in the Wilderness (10:1-13)

1. 'Our Fathers' (10:1-5)
When Paul writes, 'I do not want you to be uninformed,
brothers and sisters' (v. 1), he is introducing a new teaching

for their benefit. But it is not altogether a new topic. Rather he continues, but so as to tease out further what he has just said about himself and the need to avoid disqualification from the race (see on 9:27). The little connector 'For' shows that he is now justifying that comment about himself, except that he is now speaking directly to *them*. The burden of this passage is that they be not disqualified.

Reading ahead we may recognise at least three problems in Corinth: they believed that they could eat from the Lord's Table at his Remembrance Meal *and* eat idol-dedicated food (vv. 20-22); they somehow believed that the sacraments of baptism and the Holy Communion protected them from spiritual harm (vv. 2-4); and they believed that they were saved regardless of their behaviour (v. 12).

Accordingly Paul gives severe warnings based on the experiences of the Israelites in the wilderness. But first he demonstrates that Christians today re-live the experiences of 'our fathers', the Israelites, in their redemption from Egypt (vv. 1-4).

v.1	Our fathers were	all under the cloud
and		all passed though the sea
v.2	and	all were baptized into Moses in the cloud
and in the sea		
v.3	and	all ate the same spiritual food
v.4	and	all drank the same spiritual drink
	for	they drank from the spiritual
		rock that followed them
		and that rock was the Christ.

The experience of people becoming Christian believers was prefigured by the experience of Israel in her exodus from Egypt and her wanderings in the wilderness towards the Promised Land. Believers are baptized by water into Jesus the Christ; the Israelites were 'baptized' into Moses in the cloud and in the Red Sea. By being baptized the peoples of each covenant were joined in turn to their deliverers, Moses and Christ. Furthermore, in each covenant the people eat 'spiritual food' and drink 'spiritual drink'. Christians eat from the loaf and drink from the cup in the

Meal commemorating Christ's death. The Israelites ate manna and drank water from the rock, food and drink that signified beforehand the loaf and cup of the Eucharist.

Paul is speaking here of the two covenants or dispensations of the Bible, the old and the new, which are 'back to back'. Elements of the former repeat in, but are superseded by, the events of the latter. Redemption from slavery in Egypt for the journey towards the 'Land of Promise' in the old covenant becomes cosmic redemption from Satan, sin and death for the life's journey towards the Kingdom of God in the new covenant. The elements in the former covenant are called 'types' (*typoi* see on vv. 6, 11), which are fulfilled and surpassed by the elements in the latter covenant (which are sometimes called 'antitypes'[1]). Yet, says Paul, the new covenant completely eclipses the old[2] so that those who belong to Christ enjoy the sure hope of the Kingdom and are no longer bound by the ritual and ceremonial demands of the old, for example, circumcision, the keeping of the Jewish feasts and the food laws.

Nonetheless, there is no discontinuity between the stream of the faithful people of the Old Testament and the believers of the New Testament. The community of faith under the Old flows uninterrupted into the community of faith of the New. Paul tells the predominantly *Gentile* church of Corinth that those who came out of Egypt were '*our* fathers', Israelites though they were. Those Hebrews were 'our' spiritual ancestors to whom we belong as the one family of God, separated only by the intervening years. This remains true to this day for those of us who are Gentile Christians. The people of God did not begin with the disciples of Jesus but with Abraham. We are one people under two successive covenants.

The Israelites who fled from Pharaoh and who were led by God towards the Land of Promise were enjoying fellowship with Christ ahead of time, as it were, as they ate manna and drank water from the rock. Paul says that the 'rock that followed them...was the Christ'. The verb 'was' strongly suggests that 'the Christ' existed prior to his historic incarnation and was the source of life for the people then. They were 'baptized into

---

1   Greek: *antitypoi*; see Heb. 9:24; 1 Peter 3:21.

2   2 Cor. 3:7-11.

Moses' and they followed Moses but, though they did not know it at the time, they had actually been 'baptized' into One greater than Moses, into the promised Messiah.

But now (v. 5) comes a most dramatic contrast. This Paul achieves in two ways. First, he interjects the very strong Greek word *alla* whose force our little English word 'but' scarcely conveys. Second, having said no less than five times that '*all our fathers*' were blessed by God in the exodus and the food and drink of the early days of their journey, he then drops his bombshell, 'with *most of them* God was not well pleased'.

> *But* with *most of them* God was not pleased,
> for their bodies were scattered in the wilderness.

Following the exodus the Israelites remained at Mt Sinai for a year. It was after their departure towards the Land that their problems began. Within just a few weeks travelling north they reached the oasis at Kadesh Barnea at the southern edge of Israel, poised to enter and take possession of the land. But their unbelief, expressed in disobedience to God, who had so powerfully rescued them from the king of Egypt, condemned a whole generation to die out before they were ready to cross the Jordan and make the land their own. Yes: *All* came out of Egypt but only *two* Joshua and Caleb entered Canaan. The rest perished in the wilderness, their whitened bones scattered along the way.

What is Paul getting at in this fascinating linkage between the present believers of Corinth and the Israelites in the desert? Just this: the Corinthians must not think that the benefits of Christian baptism and the Supper of the Lord will help them if they plunge headlong into paths of disobedience against the revealed will of God. The Israelites did not make it to Canaan but perished on the journey. The Corinthians who worship the gods and fornicate may 'think that they stand' on account of the sacraments of the gospel, but the reality is they will fall, as the Israelites did. The covenants have different roles, the former prefiguring and the latter gloriously fulfilling. But the same God is the God of both and his moral character does not change. If we sin in the ways the Israelites did, then we in the churches will just as surely perish along the way.

Paul is determined not to be disqualified and so submits to rigorous self-discipline (see on 9:27). These verses encourage Christians to have the same determination for self-discipline and spiritual survival.

2. Four Deadly Sins (10:6-12)

Paul continues, 'These things were types for us' (v. 6a). By 'types' (*typoi*) he means the events mentioned above the exodus from Egypt, being 'baptized' into a deliverer (Moses), and the manna and water prefiguring the loaf and cup of the Lord's Table. These meant nothing as the people rushed to their destruction. So these *typoi* occurred for a purpose, 'that *we* [Christians] might not lust after evil things, as they lusted'. Paul's word for 'lust' means 'hot sexual passion'. The Israelites, though rescued by their holy God and though having subscribed to his righteous covenant at Mt Sinai based on the 'ten words', could not wait to sin.

Now follow four prohibitions: against idolatry, fornication, testing Christ and grumbling. In each case there is a repeating pattern of words. First, Paul begins, 'Neither be ...', then mentions the specific sin. Paul addresses the first and the fourth prohibitions directly to the Corinthians ('[*you*] do not be ...'), but in the second and the third he includes himself ('let *us* not ...'). Second, mention of the specific sin is followed by 'even as *some* of them [sinned]'. Indeed, as noted above, 'with most' God was not pleased (v. 5). Third, Paul mentions what happened to these sinning Israelites so that they perished in the wilderness.[3]

The first prohibition is against idolatry (v. 7):

Neither be idolaters
as some of them were.
As it is written,
'The people sat down to eat and drink and rose up to play.'

Paul is referring to the statue of the bull calf made of gold which the Israelites worshipped at Mt Sinai (as described in Exod. 32), from which the quotation is made (v. 6b). They ate the food sacrificed to the young bull, then they rose up and engaged in cultic dancing to this effigy. Ancient Jewish commentators

---

3   This does not appear in the first 'type', idolatry in the wilderness.

believed that this was wild orgiastic 'worship' which led to sexual acts among the people. Unlike the three 'types' following, Paul fails to mention the punishment of God. He may have felt this was unnecessary since Exodus 32:27-28 narrates how the Levites slew three thousand of their fellow-Israelites that day. Let the Corinthians who, like the Israelites, think they can worship an idol *and* the Lord be warned.

The second prohibition is against fornication (v. 8):

> Neither let us fornicate,
> as some of them did,
> and twenty three thousand of them fell in one day.

Paul's second example occurred in the plains of Moab, looking across the Jordan to Canaan. According to Numbers 25:1-2

> ...the men began committing sexual immorality with Moabite women who invited them to the sacrifices to their gods.

As in the first example we see an interplay between idolatry and fornication, a relationship that also occurred in the Graeco-Roman temples of Corinth. Paul has devoted chapters 5–7 to the problem fornication in Corinth presented for believers. Based on the Lord's judgement on Israel where thousands[4] died because of the plague, let the believers of Corinth, but also Paul, be warned to flee from the sin of fornication.

Religious worship and fornication frequently went together in pagan antiquity. But such a connection is not unknown within Christianity. An unholy relationship between the two sometimes occurs where the emphasis in Christian worship is on emotion or aesthetics rather than on the truth of the gospel and godly living.

The third prohibition is against trying the patience of the Lord (v. 9):

> Neither let us put Christ to the test,
> as some of them put him to the test,
> and were killed by snakes.

Paul's teaching springs from Numbers 21:4-7 where the people complained against God and against Moses because of the lack

---

4   Paul gives the statistic as 23,000 but Numbers 25:9 says 24,000.

of bread and water. Snakes bit the people and many died. This was during their forced journey southwards because their route was blocked by the Edomites. Paul sees the wilderness situation through contemporary eyes. He speaks about the Christ who had come in the recent half century as if he had been the leader of the exodus pilgrims twelve hundred years earlier. Evidently the Corinthians were complaining against Christ in some way that placed their relationship with him under great strain. In the Old Testament narrative the people doubted God's capacity to provide for them in spite of the repeated signs of his love and power for them. In difficult times, through which most of us must travel, we take patient Job as our example rather than the impatient Corinthians. Again Paul joins himself with the Corinthians in his appeal, 'Let *us* not put Christ to the test'.

Paul's fourth prohibition is against grumbling (v. 10):

Neither grumble,
as some of them grumbled
and were destroyed by the destroyer.

On two occasions in Kadesh Barnea people grumble against the leadership of Moses. In the first they grumble against the prospect of entering the Land (Num. 14:1-38) and in the second they grumble against Moses because of the fate that overtook the rebels Korah, Dathan and Abiram (Num. 16:41). Soon afterwards a plague struck and thousands died. Paul attributes this to 'the destroyer', most likely a reference to the destroying angel who killed the firstborn in Egypt (Exod. 12:23).

It appears that the Corinthians were grumbling about Paul, his leadership as an apostle, and teachings which they found not to their liking. The Israelites rejected Moses and the Corinthians are rejecting Paul (see on 4:8-21). They now have their own 'wisdom' teachers and are settling down comfortably in temple worship and fornication. They didn't need Paul's envoys or letters which they brought from him, or least of all a visit from him, to disturb their relaxed lifestyle in pagan Corinth!

In contemporary terms, some congregations dislike and reject the pastor who, like Paul, faces the members with their sins and the spiritual dangers they are in because of those sins. The Corinthians did not like Paul, and many professed Christians today dislike him intensely for the stand he takes on theological and moral especially sexual issues. Yet he knew, as we should, that idolatry in all its forms, fornication, trying the patience of Christ and grumbling about apostolic teaching, are deadly sins. Such sins killed the Israelites physically before they reached the land of hope and they will 'kill' us spiritually unless we turn from them.

Paul concludes his rehearsal of tragedies that overtook the journeying Israelites with a warning to the Corinthians, one that applies with undiminished force to all who belong to the dispensation of the new covenant:

> These things happened   to *them* as prefiguring examples,
> but they are written as warnings for *us*,
> upon whom the ends of the ages have descended.
> So therefore let the one who thinks *he* stands
>   take heed lest *he* fall.

This short text is one of Paul's most revealing about eschatology, the doctrine of the 'last things'. By 'the ends of the ages' Paul means the goal and end-point of the promise-laden Old Testament scriptures. The promises of God to David and about David have now been realized and kept in the recent coming of his descendant, Jesus ben Joseph of Nazareth. Jesus is the Christ of God, his Anointed One, who has died for sins and been raised alive bodily after three days, all 'according to the scriptures' (see on 1 Cor. 15:3-5). The 'age' of the old covenant has been 'ended' by Christ crucified and risen and the new begun by that death and resurrection and the outpouring of the Spirit of God on the people.

Notice that Paul moves from *them* (the Israelites) to *us* (Christians) and from *us* to *him* or *her* (the individual believer). Thus Paul places the onus on the will and conscience of the individual Christian. God's judgement on the Israelites' sins are not merely scattered and unrelated events from the past history of his people. The God of the Christians is the same God as the Lord of the Israelites. His acts of judgement then prefigure and confirm his displeasure now whenever his people sin in similar ways. God will always judge the worship of idols, fornication, testing Christ and grumbling against apostolic teaching. To be sure, that judgement may not be as physical and dramatic as that which fell upon the exodus pilgrims. Rather, it may take a spiritual form as people are quietly cut off spiritually from the source of their life in Christ. His judgement is that we will simply stop 'knowing' him. But it is a more severe judgement, because it is not merely the judgement of death, but an eternal judgement.

Evidently, arrogance was a major problem for the members of this church. Paul refers to this conceit metaphorically as being 'puffed up' (8:1). So 'bloated' and over-confident were they because of their supposed 'knowledge' and 'wisdom' (8:2-3), they believed they had outgrown their apostle (4:6, 18, 19). They were shamelessly proud of their lofty acceptance of gross sin in their midst (5:2) while being insensitively uncaring about the impact of their 'liberated' behaviour on vulnerable fellow-believers (8:1; 13:4).

But this chapter adds another dimension to their reckless pride, namely, their almost superstitious confidence that the waters of baptism and the loaf and cup of the Lord's Table would somehow shield them from the displeasure of God (vv. 1-4; cf. vv. 14, 20-22). They believed they were free to continue worshipping the gods in the temples and that the Lord would somehow protect them as they did. Paul leaves them in no doubt as to the sharp danger they are in.

'Let him who thinks he stands watch out lest he falls.'

Paul was deeply concerned that having preached to others he himself should be disqualified (9:27). He expresses this concern to sharpen the Corinthians' awareness of the grave dangers which now faced them. The apostle's warning is like a light-house beacon to all believers since. Travel into the waters of sin and shipwreck awaits you.

3. A Word of Hope (10:13)
Paul sums up this entire passage begun with his own example of self-discipline (9:24-27) with a magnificent 'word' about the faithfulness of God and the triumph of his power.

No temptation has seized you
        that is not common to man.

Paul's word *peirasmoi* can mean either or both 'temptations' and 'trials'. Let all believers understand that 'temptations' and 'trials' are part of general human experience. As fallen people in a fallen world we are all subject to moral temptation and prone to trying circumstances right through our lives, from the cradle to the grave. It is not helpful to think that God has cursed us or singled us out for special punishment.

> God is faithful
> who will not permit you to be tempted (or tested)
> beyond your power.

Several times Paul asserts that God is faithful, that is, true to his promises and constant in his love to his people (1 Cor. 1:9; 2 Cor. 1:18; 1 Thess. 5:24; 2 Thess. 3:3). God is not fickle, petulant, arbitrary or vacillating like the gods of Greece and Rome, or for that matter deities generally. When Patrick preached in Ireland he emphasised the constancy of the character of God as against the perverse changeability and capriciousness of the local gods. It is a huge relief to know that the God of the universe is a moral, constant and good Being, who is unchanging in his faithfulness.[5]

And, assures Paul, the faithful God simply will not allow you to be tempted or tried beyond what you can bear. In context Paul is addressing the moral crisis in Corinth at that time. The people may have felt that the strength of temptation was too great and that they must succumb to it. Not so, Paul promises. The sovereign God is not absent from his world. His loving hand will be there to shield you, but only if you desire him to.

On the contrary ('But' *alla*) God will not only allow you to escape by the 'skin of your teeth', as it were. In his strength you will be empowered to resist whatever pressure that temptation or trial places you under.

> But with the temptation [or trial]
> he will make for you a way of escape
> that you may bear up under it.

God, who is powerful as well as faithful, will not allow you to be shut in a room with no exits. Whatever the temptation we face or the trial we must endure we are not locked in by it.

---

5   Every good and perfect gift is from above,
    coming down from the Father of the heavenly lights,
    who does not change like shifting shadows (James 1:17).

Rather, God will always also provide us with at least one door through which to make our escape. Paul does not say that we are enabled by God merely to 'bear' the temptation or trial, but that he will empower us to 'bear up' under it, that is, prevail in it. Paul is, of course, speaking of matters from an eternal perspective. In this life believers, like all others, are caught in the sufferings and disappointments of life which none of us in the end can regulate or control. But in the long term and in the eternal perspective we place ourselves with confidence and quiet trust in the loving and faithful hands of our God.

One final observation. The 'way of escape' may often prove to be by means of a human agency. It may be a friend who will hold me morally accountable or one who stands with me in my trial. Clearly, then, we should seek to be such true friends to others in their temptations or trials. There is a significant role for the pastor who faithfully and wisely teaches the Word of God to the people, through which God's 'ways of escape' are frequently discerned. Such a friend, as well as pastor, Paul proved to be for the Corinthians.

2. Flee From Idolatry (10:14-22)
The passage following is a direct application of its immediate predecessor (10:1-13), where Paul established that God's judgments on redeemed Israel journeying to the Land of Promise continue to apply to those redeemed by Christ who are travelling to the Kingdom of God. The waters of baptism and the loaf and cup of the Table of the Lord are not religious talismen or magical charms shielding us from God's displeasure on idolatry, fornication, testing Christ or grumbling. That passage in turn followed from his passionate concern not to be disqualified from the race due to a lack of spiritual self-discipline (9:24-27).

Going back even further, the present passage completes his pastoral advice about going to the temples. Earlier he had admonished them not to attend the dining rooms attached to the temples where meals were eaten from food sacrificed earlier to the god of the temple (see on 8:7-13). Now he tells them in the most direct terms to avoid temple attendance altogether, indeed, to 'flee from' such religious services.

Naturally it strikes us as rather odd that Paul deals with these issues in such a roundabout way, especially since he interpolates the long passage about his apostleship and the relinquishing of his rights and freedoms as an apostle (see on 9:1-26). The reason, of course, is that he is not writing such pastoral advice in a vacuum, as it were. Rather, he is responding to their letter in which they were not merely asking for clarification but arguing for their rights and freedoms to continue to attend the temples and to eat the idol-sacrificed food.

He begins his closing exhortations with love, yet with firmness and an appeal to good sense. His love emerges from his appeal to 'my beloved ones' (v. 14), which follows his stern warnings of Israel's tragedy at the hand of her God.[6] His firmness is heard in the unequivocal command, 'Flee from idolatry'. The use of the preposition 'from' suggests the concrete act of physically moving away from the temple itself. Our word 'flee' translates a Greek word (*pheugō*) from which we derive the word 'fugitive', one who desperately escapes from life-threatening danger or an enemy. He says the same about fornication (see on 6:18). Both idolatry and sexual sin are dangerous enemies from which the believer must take flight immediately. Pastoral experience endorses Paul's sober sense of the danger these sins represent to Christians. Life in this age may go on for the idolater and the fornicator, but unless that person turns decisively from his or her ways that person will not inherit life with God in his Kingdom (see on 6:9-11).

But he also appeals to their good sense (v. 15), informed by the gospel and sanctified by the Holy Spirit:

I speak as to sensible people.
You judge what I say.

This is no postmodern invitation for them to regard their opinions to be as valid as his on this issue. On the contrary, he is giving his teaching for them to reflect on its rightness, which he does by three arguments.

First, they must understand the nature of the Lord's Table and the loaf and cup which Jesus instituted for his covenant people on the night he was betrayed.

---

6   Cf. 4:14 where similarly warm tones follow stern ones.

> The cup of blessing which we bless,
> is it not our participation in the blood of the Christ?
> The loaf we break,
> is it not our participation in the body of the Christ?

This is a mere glancing reference to the Lord's Supper. Apparently Paul mentions the Meal here only because of their superstitious confidence that they can sin with impunity because of it (see on 10:1-4).

We glean from these few words some ideas about the early practice at the Supper of the Lord, which occurred when the 'whole church gathered' (11:18, 33-34; cf. 14:23).[7] We need to read Paul's words here along with his account in 11:23-26. The 'actions' which are only barely described here are three: *blessing* God for 'the cup of blessing', *breaking* 'the loaf'[8] and '*participating*'. As the 'body of believers' eat and drink we 'participate' together in the broken loaf and the outpoured cup. But we also 'participate' together at an emotional and spiritual level in our love, faith and commitment to the Lord Jesus, whose broken body and shed blood have redeemed us. In our eating and drinking together spiritually we participate 'in him'.

Regrettably, many churches place all the practical emphasis on the third action, the 'participating' (eating and drinking) but not 'all together' but individually, usually of a tiny piece of bread or wafer and a sip of wine. We have made the Lord's Supper a highly individualistic and private ceremony. Furthermore, we have readily conveyed the false impression that the blessing of God somehow resides in those fractional quantities of bread and wine which the individual consumes. Nothing could be further from the intention of Jesus. The 'participation' (eating and drinking) is to be dependent on 'breaking the loaf' (for which we have given thanks) and the 'blessing (of God) for the wine cup'. The first two actions (breaking the loaf and blessing God for the wine cup) display the broken body and shed blood of Jesus in his death for us. The third action (eating

---

7   On the assumption that the head of the house then led the family in prayer it is held that in the 'household of faith' the most senior elder present would lead the people at the Table of the Lord.

8   Evidently the loaf was 'broken' first, then the cup 'blessed'. That is the order given later in a more complete description (see 11:23-26); the loaf is mentioned second here as a foundation for what Paul will go on to say in the next verse.

and drinking) expresses the unity 'in Christ' of the people as together they 'participate' in him. All three actions are to show forth the death of the Lord until he comes (11:26).

Through Paul's words here and in 11:23-26 we see silhouetted the Lord Jesus in the upper room eating the Passover with his disciples at night shortly before his arrest. At the conclusion of the Passover meal, which was to bring to mind annually the Israelites' escape from Egypt, Jesus pointed to the new exodus, the redemption of a people by means of his death and the resurrection which will follow in three days. Upon taking the loaf, and giving God thanks for it, Jesus broke it, saying, 'This is my body', and he gave it to them to eat. Then taking the Passover 'cup of blessing' and blessing God for it, saying, 'This is the new covenant in my blood', Jesus gave it to them to drink. To bring to mind regularly[9] his great work of redemption at the First Easter Jesus instructed them to 'do this in remembrance of *me*'.

What was in Jesus' mind when he broke the bread and blessed God for the wine cup? He said that the bread broken is his 'body' and that the wine cup blessed is his 'blood', as Paul's text clearly shows. That body broken and that blood outpoured point to one thing, the atoning death of the Messiah when his body was broken by nails and spear and his blood poured out in the dust at Golgotha.

This, then, is Paul's first consideration which he advances for their agreement. As they eat at the Lord's Table following the breaking of the bread and the blessing for the cup, they are 'participating in the blood of Christ and in the body of Christ' by a corporate act of recollecting his saving death for them. There is no question, of course, that the loaf and the wine somehow become Christ's body and blood objectively. This view began to emerge within a century of Paul's Letter to the Corinthians and developed into the doctrine of transubstantiation in late antiquity, when Jewish prophetic symbolism was no longer understood in a predominantly Gentile church. Symbolic actions like the Passover in the tradition of Israel to which Jesus belonged gave way to a superstitious adoration for the transubstantiated body and blood of Jesus in the loaf and cup. However, these

---

9   It is not altogether clear how frequently New Testament believers commemorated the Lord's death in this way. Was it daily (Acts 2:46), weekly (Acts 20:7) or periodically (1 Cor. 11:18)?

foods, bread and wine, remain the 'loaf' we break and the 'cup' for which we offer blessing. They are a 'participation' together in the 'body' and 'blood' of the Lord, that is, in the benefits of his death, in the hearts and minds of the community of faith gathered in his name. This is a potent shared experience, calling to mind, bringing alive in the memory, the love of Jesus for his people.

His second 'word' for their acceptance flows from the first, namely that they are 'one body' (v. 17). This is because the 'body' of believers shares in 'one loaf' broken at the Lord's Table.

Because there is		one loaf,
we who are	many are	one body,
for we all	partake of	one loaf.

The 'many' members of the congregation are made 'one body' as they share together in the 'one loaf.' The members of the assembly find a profound unity at the Table of the Lord. So, argues Paul, how can some of the members fracture that unity by going to an idol-temple and worshipping the god?

In passing, we cannot but observe the degree to which the point of the Lord's Table is often missed in church practice. What is portrayed in most churches is not the unity of the body of believers as set forth by the 'one loaf' on the Table which is then visibly broken for all. Rather, we present our individualism by tiny pieces of bread distributed at the Lord's Supper, which had been neatly diced the night before in the minister's or elder's kitchen and kept fresh in a plastic wrapper! The apostle would have us find unity in that 'one loaf' visibly broken for all and shared by all, rather than in the distribution of *pre*-broken pieces.

Paul's third argument is an appeal to the practice of sacrifices in the Temple of Jerusalem (v. 18).

Surely those who eat the sacrifices participate in the altar.

By the 'altar' Paul most likely means the Lord God of Israel himself *to whom* the sacrifice had been offered. Even though an altar is merely a piece of stone and the sacrifice a mere sheep, goat or calf, yet those who eat the altar sacrifice drew near to the Lord at that moment. Those sacrifices are now superseded and irrelevant through the one final sacrifice of the Messiah crucified, the Passover lamb of God. Yet, looking back, those worshippers were indeed drawing near in fellowship with Yahweh under that dispensation.

This is a potent argument against the Corinthians, who loftily believed that one could attend pagan sacrifices with impunity 'knowing' that there was 'no God but one' (see on 8:4). If eating the sacrifice in Yahweh's Temple was no empty act, but a living, dynamic and fellowship creating act, then the same must be true of the worship of the god in the pagan temple.

Yet this is a rather risky line to run. So Paul immediately corrects any possible misunderstanding (v. 19). 'What am I saying?' he asks. 'That idol-sacrificed food is anything or an idol is anything?' His very way of posing the question grammatically shows how preposterous the question is. 'Of course idol-food is nothing and an idol is nothing.'

So what is the problem about going to these temples, whether the temple precincts or one of its small dining rooms for a meal? Simply this. 'What you sacrifice you sacrifice to *demons* and not to God' (v. 20). True, there is no god there, for 'there is no God but One'. There is no Apollo. No Zeus. No Aphrodite. No Demeter. No Artemis. There are no gods or goddesses. They do not exist. In this you are right. But there is not therefore *nothing* there. There are *demons* there. For demons exist and they are present in the temples of the gods as the priests offer sacrifices and the people eat the sacrifices. They worship demons. They are in touch with demons. They open their lives to demons. So Paul says, 'I do not want you to have fellowship with demons'.

Of course many intellectually attuned Christians would join the Corinthians in scoffing at the gods, the priests, the sacrifices and the temples, not knowing the spiritual danger inherent in such a dismissive attitude. 'Your theological knowledge is dangerously incomplete', Paul says to them and to us if we are so foolish as to think the Corinthians' thoughts after them.

Now for some 'home truths' to clinch the arguments in their minds (v. 21).

You are not powerful enough to drink   the cup of the Lord
                                and   the cup of demons.
You are not powerful enough to share in the table of the Lord
                                and   the table of demons.

They wanted to have it both ways, that is, drink the cup of the Lord and eat from the table of the Lord in the remembrance meal and also go to the temple of the god and drink and eat the sacrificial offerings. They thought they could do both. Most likely they thought the emblems of the Lord's body and blood would somehow protect them like a magical charm from spiritual harm. In other words, Paul is saying that the demons are strong, more powerful by far than you. Go to the temple, eat and drink the sacrifices and you run the real risk of being captured by the demons. Had they remembered the stories in the Gospels of the destructive power of demons in the lives of men like 'Legion' they may have recoiled from any step that would open the door to the 'unclean spirits', as the Gospels call them.

Finally (v. 22), do they think the Lord is unconcerned that they who have been redeemed at such a price would now expose themselves to infestation of demons? Do they think the risen Lord has no opinion of such an eventuality? How foolish they are. Again, do they not recollect the accounts of the fierce 'search and destroy' mission of Jesus against the 'strong man' who held spiritual captives in his dungeons of fear and darkness (Mark 3:27)? Paul soberly cautions against provoking the jealousy of the Lord against those who worship the gods instead of him and who allow themselves thereby to become the haunt of demons. Do they think they are stronger than the Lord?

This is an urgent warning from Paul to these confused believers in Corinth and their counterparts today who think they can worship Christ *and* other gods. 'You will provoke righteous anger in One who is infinitely stronger than you', Paul is saying. Let us call to mind the power of Jesus as he broke open the prisons of the strong man and set his captives free. But that Lord will be against us if we turn aside to worship other gods.

3. Eating Market-place Meat at Home (10:23–11:1)

This short passage displays Paul's verbal artistry. It is worth pausing for a moment to take in the layout of his words.

He begins by twice quoting the Corinthians' commitment to 'freedom' ('all things are lawful') which he answers by 'but not all things are helpful...but not all things build up' (v. 23). These two qualifiers later become the principle governing Christian behaviour ('Let no one seek his own, but the other person's good' v. 24) which he will think through with them for two practical situations involving 'temple-sacrifices' (vv. 26-28). The first is when you go to the meat market where these goods are on sale and the second is what are you to do when confronted with this food in the home of an unbeliever. Paul turns briefly to answer criticism about his policies and practices before concluding the passage with three staccato principles of behaviour (vv. 29-11:1). One cannot but be impressed by Paul's economy of words and the effectiveness of his communication. No wonder the Corinthians thought that his letters were 'powerful and strong' (2 Cor. 10:10).

By twice repeating the Corinthians' slogan 'All things are lawful' (v. 23) Paul is repeating the attitude they had about 'market-place meat'. Much of the meat sold in the markets of Corinth had previously been 'sacrificed in a temple to the god' (see on v. 28). Was it 'lawful' for Christians to eat that meat? Were they 'free' to do so? This is the second occasion Paul had quoted their deeply held views about their 'authority' and their 'freedom' (see on 6:12[10]). Clearly 'freedom' was their guide in all things!

How will the former Pharisee respond? Pharisees had a rule for every small detail of life. Theirs was religious legislation taken to extremes. The *Mishnah*, written a century or so after the close of the New Testament age, is larger than the whole Bible. Its collection of minute rules and regulations for every aspect of behaviour reflects the way Pharisees multiplied rules and regulations. In turn this approach threw up a class of legal experts in Jewish Law. Clearly, the Gentile Corinthians were taking an opposite view. But how will Paul respond to complex moral and ethical situations?

His response is instructive for us today. The cultural circumstances for most will be different from those of the Corinthians, but the principles of his advice remain. Significantly, Paul emerges here neither as a Pharisaic legalist nor as a Corinthian libertarian. Rather, he sets down the example of Christ for them and us to follow (see on chapter 11:1). But this is to anticipate his last word. First we must think through the issues with him as he responds to the Corinthians.

---

10   In the earlier reference the words were, 'All things are lawful for *me*'.

They say:	'All things are lawful.'
He replies:	'But not all things are helpful.'
They say:	'All things are lawful.'
He replies:	'But not all things build up.'

Their simple principle was 'freedom', *their* 'freedom'. This has a curiously modern ring to it. 'My rights', 'my freedom', we hear all the time in the modern secular society. But in sharpest contrast Paul urges the consideration of *others* what is 'helpful' to *others*, what 'builds up' *others* in true understanding of the mind of God. For the Corinthians it was '*me* first', but for Paul it was '*others* first'.

This Paul sums up in a brief 'word' (v. 24):

| Let no one seek his own | [good] |
| but [each] his neighbour's | good.[11] |

Such 'good' is found in actions which are 'helpful' and which 'build up' (v. 23), or as he will say later, actions which will 'save the many' (see on v. 33). Having laid down the 'seek-the-good-of-others first' principle in a word, 'love' Paul now thinks through with his readers two different situations.

The first is when the Christian is in the market place of Corinth and the question is whether or not to purchase meat that may have been sacrificed in a temple (v. 25). Paul's word *makellum* ('meat market')[12] has been found inscribed on the remains of a shop in the main public square (*agora*) in Corinth. This would have been one of the shops Paul has in mind as he writes. So what is Paul's practice and what does he advise?

Eat everything sold in the meat-market
without asking questions on account of conscience.

'Conscience', as used by Paul, does not mean 'guilty' or 'clear' conscience, a subjective sense of right and wrong that varies from person to person. Rather, he means the believers' theological understanding, based on the teaching of the gospel, as it issues in ethical living. We might call it 'commonly held values'. In short, 'without asking questions on account of con-

---

11 'Good' is inferred, it does not appear in Paul's text.

12 *Macellum* is a Roman word taken into Greek.

science' means that believers are free to buy the meat, take it home and eat it.

Immediately (v. 26) he justifies this 'freedom' by giving a text from the Old Testament, Psalm 24:1.

> For the earth is the Lord's
> and everything that is in it.

The 'earth' and 'every part of the earth' comes from and belongs to the Lord, including the meat in the butchers' shops in Corinth. Since believers have acknowledged this meat to be God's 'gift' for which they eat in 'thanksgiving', they are, indeed, 'free.'

Paul stoutly defends this 'freedom' for himself and others, though as we shall see he was subject to criticism for it, most likely from a Jewish Christian quarter (see on vv. 29b-30). This may have been because Paul's present advice seemed at odds with the judgement of James at the Jerusalem Council where a ban was placed on *eidōlothutos*, 'idol-sacrificed meat' (Acts 15:29; 21:25). It is by no means clear whether the prohibition of the Jerusalem Council was restricted to such food eaten at the pagan temples or whether it also included eating idol-dedicated food in one's own home.[13] Furthermore, Paul faced two practical problems in cities like Corinth. One was that there may have been no way to tell which meat had been offered in sacrifice and which had not. The other was that believers ate this food at home and in privacy, as it were, giving no overt offence to others. Whatever the circumstances at the time Paul did not apply the Jerusalem Council's prohibition to eating at home.[14] In this case, then, Paul upheld the Corinthians' view that 'liberty' should apply.

But there is a second situation, that is, where an unbeliever invites you to his home and places 'temple-sacrificed' meat before you (v. 27). What are you to do when that happens? asks Paul. If nothing is said, go ahead and eat, is his advice. Once again he adds, 'without asking questions on account of

---

13   The same dilemma applies to the very negative reference to 'idol-sacrificed' food in Revelation 2:14, 20.

14   As he also ignored the decree that Gentiles must eat only kosher-slaughtered meat.

conscience' (see on v. 25). This is a mandate to eat as a matter of Christian 'freedom'. In passing, we note that Christian believers, unlike Jews, were free to mingle socially with unbelievers and to visit their homes for a meal (see on 5:9-10).

If, however, someone present observes that this food is 'temple-sacrificed', Paul advises, 'do not eat it' for the sake of the one who pointed this out, that is, 'for his conscience' (v 28). It is not made clear who this person is. Is it an unbeliever, either the host or another guest? Is it a fellow-guest who is also a Christian? On balance, most probably it is the unbelieving host who has made the observation about the meat. But why would he make his comment? Did he suddenly think, perhaps, that Christians had the same scruples as Jews who, for their part, would never eat such food? Was he being considerate to the scruples of his Christian guest? We simply do not know.

More to the point we must ask why Paul seeks to protect this unbeliever's 'conscience' and in these circumstances firmly discourages the eating of the 'temple-sacrificed' food. Almost certainly the answer is that Paul does not want this unbeliever to be confirmed in his 'conscience', his 'theological understanding', about the gods, idols and the sacrifices. For unbelievers typically held that the gods did exist and on that account they sacrificed to them in their temples. By his behaviour Paul wants fellow-Christians to be stepping-stones to faith in the God of Israel and his Son, the Messiah Jesus. Under no circumstances does he want Christians to be stumbling blocks to faith by confirming unbelievers in their idolatry.

Paul, however, establishes that it is on account of the conscience of the unbeliever, not the conscience of the Christian (v. 29a).

> But I say the conscience of the other man
> not your conscience.

Here he returns to the 'freedom' of the individual Christian to buy, take home and eat meat, whether 'temple-sacrificed' or not (see on vv. 25-26). The only reason to qualify this freedom is the conscience of the unbeliever in whose house the Christian is a guest. It is not on account of his own conscience that the Christian will decline to eat, but only out of consideration of the impact of his or her behaviour on the unbeliever.

In the next few sentences (v. 29b-30) Paul's language betrays a degree of agitation.

> For why should my freedom be judged by another's con-
> science? If I share in a meal in thankfulness
> why am I blasphemed for that for which I offer thanks?

On the face of it Paul seems to be contradicting himself. On the one hand he urges that one not eat on account of the conscience of the unbeliever (vv. 27-29a). But now he asserts that the 'freedom' of the Christian is not to be judged by the conscience of another person. But the contradiction is only apparent. The decision not to eat for the sake of another is entirely voluntary; it is not a matter of theological obligation. But this does not mean the unbeliever or anyone else can stand in judgement over Paul or others and demand abstinence from such food.

Paul's unusually sharp language may indicate that he was sensitive to criticism over his policies and practices in eating 'temple-sacrificed' meat at home. Was it the case that local Jewish Christians took exception to Paul's openness to 'living like one not having law...so as to win those not under law' (9:21)? Did they interpret his Gentile-type living as some kind of evidence that he was not a true apostle (see on 9:3)? In practice this probably meant that when present with Gentiles Paul did not uphold Jewish scruples about idol-sacrificed food, unless of course someone pointedly referred to the food as 'temple-sacrificed', as in the example above. Paul is 'free' in principle to eat because he has offered thanks to the Lord for the food. But Paul's words about 'being judged' and 'blasphemed' are so strong as to suggest that this was precisely what was happening in Corinth.

In short, Paul defends the principle of 'freedom' for himself and others to eat 'temple sacrifices' in a domestic situation. In his own home the freedom is unqualified (vv. 25-26), but as a guest of the unbeliever the freedom is qualified if attention is drawn to the fact that the food has been sacrificed beforehand (vv. 27-28). The believer's relinquishment, however, is volun-tary and it is only for the sake of the unbeliever's 'conscience', that is, his need to understand the truth that gods made with hands are no gods. That said, however, Paul will not allow the believer's conscience to be held hostage to those believers, who we suppose were Jewish Christians (vv. 29-30), who held there was no such freedom.

The passage is drawing to its close. Paul initially advanced the principle of 'seeking the good of others' to qualify the 'freedom' demanded by the Corinthians, and he has applied this to 'temple-sacrificed' meat in two domestic situations. Now, signalled by the important word, 'Therefore' he draws three conclusions from these case studies.

First, he declares that the 'glory of God' should be uppermost in informing and directing all decisions about these matters (v. 31).

Therefore
whether you   eat
or   drink
or whatever you   do
                      do everything to the glory of God.

Here we may discern the depth of Paul's devotion to God, revealed first as creator and saviour in the pages of the Old Testament, but now more fully as the gracious Father through the incarnation, death and resurrection of his Son, Jesus the Christ. The Christian's greatest concern in life is to attribute honour and praise to the God of the universe. Nothing the believer does is to diminish the brightness of God's goodness and kindness. In Paul's advice for these situations, mundane and seemingly trivial though they are, Paul wants believers to demonstrate the grace and others-centred character of God. To be sure, believers are to enjoy their 'freedom' as an expression of the grace of God to them. Yet by their thoughtfulness and practical consideration for others they are to point to God's kindness to those 'others'.

There is a second conclusion which arises out of the first (v. 32):

Be no stumbling-stone   to Jews,
                        to Greeks,
                        to the church of God.

Paul is reflecting with his readers about his own policies and practices towards different cultural groups. With Jews 'those under Law' Paul avoids offence by accommodating to Jewish

scruples (see on 9:20). As a Jew Paul could do this readily
enough, though he does not explain in detail how a Gentile
might avoid bringing offence to Jews. Perhaps it is enough for
Paul to state the principle that Christian behaviour calls for an
accommodating spirit in cultural matters. Paul, however, would
never countenance watering down the gospel.

His brief admonition not to cause 'Greeks' (that is, Gentiles)
'to stumble' merely summarizes what he has said about going
to the home of the unbeliever (v. 27-28). The decision to eat
or not to eat is entirely settled by the believer's perception of
the effects of whatever action is taken. But this principle is to
inform all relationships with 'Greek' unbelievers.

In urging against causing the 'church of God' to stumble Paul
is most likely returning to the original presenting circumstance,
the spiritual vulnerability of the 'weak brother' (see on 8:7-13).
The life and speech of mature Christians is to be crafted so as
to 'build up' the fellow-Christian and to do nothing to bring
about his spiritual downfall.

In short, Paul affirms the 'freedom' of the Christian as a matter of principle, but that 'freedom' is not to be exercised so as to
cause any to 'stumble' away from Christ, whether Jew, Greek or
fellow-Christian.

Paul's third conclusion follows from the previous two
(vv 33-1). He puts it in positive terms, however, and he states
it in terms of his own example:

Even as I also seek to please all people in everything I do,
> not seeking my own good
> but   the good of many
> > that they may be saved.
> > Be imitators of me
> even as I also am [an imitator] of Christ.

Paul's Spirit-inspired genius is seen in these words. He picks
up his first principle stated at the beginning, that Christians
should 'seek' the 'good' of others not their own 'good' (v. 24). He
also returns to re-state his policy of cultural accommodation to
'save' as 'many' as possible (9:19, 22). Clearly a person's 'good'
is that he or she be 'saved'.[15] Paul was truly 'free' in Christ from

---

15   Paul's teaching about being 'saved' is important in this letter (see also 1:18, 21;
3:15; 5:5; 7:16; 9:22; 15:2).

his own cultural scruples to present the gospel to those who were as yet 'unfree' from cultural restraints.

Hence he invites his readers to enter into the same genuine 'freedom', a 'freedom' not to be 'free', that is, to be the 'slave' of others. He asks them to imitate him. In this, however, he points to the true and ultimate model who is not Paul, but Christ. Christ was the authentically 'free' person who laid aside his liberty for others. Christ truly represents and incarnates the God from whom he comes. God is a gracious and kindly self-giver for others and Christ is a gracious and kindly self-giver for others.

Nowhere is this more clearly expressed than in a saying of Jesus that seems to have inspired Paul's choice of the words 'seek' and 'save' in these verses, but also at the beginning of this passage (v. 24):

> The Son of Man came to *seek* and to *save* the lost (Luke19:10).

'Seeking' to 'save' the lost was the mark of Christ in life, but particularly in death. The scoffers at Golgotha said with more truth than they realized, 'He saved others. Himself he cannot save'. The Messiah Jesus was 'free' to lose his life that others might be 'saved'. Paul grasped something of that 'freedom' to set aside cultural 'freedom' that 'many' might be 'saved' and he invites the Corinthians and us to copy his example. Yes, 'freedom' is important. But it is the 'freedom' to forget oneself, a 'freedom' not to be 'free', 'seeking' what is ultimately important, the eternal salvation of the lost. That is what Jesus came to do and in this he was followed by his devoted minister, Paul the apostle.

Throughout chapters 8–11 Paul has been teaching about temple culture in Corinth. Their initial question related to 'idol-sacrificed' meat (8:1), which they believed they had the 'freedom' and 'authority' to eat as they attended the sacrifices. They held that their theological knowledge about 'no God but One' gave them 'freedom', both to attend the temples and to eat the sacrifices. Paul makes quite clear that believers must not participate in any activities of the temples, whether in the attached dining rooms (8:7-13) or in the temple proper (10:14-22). Eating 'temple-sacrificed' meat at an unbeliever's home was another matter (10:23–11:1). Believers need to offset their 'freedom' to eat at home against the greater 'good' of others, that is, their salvation.

Throughout chapter 9 Paul offers a lengthy defence of his apostleship against those (Jewish Christians?) who called it into question (9:1-22). It was a problem for them that, unlike other apostles, Paul steadfastly declined to be paid for his ministry. Furthermore, his openness to eating 'idol-sacrificed' meat when in the company of Gentiles also seemed to them to disqualify him.

Paul powerfully describes the steps he took in personal self-discipline and lays before the Corinthians the solemn fate of those Israelites who thought they stood but who were overturned in the wilderness (9:23–10:13).

The cultural setting Paul addresses in chapters 8–10 is remote from readers in modern secular societies. Yet the circumstances are similar for many in Asia and Africa, where temples, priests and sacrifices are still to be found. Either way, Paul's principles of behaviour continue to instruct, encourage and build up.

SOME QUESTIONS FOR PERSONAL REFLECTION:

1. Think through how the four deadly sins for the Corinthians might apply to you.

2. Do you agree/disagree that there is spiritual danger in worshipping other gods?

3. Think of an example where you did not seek the spiritual good of someone.

4. What is Christian 'freedom'?

STUDY QUESTIONS:

1. What is the connection between the 'fathers in the wilderness' and the Gentile believers at Corinth?

2. What are the four prohibitions which Paul states? What is their connection to the Israelites in the desert?

3. Why does Paul stress the faithfulness of God in the context of their behavior?

4. What was the superstitious confidence the Gentiles had in regards to the Lord's Supper?

5. What does Paul mean by 'conscience'? Is it subjective or objective?

6. Why is the concern for others so important? What does this hope to accomplish?

I I

Traditions Corrupted
(I Cor. I I:2-34)

In this chapter Paul addresses two departures from his teaching since he left the church three years earlier. These teachings he calls 'traditions', a technical word the rabbis used for 'blocks' of teaching they would 'hand over' to their disciples. In this case, however, Paul is the 'rabbi' and the congregation in Corinth is the 'disciple'.

How did Paul hear about these recent practices in the Corinthian church? Most likely these were among the 'reports' brought to Paul in Ephesus by Chloe's people (1:11), or by Stephanas (16:17). These represent further evidence of division within the Corinthian assembly. The act of bringing these matters to Paul's notice implies disapproval by some in regard to the actions of others. Clearly, too, those who reported to Paul were among those who remained loyal to him (cf. 1:12), who knew that he would share their disagreement. Furthermore, these departures from the founding apostle's 'traditions' add weight to the suggestion that since Paul's departure local leaders had arisen who wished to take the church in rather different theological directions from his.

The first 'tradition' related to man-woman relationships within the assembly of believers. At the time Paul established his churches he laid down important principles governing such relationships. The second 'tradition' was the procedure to be followed in remembering the death of the Messiah at the thanksgiving meal (v. 23).

Presumably there were other 'traditions' that the apostle 'handed over' which the Corinthian and other churches 'received'. Where the 'traditions' continued to be observed Paul would have no reason to refer to them in his letters. Only when the 'tradition' was departed from would there be any need to raise the matter with the church in a letter. This is the case here. We may regard the Corinthians' departures from Paul's 'traditions' as providential since otherwise we would not have the benefit of these important teachings.

Paul introduces the first departure with a note of 'praise' (v. 2). Yet there were difficulties to set right. No such encouragement is signalled at the head of the second matter, the Remembrance Meal (v. 17). Rather, he says, 'In the following...I have no praise at all'.

These two 'traditions' relate to life within the church meeting. When it is understood that chapters 12–14 also relate to the gathering of the believers it can be readily agreed that chapters 12–14 belong with chapter 11, forming one block of teaching. Once more, therefore, we see Paul allowing the circumstances of this church to provide occasion for him to provide systematic teaching, but organized thematically. Thus to the topics of 'wisdom' (1–4), 'the sexual holiness of the saints' (5–7), 'temples and sacrifices' (8–10) we now add 'life together in the church' (11–14).

1. Man–Woman Relationships (11:2-16)

This passage is controversial. Many condemn its teachings as 'patriarchal' and 'hierarchical' and therefore essentially irrelevant and unhelpful to the modern world. Many congregations do not hear this passage in church since it does not appear in the *Revised Common Lectionary*. Some commentators will accept only some parts of Paul's argument, dismissing the rest as 'strained' and to be ignored. This raises serious questions about our attitude to and use of the Bible. By what canons are we able to relegate sections of the text? If we do so here we must be free to do so at other points that seem difficult. Do the principles of 'political correctness' now overrule the principle of biblical authority? This passage proves to be a critical test case for biblical authority.

1. Preliminary Questions

Three preliminary questions must be answered.

First, is this passage primarily about 'men' and 'women' or about 'husbands' and 'wives'? Our problem is that Paul's words can bear two meanings. 'Man' (*anēr*) can mean 'male' or 'husband' and 'woman' (*gynē*) can mean 'female' or 'wife'. Greek had no separate words for 'husband' and 'wife'. In my view, this passage points primarily to a 'husband' and 'wife' situation, rather than to a 'man' and 'woman' one.

It is clear that the 'marriage' of Adam and Eve in Genesis 2 is the background of this passage. 'Man is not *of* woman, but woman is *of* man', he observes (v. 8), reflecting on the Lord forming Eve *from* Adam's rib (Gen. 2:22). He adds, 'man was not created *for* woman, but woman *for* man', (v. 9), pointing to Eve as Adam's God-given 'helpmeet' (Gen. 2:21-22). His qualifier, 'Yet in the Lord woman is not independent from man, nor man from woman', echoes the 'one flesh' unity of Adam and Eve (Gen. 2:23) and clinches the case for husband-wife relationships rather than man-woman relationships. His insistence that 'woman is *for* the man' (v. 9) but also that 'the man is *for* the woman' repeats exactly the reciprocal husband-wife obligations of 7:3-5 and firmly establishes that Paul is writing primarily about 'husbands' and 'wives'.

Second, what does Paul mean by 'head'? Scholars have debated whether 'head' (*kephalē*) means 'head over' or 'source of' (e.g., the 'head' or 'source' of a river). Both positions have their competent and passionate advocates. It is safe to say that the debate has been coloured by the modern debate over 'women's rights'. If the current medical understanding of 'head' were followed it would mean that the head as the seat of the brain pointed to 'head *over*' as the correct interpretation. Ancient anatomy, however, saw the 'head' as a 'source' of various fluids emanating from ears, eyes and mouth. The human 'head' was seen as such a 'source', but the 'heart' was the location of thinking and feeling. There are many instances, however, where 'head' carried the metaphorical sense of 'head over'. After all, the 'head' is the highest part of the body. Furthermore, the 'source' view makes little sense of Paul's opening words that 'the head of every male is Christ' (v. 3). In my view Paul's use of 'head' in this passage points to a 'hierarchical' meaning.

Thus Paul is using the imagery of 'top down' authority, of Christ as *head* to every man, of a man as *head* to his wife, of God as *head* to Christ (v. 3). To be sure, there is some reference to the 'source' idea in his words, 'woman is *from* man...but all things are *from* God' (vv. 12, 8). But this does not support the 'source' hypothesis over hierarchy, rather it gives 'source' as the basis for the hierarchical teaching that God is head of man and man is head of woman.

Third, is Paul speaking about the 'covering' of the head (e.g., by a hat or a veil), or is he referring to a woman having her hair 'bound up' and 'covered' rather than 'uncovered' and 'let down'? Probably it was the latter, 'hair up' or 'hair down'. In that case earlier Bible translations may have misled us; the word 'veil' appears nowhere in Paul's text, neither as a noun or a verb. I believe Paul is referring to the arrangement of a woman's hair, not the wearing of hats or veils.

In Graeco-Roman culture women typically had long hair and men short hair. A woman whose hair was cut very short was probably passing herself off as a man, whether as the 'male' partner in a lesbian relationship or as a fugitive woman seeking to avoid abduction and rape in times of war. It was a matter of shame for a woman to be of 'mannish' appearance by being shaved or shorn (v. 6). Thus the length of hair at that time denoted a person to be a man or a woman. Paul said that long hair dishonours a man, whereas a woman's long hair (when arranged 'up', as a 'mantle' v. 15) is her glory (vv. 14-15). Part of Paul's concern in this passage, then, is to preserve among believers a visible distinction (consistent with that culture) between men and women. Here Paul is seeking to uphold the Creator's creation of the polarities of human sexuality. The Old Testament rules against a man wearing a woman's clothing and vice versa gave expression to God's creation of humans as 'male and female' (Deut. 22:5; Gen. 1:27). In Corinth hair length was a mark of 'male-ness' or 'female-ness', a distinction Paul did not wish to see blurred within the church community.

A woman's hair arrangement, however, symbolized something else that was closely related to her femininity. Women typically had long hair which was arranged neatly 'up' often with a partial cloth cover, as the many sculptures of women from those times indicate. Surviving sculptures of wedding ceremonies from that era portray wives with bound and covered hair. Hair that was neatly 'up' and covered was a sign of decorum and dignity for all women married and single, but in all probability, a particular cultural symbol of wifely domesticity. Among the women who wore their hair 'down' were ecstatic, out-of-control priestesses speaking prophetic oracles at the temple of Apollo at Delphi (to the near north west of Corinth).

It is evident from this passage that women in Corinth were now praying and prophesying in the church with heads 'uncovered', with hair 'down' (vv. 5,6, 13). In so doing they were presenting themselves as if unmarried and so were dishonouring their 'heads', that is, their own husbands as well as other men (vv. 3 and 5).

This was a dramatic departure from the 'tradition' Paul had 'handed over' to the Corinthians and the practices that were followed during his time with them. What had arisen in the past three years to bring about these changes? Paul speaks of 'contention' over this issue (v. 16). What was its source? Most likely such 'contention' was a further example of the 'eschatological madness' Paul addressed earlier in the Letter (see on 7:17-24). Paul had preached that with the death and resurrection of Jesus the Messiah the new age of the Kingdom had come. The Corinthians' experience of 'gifts' of prophecy and tongues-speaking within the church had confirmed that great reality. Yet they appear to have been so caught up with the 'gifts', the Spirit and the new age that they have forgotten that the present age continues until the Return of Christ. To be sure, male and female distinctions will be no more when the Kingdom is revealed in its fullness. But until then those distinctions remain, and with them the God-ordained submission of a wife to her 'head', her husband.

2. The 'Tradition': Man is the 'Head' of Woman (vv. 2-3)
Paul begins with a note of praise which, however, he quickly qualifies. 'I praise you...*But* I want you to know...' (vv. 2-3). This is good pastoral method. He is genuinely able to commend them for 'remembering' him, that is, for 'holding to' the 'traditions' which he originally 'handed over' to them when he established the church. Yet this is now a matter of 'contention' (v. 16).

This is the language of the rabbi to his disciples. Here Paul
speaks as one who had been a disciple of Rabbi Gamaliel
but who, at the time of his conversion to Christ, was himself
a young rabbi (probably) ministering to the Greek-speaking
synagogues of Jerusalem. More particularly, however, Paul
knew that Jesus was Rabbi to his disciples. They 'followed after'
him, were 'with him' and 'learned from' him as a disciple did
from his master and teacher. Characteristically Jesus taught
parables in public and debated with the scribes in public, but
explained his teachings in private to his disciples. Immediately
following the resurrection and ascension the apostles adopted
a rabbi-to-disciple relationship as teachers to the many hundreds who accepted the word of God and submitted to baptism
in the name of the Lord Jesus Christ. Paul adopted this way of
speaking in relationship to congregations brought into being
through his preaching of the gospel. There were a number of
'traditions' that believers were to follow, including between
husbands and wives.

As noted above (1:1), the Corinthians (or some of them) have
left these teachings behind them. Paul is addressing the women,
specifically *wives* (as I see it) in relationship with their husbands.
Before addressing the present pastoral problem Paul reminds
them of the 'tradition' he 'handed over' to them initially.

> I want you to know that
>
> | the head of every man | is | Christ |
> | the head of a woman | is | the man |
> | the head of Christ | is | God. |

The critical assertion of these three statements is the centre one,
'the head of a woman is the man'. From this will spring his
following argument. Paul, however, must locate this assertion
within a broader theological context. Thus he begins, 'the head
of every man is Christ' and he ends, 'the head of Christ is God'.

His opening statement is rather narrow. He does not say here
as he could have that Christ is 'head' of the Church (Eph. 1:22;
4:15; 5:23; Col. 1:18; 2:19) or 'head over everything' (Eph. 1:22),
the ultimate governor (Rev 5:5) who 'must reign' until history
will come to its God-appointed 'end' (1 Cor. 15:24-25). Since
his concern in the passage following is concentrated on man-
woman relationships, especially husband and wife relation-

ships, he makes the limited statement, 'the head of every *male* is Christ.' (Paul carefully uses the word *anēr*, male, rather than *anthrōpos* which means 'man' but in the generic sense of 'man and woman'.)

His closing statement serves to complete the cluster of three. God (i.e., God 'the Father') is 'head of' Christ. This is consistent with the 'Father' and 'Son' language used by Jesus and found throughout the New Testament. The words 'Father' and 'Son' imply what early theologians called the 'eternal generation' of the Son of God. The Son was and always will be equal in *being* with his Father. Yet he was and always will be 'under' the 'headship' of God his Father. His 'eternal generation' as the Son of God also implies his 'eternal subordination' in ready obedience to the will of his Father.

In short, Paul is making a powerfully hierarchical statement. God is the 'head of' Christ; Christ is the 'head of' every man; man is the 'head of' woman. By 'every man' Paul means 'every *male*'. As noted above (1:1), while Paul's original words can mean 'male' and 'female', the context as it unfolds points to a conjugal understanding, 'husband' and 'wife'. Paul is thinking of a husband's 'headship' in marriage.

This is the vocabulary of hierarchy, vocabulary that is both strange and unwelcome to modern ears accustomed to convictions about equality. Three comments may be made in passing. First, the subordination of wives to husbands is taught by both apostles, Paul and Peter. Most likely it was a pre-Pauline, pre-formed tradition, for which his modern critics blame him but which he did not originate but merely reiterated and applied. Second, the 'headship' of the husband is one of sacrificial, self-giving love for his much cherished wife, based on the example of Christ's saving sacrifice of his body, the Church (Eph. 5:25-32). Third, the wife's 'submission' to her husband is nowhere spelt out in detail, whereas the duty of the husband's love is explained at some length (Eph. 5:25-32; 1 Pet. 3:7). By 'submission' Paul and Peter appear to mean that a wife is to respect her husband's God-given 'role' or 'office' in the ordering of human affairs in that most important of human associations, the family. For their part, husbands are to prove themselves worthy of this high calling by following the example of Christ's sacrifice for his people.

In the passage following Paul is chiefly concerned that women in general, but wives in particular, express in practical ways their respect to the God-given role of men as husbands. This they were tending not to do by praying and prophesying in the assembly with hair 'uncovered' and 'down'.

3. Praying and Prophesying in the Assembly of Believers (vv. 4-6)

By his next words Paul takes us inside one of the meetings typical of churches established by him in Galatia, Macedonia, Achaia and Asia, and in all probability the church of Syrian Antioch which he did not found (cf. Acts 13:1-3). These assemblies were led by presbyters among whom were those who taught and catechized the congregations in the Scriptures of the Old Testament and the New Testament (at least as much as was written by then), but also in the oral 'traditions' like those Paul mentions in this chapter (see Gal. 6:6). Alongside the teaching offered by presbyters and formal liturgical elements (e.g., a 'benediction', a *eucharistia*, 'thanksgiving', or a 'grace') the proceedings also allowed free and extempore ministry of 'prophesying' and 'praying' by those 'gifted' to do so. Whereas presbyters (also called *episkopoi*, 'overseers') who taught were men (1 Tim. 2:11-3:7) probably based on the practice of the synagogue there was also free exercise of other 'gifts' open to both men and women. The Spirit had come with the hearing of the gospel. The people as a whole, both men and women, were now 'gifted' by the Spirit and gifted in various and diverse ways (1 Cor. 12:4-11, 27-31; 13:1-4). 'Prophesying' was the Spirit-inspired application of the gospel, the oral 'tradition' and the Scriptures to the life of the gathered people. Unlike the presbyter-teacher whose ministry was a matter of 'office' and regularity, those who prophesied did so on an occasional basis, as the perceived need arose.

But this free exercise of praying and prophesying by (some of) the women of Corinth had now been expressed in ways that subverted the order of man-woman relationships established by God for the present age. Paul could easily have brought such praying and prophesying to an end by simply insisting that ministry in the church be confined to the presbyters. Legalistic restrictiveness has typically been the approach adopted throughout Christian history when difficulties are encountered.

But this is part of the glory of God's Spirit-inspired apostle. He does not forbid women 'praying and prophesying', but reminds the men and women concerned of the theological guidelines within which such ministries are to be exercised. Paul is ever the teacher of godly principles rather than the legislator. Having laid down those principles he does not instruct them (or us) what to think, but *how* to think. This is a major reason why Paul's letters are as long as they are. Had Paul merely wanted to tell the readers what to do and what to think his messages to the churches could have been in each case a one or two page encyclical.

For men, the governing principle is: 'the head of every man is Christ' (v. 3). The first outworking of this is in verse 4:

> Every man praying or prophesying
>   having [a covering] upon   his head
>   dishonours   his head.

Paul points to two levels of meaning. Such a man dishonours his own head, but more to the point he dishonours his 'head', Christ. As he explains later, a man ought to be bareheaded since he is 'the image and glory of God' (v. 7). Paul is here thinking back to Genesis 2:7 where the man Adam is created first as the image bearer of God. Only later is the woman created *from* him and *for* him (Gen. 2:22-24; 1 Tim. 2:13).

The closely related principle is: the head of a woman is the man. The outworking of this principle is in verse 5:

> Every woman praying or prophesying
>   with uncovered   head
>   dishonours   her head.

Paul is now getting to the point of the entire passage. It is a moot point whether or not the men in Corinth had departed from the 'tradition'. In Graeco-Roman culture the men were ordinarily short haired and presumably uncovered and the women long-haired but with tresses arranged 'up' and in some way covered. By praying and prophesying with hair 'down' and uncovered the women appear to have been the ones who were departing from the apostolic 'tradition'. Of course, the length and arrangement of hair in itself was and is of no theological importance. But such hair arrangement can 'make a statement' about a woman's relationship with her husband. A woman could be saying, 'I am praying and prophesying in my own right, as if I am now unmarried, no longer subject to my husband as head'. In short, she could be saying that with the Spirit, who enabled her to pray and prophesy, has come the new age in all its fullness when there will be no marriages and therefore no submission. It is possible that the experience of the Spirit suggested that the age of the unmarried, an angelic age had now come, when all signs of authority could be cast off. Perhaps the Corinthians were influenced by Jesus' words that in the age of the Kingdom people would be unmarried, like the angels (cf. Mark 12:25). But Paul is saying that such thinking is *over-realized* eschatology. The present age continues and with it God's ordering of husband-wife relationships.

In verse 5 Paul gives a tangential illustration pointing out the shamefulness of this behaviour. 'Do you not see that your hair "up" and "covered" is a sign that you are married and that to let it "down, uncovered" in ministry in the assembly is publicly to "shame" your husband and other men? It would be like cutting all your hair off as men do, as women do who are embarrassed or ashamed of being women (like fugitive women and lesbians). Your femininity and your relationship with your husbands are inseparable. Do not deny the one or the other. Keep looking like a woman, a *married* woman. Keep your hair "up, covered" in the assembly, including when you pray and prophesy.'

The background to this notion of 'shame' may be Genesis 2:25 where the husband and wife were naked but 'felt no shame'. Paul uses exactly the Greek word (*aischros*) found in Genesis 2:25, which however is exceedingly rare in the Greek Old Testament (the Septuagint). In the marriage bond there is no sense of 'shame' in one aspect of life, nakedness. So let a woman feel no 'shame' at her husband by denying in the public meeting the cultural symbol of her 'submission' in marriage to him, her hair arranged 'up' and 'covered'.

We must again note that Paul does not resolve this pastoral problem by forbidding the ministry of women in praying and prophesying. In this regard we do well to notice how important was the ministry of prophesying for the health of the church (see 12:10,28; 13:2,8; 14:1-5, 22-25, 29-33a, 39). This high ministry was and remained open to women. We know that the four daughters of Philip the Evangelist exercised the ministry of prophecy (Acts 21:9). Those today who are troubled by the creeping power of women over men in the church must not overreact by silencing the voice of women in the public life of the church. Paul did not do this nor should we.

4. Woman the 'Glory' of Man (vv. 7-10)

As noted above (1:1) underlying verses 7-10 is the 'marriage' of Adam and Eve in Genesis 2:20b-24. Running through these verses is Paul's teaching on husband and wife relationships arising from the passage in Genesis.

He begins (v. 7) by giving the reason, stated negatively, why a man praying or prophesying with head covered brings 'shame' to his 'head' (v. 4). It is because, as he now states, 'a man ought not to cover his head, since he is the image and glory of God'. Once more early chapters of Genesis help explain Paul's teaching. God formed the man Adam from the dust and breathed life into his nostrils (Gen. 2:7) as one who bore the 'image' of God (Gen. 1:26), and therefore his 'glory'. 'Glory', however, is not to be found in the creation texts. I presume this is Paul's reflection on the 'brightness' of the man's role tending God's garden in Eden and his naming of the animals that God brings to him (Gen. 2:8-20a).

For Paul, however, it is 'glory' not 'image' that is the focus of his attention. 'Image' is his stepping stone from the text of Genesis to his word 'glory', as he now proceeds to say:

> For
> the woman is the *glory* of the man.

But how can he say this and what does he mean?

In verses 8-9 Paul gives two explanations why 'woman is the glory of man', each introduced by the explanatory 'for' contrasted with 'but'.

For man	is not	of woman
but woman	[is]	of man (v. 8)
For man	was not created	for woman
but woman	[was created]	for man (v. 9).

A man is the glory of God and a woman is the glory of a man. Originally she was made *from* him and *for* him. Nothing could be clearer but that Paul is drawing his teaching from Genesis 2:20b-24. How is a woman the 'glory' of a man? It is because, as the Genesis passage teaches, the woman whom God brings to man in marriage brings him so much joy. His days of loneliness are past. What the animals could never be for him this beautiful fellow human of opposite sex is, his glory. He sings:

> She is bone of my bone
> > flesh of my flesh.
> 'She is "woman"
> because she is taken
> > from "man."'

Adam's love song when confronted by God's gracious gift to him is but the first of millions of love songs in all cultures inspired by the beauty of a man and a woman in one another's eyes. She is his 'glory' since she fulfils him at his deepest wellsprings of companionship, sexual fellowship and shared procreation.

Her physical head needs to reflect submission to her husband, her metaphorical 'head' whose 'glory' she is, just as the man bareheaded ought to point to God whose 'image' and 'glory' he is. If the man 'ought' to be bareheaded, the head of the woman 'ought' to be with hair 'up' and 'covered' (see on v. 5). This must be what Paul means by these unusual words (v. 10):

> For this reason
> the woman ought have authority on her head,
> > > on account of the angels.

The word 'authority' was used of the 'right' a Roman emperor gave someone to govern a province. A governor like Pilate exercised 'authority' on behalf of and in place of the Emperor Tiberius. The woman praying or prophesying in the assembly did so because of and under the 'authority' of her husband. And the sign of his 'authority' as husband was that her hair was 'up' and 'covered'. The angels are God's messengers and ministers who represent God and who are present when the people gather in worship. They need to see that the woman who prays or prophesies does so under the 'authority' of her husband, that is, by the appearance of her head. The angels are custodians of the God-ordained hierarchies for this present age which are to remain in place until the advent of the new age. In that culture, the licence for her ministry for the Spirit-gifted woman was her hair arrangement. In subsequent situations such as ours the 'sign' of that authority will probably be different, perhaps the wearing of the marriage ring. Whatever the case women should continue to look like women!

5. Corrective Words (vv. 11-12)
Ever careful Paul cannot leave his teaching on that note. He must ensure that his words are not taken as a mandate for some kind of male oppressiveness.

Verse 11 begun by 'Nevertheless' (*plēn*) introduces a strong qualifier and corrective to his exposition. To be sure, a woman is the glory of a man, being created *from* him and *for* him, and therefore bearing the mark of his authority on her. Nevertheless...

> *Nevertheless*
>   neither is a woman independent of a man
>   nor   is a man   independent of a woman
>   in the Lord.

'Independent' conveys a poor impression of Paul's word (*chōris*), though it is not easy to improve on it. By it Paul means that in Christian marriage a man and a woman are closely knit together. If they are 'one flesh' in human terms how much more truly united are they 'in the Lord [Jesus]' in spiritual terms. She is his glory and she bears his authority, yet they are inseparably one.

Sexuality, support and companionship in marriage are implied by Paul's words. Conjugal relationships in all their forms are a two way street. The man and the woman are profoundly one because he is 'for' her and she is 'for' him. As Paul taught earlier, the husband's sexual obligation is not to provide for his satisfaction but rather to serve his wife, and the wife's sexual obligation is not for her fulfilment but for his (see on 7:3-5). Each lives for the other. Such is the mutuality of their relationship.

But in conclusion Paul must acknowledge that God is the ultimate source of all things, including men and women and their relationships with each other. Based on Genesis chapter two Paul must affirm that woman is from man and man is from God.

6. *Judge What is Fitting (vv. 13-16)*

Paul draws his pastoral teaching to a conclusion.

He begins (v. 13) with a challenge for them to 'judge this matter for themselves' followed by a question, 'Is it fitting for a woman to pray to God uncovered?' Clearly from his previous explanations Paul thinks that it is quite *un*fitting.

We might think that he would repeat his arguments that in such a situation the woman would dishonour her 'head', that is, her husband. Somewhat to our surprise, however, he canvasses an argument from 'nature' (*physis*). The Stoic philosopher Epictetus (AD 50-120) was to observe:

> Can anything be more useless than hairs on the chin? Well what then?
> Has not nature used even these in the most suitable way possible?
> Has she not by these means distinguished between the male and the female?...
> Wherefore, we ought to preserve the signs which God has given. We ought not ... confuse the sexes which have been distinguished in this fashion.

Unlike the Stoics who had a passive concept of creation by an impersonal creator, Paul asks his questions as a son of Abraham who worships the Creator of the Universe according to Biblical revelation. By 'nature' Paul means God who created and sustains nature. In that vein Paul asks (v. 14-15a):

> Does not nature herself teach you
> that it is a disgrace for a man to have long hair
> but if a woman has long hair it is her glory?

He adds (v. 15b):

> Because her hair has been given her in place of a mantle.

A woman's femininity and beauty is enhanced by her long hair, which is given her (by God, that is) in place of a handmade mantle. The word literally means a decorative woman's garment that is 'cast around' (*peribolaion*) her. But a man is not beautiful, at least not in the way a woman is. A man's 'beauty' lies in his true masculinity. Long hair, according to Paul, has an aesthetic character consistent with femininity. It is inappropriate (a 'disgrace') for a man to present himself effeminately.

Why, we ask, does Paul appeal here to the short hair-long hair (male-female) argument rather than to the head uncovered-head covered (husband-wife) consideration back in verses 4-5, 7? The answer is that the two arguments are so intertwined as to be inseparable. Hair of long length and its orderly arrangement pointed to (1) a woman's 'female-ness', and (2) to her conjugal relationship as subject to a husband. Hair that was short and a head that was uncovered pointed to a man's 'male-ness', to being the image and glory of God and to being the 'head' to a wife.

Paul concludes with an appeal to the universal practices of 'the churches of God'. As well as the churches Paul founded in Galatia, Macedonia, Achaia and Asia he is also referring to the churches in Judaea (cf. Gal 1:22; 1 Thess 2:14) established by Peter many years earlier. This was a universal practice in the churches of the apostles.

What do we learn from this passage?

First, in whatever culture we find ourselves it is important that distinguishing marks for men and women are expressed. Paul clearly cherished sexual differences as God-given and to be appreciated with thankfulness. Women have their distinctive 'beauty' in appearance and temperament but men, too, have theirs. These are not to be shrunk from nor blurred. Needless to say he is by no means advocating sexually suggestive dress or posture by men or women. But human beauty in men and women can be presented decently and modestly.

Second, Paul is concerned that wives acknowledge their husbands as 'head'. The apostles do not give much detail as to how this is to be done in regard to decision making, for example. The Bible is silent on issues like that, as it happens. We do well not to extrapolate demands and rules that are not set forth in Holy Scripture. But this passage does point to a wife so conducting herself that she respects her husband and other men and that she does not bring shame on them by the way she presents herself and conducts herself in public, including in the public life of the church.

Third, there is no basis in this passage or in any other for the idea that women as a gender were under the headship of men as a gender or that women in general were to be subject to men in general inside the church. The 'headship' and subordination passages all relate to husbands and wives. This passage is saying that a woman must not diminish her wifely submission to her husband as she exercises ministry within the church.

Fourth, it is clear that women as well as men exercised the 'gifts' of Spirit-inspired praying and prophesying within the community of faith, provided they did so under the 'headship' of their husbands. That freedom, however, did not extend to assuming the role of presbyter-teacher within the congregation, which was restricted to men (1 Tim. 2:11-3:7).

Pastorally this is a vexed issue in modern societies where women take their place alongside men in every area of life. The limiting of women's leadership within the congregation was not based on any implication about male superiority or female inferiority but on the distinctive role of the husband in marriage and family life (Eph. 5:22-33).

At the same time, we have in this passage where women pray and prophesy a basis for the voice of women to be heard in the church.

2. The Supper of the Lord (11:17-34)

1. Background in Corinth
The background to Paul's words here is the 'last supper'. This issue is what is commonly called 'the Lord's supper' but which I am referring to as the remembrance meal or the dinner of the Lord.

The remembrance meal occurred when all the believers in the city assembled for some kind of communal meal. But it is evident from Paul's comments that things were seriously wrong with the Corinthians' behaviour towards one another when they 'came together'.

2. 'Coming Together' but for the Worse (vv. 17-22)
This passage is 'framed' with the words, 'I do not praise [you]' and it is an example of 'ring composition' forming what is called an *inclusio*. The benefit of recognising this is to establish it as a discrete passage. These are amongst Paul's most severe words to any congregation. Why does Paul censure these people?

Verse 17 begins with a contrastive, 'But'. The 'instruction' he is about to give is prompted by a more serious problem than the women's failure in submission addressed in the previous passage. This new problem related to their 'coming together' (*synerchesthai*) as indicated by the fivefold repetition of that verb in this passage (vv. 17, 18, 20, 33, 34). The word can mean either 'to assemble' or 'to meet *together*', though it is likely that Paul has both meanings in mind. The Christian gathering is no mere assembly but it is to be a 'meeting together in unity'. But the Corinthians' 'coming together' did not issue in such unity but in division. It was, therefore, 'not for the better but for the worse'. Paul is saying, in effect, it would have been better if they had stayed at home!

The explanatory 'For' at the beginning of verse 18 immediately gives the chief reason he withholds his praise from them. Ordinarily they met by 'houses' as sub-groups of the congregation. From time to time, however (and we do not know how frequently), they 'came together as church', that is, as he will say later, when the 'whole church' came together (14:23). Most likely this was in the house of Gaius, 'the host of [Paul] and of the whole church' (Rom. 16:23; cf. 1 Cor. 1:14). But Paul 'hears' that there are 'schisms' (*schismata*) among them and he is inclined to believe it. Perhaps this 'report' came also from Chloe's people who told him of the 'schisms' (1:10) which, in our view, were associated with unnamed local leaders (see on 4:6). Be that as it may, these were different 'schisms' arising not so much from personalities as from selfishness and insensitivity. Paul is aggrieved that the 'church' should be 'torn apart' for whatever reason.

In passing, however, he comments that 'there must be divisions among you' (v. 19). Here he uses a different word (*haeresis* 'heresies') which in the following centuries would mean departure from orthodox belief. In the unfolding history of the church a 'heresy' often became a 'schism' even though the words used here are synonyms. Paul teaches that 'division' within the congregation at Corinth served to 'show up' those who were 'approved' or 'tested'. Doubtless he is reflecting on those aggrieved persons from whose 'reports' Paul came to 'hear' about the current 'schisms' in Corinth. We are reminded that God is more concerned with the quality of faith and life in 'tried and tested' individuals than mere numbers of professed adherents. Paul's word 'must' tells us that evil as they are, 'heresy' and 'schism' are divinely sanctioned. They have the effect of demonstrating those who are 'tested' by those circumstances and therefore who are 'approved' by God.

After that brief digression the apostle returns to his argument (v. 20). This he introduces with a summarizing, 'Therefore'. He is saying, 'There are schisms when you meet as the church. *Therefore* it is not the "dinner of the Lord" that you eat'. A *deipnon* is an evening meal. 'Supper' is an old fashioned word so I have preferred to use 'dinner'. This is a 'dinner' that 'belongs to the Lord (*kyriakos*)' because it was instituted by the Lord, made possible by the death of the Lord. We must emphasize that this 'dinner' is the Lord's in the same way as, we noted earlier, the 'cup' is the Lord's and the 'table' is the Lord's (see on 10:21). The Lord established this 'dinner', provided for it by his death and is the host who invites his people to it.

The 'dinner of the Lord' consists of a small quantity of bread and wine. Those present are to find their unity and fellowship in their participation together in that 'dinner'. But in their 'coming together' the wealthy ate a full meal, including overflowing wine, while the 'have nots' had only a fragment of bread and a taste of wine (see v. 21). Thus the community which was intended to find unity in sharing a loaf of bread and wine cup found only disunity, and was torn by schism owing to the rudeness and insensitivity of the wealthy. It was not the Lord's dinner that the Corinthians ate but merely 'any old' dinner.

With verse 21 Paul gets to the point, as explained by the introductory 'For'.

> *For*
>> each goes before [others]
>> in eating his own dinner.

Some scholars suggest that Paul is critical because a small number of wealthy members ate and drank fine food within the *triclinium* or dining room inside the house (that would accommodate only about ten persons), whereas the rest of the members ate inferior food separated from them in the *atrium* or outside courtyard. Attention is drawn to a description of a meal given by a wealthy host found in the letters of Pliny the Younger:

The best dishes were set in front of himself and a select few,
and cheap scraps of food before the rest of the company.
He had even put the wine into little flasks,
divided into three categories....One lot was intended for
himself and us,
another for his lesser friends...and a third lot for his and
our freedmen.

Does Pliny's account point the way to understanding Paul's displeasure with the Corinthians, especially when understood in terms of a small *triclinium* for the wealthy separated from an *atrium* for the poor? To be sure, there were 'have nots' among them (v. 22) which implies that there were also rich members. The 'have nots' were 'hungry' and, presumably (some of) the wealthy were 'drunk', so well furnished were they with wine.

This reconstruction of the situation, however, depends too much on our limited grasp of the size of houses in Corinth. There are only a few houses in the Achaian capital which have been unearthed by archaeologists. The few excavated villas in Ephesus, however, are significantly larger than those investigated in Corinth. In any case it is only speculation to say that the wealthy ate in the *triclinium* and the poor in the *atrium*. It is equally possible that all ate in Gaius' *atrium*.

A better understanding is based on critical words which appear later: 'When you come together to eat, *wait* for one another' (v. 33). So the 'sin' of the Corinthians was that some began eating the meal 'before' others. It follows that those who began before others may have been the wealthier members who had time not only to eat but also to drink enough to be intoxicated, and those who came later were the 'have nots' who were hungry. Possibly the late comers were slaves as well as poorer members, whose only 'food' on their eventual arrival was the bread and wine of the remembrance meal.

In Paul's mind the better endowed members should have waited till others arrived and, moreover, shared their food and drink with them. That some were 'drunk' while others were hungry points in this direction.

Paul's anger at the selfishness of the wealthy is probably to be understood against the background of the drastic food shortage in Greece as a result of the grain famine that struck the eastern Mediterranean during the latter years of Claudius' principate. These were times of great hardship for the poor who were unable to afford the steeply increased food prices and who were dependent on the erratic welfare provisions of the emperor.

In verse 22 the heat of Paul's anger at the wealthy can be felt even from this distance as he fires off question after question to them.

> You [wealthy] have houses to eat and drink in. You do, don't you?
> Or, do you despise the church of God
> and humiliate those who have nothing?
> What shall I say to you?
> Shall I heap praise on you?
> In this I praise you not.

The wealthy had 'houses' in which they certainly 'ate and drank'. By bringing their wealth into the meeting of the saints and flaunting it before the poor, by eating and drinking lavishly, and doing so without waiting for the poorer members, and without sharing with them, they have 'despised' the church of God and mocked the poor among them. Paul is almost speechless in disbelief at their behaviour.

Here we see something of Paul's passion for the poor (cf. Gal. 2:10), a passion he shared with James (James 1:9; 2:1-7; cf. 1:10-11; 5:1; 1:27) and which he expressed elsewhere for the 'weak' (2 Cor. 11:29). In this both apostles were following the example of the Lord (e.g., Matt. 11:28; Luke 6:20; Mark 9:42; cf. Isa. 11:4), and the prophets before him (e.g., Is. 2:17; Jer. 22:16; Amos 4:1).

3. The Dinner of the Lord (vv. 23-26)

Paul must go back to basics, which is why he rehearses the 'tradition' about the dinner of the Lord. Perhaps they have forgotten what it is about, so that he must remind them. Above all, it is not a dinner 'party' at which people are gorged and drunk. It is a metaphorical dinner, a 'dinner' whose only food is a small quantity of very simple food, from a shared loaf of bread and from a shared cup of wine. Had the Corinthians eaten this 'dinner' in the context of a meal that was shared and at which the members treated one another with courtesy and respect regardless of wealth or status Paul would not even have raised the subject. Since they do not eat the dinner of the Lord when they 'come together' (v. 20) he must tell them once more what it is.

In verse 23a we meet again Paul's rabbi-to-disciple language (see also 11:2; cf. 15:1,3). The 'tradition' Paul 'handed over' to them five years earlier he 'received from the Lord'. He is referring here (almost certainly) to the time of his conversion near Damascus and to Ananias' preparation of him for baptism there. I presume that Ananias instructed Paul and 'handed over' this 'tradition'. That teaching went back to the Passover meal when Jesus established his 'dinner' by which his followers could 'remember' him in the time ahead until his Return. Thus the 'tradition' came 'from the Lord', was 'received' by the Twelve who 'delivered' it to members of the Jerusalem Church, from whom (somehow) Ananias 'received' it and taught it to Paul. A decade and a half later Paul 'delivered' this 'tradition' to the Corinthians.

In verses 23b-25 Paul repeats the 'tradition' that narrates what occurred on the night Jesus instituted the remembrance meal. It was during and 'after' the Passover dinner (v. 25) which Jesus shared with the Twelve, the 'night he was delivered' by Judas Iscariot. This brief narrative dovetails exactly with the Gospels' accounts of that fateful Passover evening when Judas 'delivered' Jesus to the chief priests who 'delivered' him to Pontius Pilate.

> The Lord Jesus...
>   took a loaf
>   and giving thanks
>   broke it
>   and said
>   'This is my body which is [broken] for you.
>   Do this to remember me.'
> Likewise after the Dinner
> [he
>   took] a cup
>   [and giving thanks]
>   said
>   'This is the new covenant in my blood.
>   Do this to remember me
>   as often as you drink it.'

Earlier, Paul referred to 'the cup of blessing which we bless' and the 'loaf we break' (10:16). Jesus spoke of his body 'broken' and also 'gave thanks for the cup' (Matt. 26:27; cf. Luke 22:17). Although Paul omits these details in his rehearsal of the 'tradition' their inclusion above in square brackets is justifiable.

At that Passover meal Jesus took in his hands a loaf which he broke and a cup with outpoured wine. By his accompanying words he explained that these actions depicted his death the next day. His body is broken and his blood is shed. But his body is broken 'for' his people and his blood poured out to establish the new covenant, as prophesied by Jeremiah (31:31-34). Jesus died to establish God's new covenant based on his divinely bestowed righteousness on his people and the working within them of his powerfully transforming Spirit (2 Cor. 3:8-9, 18). The apostles and all subsequent preachers of the gospel are 'ministers of a new covenant' (2 Cor. 3:6). A 'new covenant' means a 'new people', God's family, whose members are brothers and sisters in the Messiah crucified and risen. Paul's anger was directed towards the wealthy Corinthians because in the remembrance meal they did not act towards their fellow-members as brothers and sisters in the covenant of God but treated the poor among them with disdain.

But Jesus' actions and words were not merely prospective, to explain to the Twelve that night the meaning and significance of what would happen the next day. Rather, what Jesus did and said was to be repeated into the future as a way of bringing *him* to the 'memory' of his people. This matches exactly the Lord's institution of the Passover meal in Egypt. The Lord instructed Moses and Aaron that it was to be 'a day of *remembrance* for you. You shall celebrate it as a festival to the LORD' (Exod. 12:14, NRSV). By the actions, the words, and the eating and drinking at the dinner of the Lord, the new covenant people 'call to mind' the death of their Lord on their behalf. Jesus intended his people corporately to 'remember' him, which they do when they eat his 'dinner' together. Jesus offered his sacrifice on the cross for his people once. He achieved an eternal salvation by this never to be repeated act (see Heb. 9:26-10:10). There can be no re-offering of that sacrifice, but only the 'remembrance' of it.

Jesus, we thus obey
Thy last and kindest word;
Here in thine own appointed way
We come to meet our Lord...

Thus we remember thee,
and take this bread and wine
As thine own dying legacy,
And our redemption's sign.
                                    Charles Wesley

Regrettably for many people the emphasis in the Lord's dinner is directed towards the tiny elements of bread and wine, that is, in the *objects* that are consumed. But this is only part, and the latter part at that, of what Jesus instituted. *Watching* the actions and *listening* to the words go before the *eating* and *drinking*. When Jesus said 'do this', he meant his people are to do *all three things* in 'remembrance of me'. This is done together by all present and it is a subjective act of 'remembering' the Lord Jesus himself. Any notion of the 'real presence' of Jesus in the actual bread and wine misses the point completely. If the focus is on the elements to be consumed and them alone the whole point of the 'drama' that Jesus said was to be re-played is lost. In its place there is the mere preoccupation with what is eaten and drunk as a means to enjoying God's blessing. For the dinner of the Lord to be restored to Jesus' intention it requires the involvement of the *eyes* and the *ears* as well as the *mouth*. But not merely my eyes, my ears, my mouth, but mine in fellowship with those others who are present. It is an act of 'remembering' *together*.

In verse 26 Paul adds his own explanation of this tradition.

For as often as   you eat   the loaf
                       and drink   the cup
    you proclaim the death of the Lord
    until he comes.

The Corinthians have corrupted the dinner of the Lord. They have made it into a party for the rich. Rather, it should be a sparse 'meal' of a loaf of bread and a cup of wine, which those present, having seen the actions and heard the words, then 'eat' and 'drink'. By the totality of watching, listening and eating together at this 'dinner,' says Paul, 'you proclaim the death of the Lord until he comes'. Thus the 'dinner' is (1) for 'remembering the Lord' (vv. 24-25) and (2) to 'proclaim' his death until his return. In short, at the dinner of the Lord the members tell one another the gospel, centred in the death of Christ and his second coming.

In his explanation of the 'tradition' Paul states that those present 'eat the *loaf* and drink from the *cup*', which point in turn to the *broken* body and *shed* blood of the Lord. In sharing that loaf and wine cup they share together in the 'body of Christ' and the 'blood of Christ', that is, in the benefits of his death.

In itself the bread remains bread and the wine remains wine. Within a century, however, Christian leaders were referring to the bread and the wine in realistic terms as the flesh and blood of Christ. Ignatius, Bishop of Antioch, referred to these as 'the medicine of immortality and the antidote to prevent us from dying' (Ephesians xx). The sense of dramatic action from the Old Testament prophetic tradition in the remembrance meal as intended by Jesus soon began to be lost in an increasingly Gentile church. In time the bread and wine would be venerated in worship.

With the Reformation came a return to a truer understanding of the dinner of the Lord. Many Protestants, however, in reacting against unreformed practice of the holy communion have tended to downgrade the significance of the remembrance meal. Yet Jesus said, 'Do this in remembrance of me', and Paul declared that by it we 'proclaim the death of the Lord until he comes'. The words of Christ and his apostle suggest that we think very highly of the supper of the Lord.

Who presided at the Table of the Lord in the house of Gaius when the whole Corinthian community of faith gathered? Paul gives no clue as to the identity of the president. It is a reasonable conjecture, however, that the most senior presbyter present repeated the actions and spoke the words of remembrance. At the Passover Meal the father of the household took the place of leadership and in the synagogue the place of honour was given to the most senior elder. It is probable that the early churches followed the same general principle in order to secure the dignity and significance of the dinner of the Lord. The idea that the remembrance meal is only valid and effective if an episcopally ordained person presides at the table has no basis in the teaching of the apostles. This, too, however, soon gave way to a priestly and sacerdotal view of the remembrance meal. In short, if the dinner of the Lord is to retain the meaning and significance intended by Jesus, the teaching of the Apostle Paul must be closely adhered to.

4. The Lord's Discipline (vv. 27-32)
Paul now returns to the scandalous behaviour of the Corinthians at the remembrance meal (see on vv. 17-22).

In verse 27 Paul cautions the readers concerning the consequences of their action. To eat the bread and drink of the cup of the Lord unworthily, that is, in circumstances of greed, selfishness and insensitivity, as the wealthy Corinthians have done, is 'therefore' to be 'guilty of the body and blood of the Lord', that is, his death. It was precisely those attitudes that brought about the death of Jesus. To repeat them on the occasion of the meal at which his death is recalled means nothing less than to share in the guilt of those who killed him.

With so weighty a possibility in mind Paul exhorts them one by one in verse 28, 'Let each person test himself or herself'. By 'test' (*dokimazein*) Paul uses the blacksmith's term for testing so as to approve a piece of metal for strength. Only when I have passed that 'test' am I ready to eat from the loaf and drink from the cup. In other words, Paul calls on his readers then and now to reflect seriously before sharing in the meal. For the Corinthians this would mean 'coming together' in a spirit of genuine brotherly and sisterly love towards all those present, rich or poor.

In verse 29 Paul issues a specific warning:

For whoever eats and drinks [unworthily]
   eats and drinks condemnation to himself
since he does not discern the body [of the Lord].

The Corinthians have 'despised the church of God' and 'humiliated the have nots' among them. That is, they have failed to 'discern' that this is no mere collection of people but the 'body' of the Lord Jesus Christ (see on 12:12-31). Here, though, it is a Pauline play on words. It is the 'body of Christ' that participates in the 'body' of the Lord as they eat from the loaf at the Lord's table (see 10:16). Both the people and the loaf are highly significant, the people for who they are ('the body of Christ') and the loaf for what it points to ('the body of Jesus' broken in death for his people). Let the reader take great care as he or she approaches this meal. For to eat unworthily in our relationships with others, as some of them were doing, secures the displeasure of the Lord.

The apostle points (v. 30) to recent tragic circumstances in Corinth in which 'many are weak and sick and not a few have died'. It seems likely that an epidemic had struck Corinth, though we have no external evidence of it. Ancient cities were so unsanitary, however, that in a pre-immunization age, disease frequently caused the deaths of many. As noted earlier Corinth was affected by famine and food shortages at that time (see on 7:25-35). Paul saw sickness and death as a consequence of the Corinthian behaviour at the remembrance meal. By no means did Paul see other sufferings as a consequence of disobedience to the will of God. Many difficulties he and other Christians faced were due to hostility towards the message of Christ crucified and risen (see e.g., Rom. 8:36-38; 2 Cor. 1:3-7). But in this case Paul, with apostolic insight, attributed these illnesses and deaths to the Corinthians' failure to 'discern the body' of Christ at the supper of the Lord.

Paul calls for self-discernment (v. 31). Earlier he urged the Corinthians to 'discern the body [of Christ]', that is, to reflect on the impact of their actions on the others in the church. But this cannot be separated from discerning oneself and one's attitudes and motives. What do I think about others in the congregation, especially those who may be less well educated or poor? Do I regard them as in some way inferior? Do I prefer the company of the clever, the accomplished, the articulate, the wealthy? Do I avoid those who are at the other end of the spectrum? Better by far, suggests Paul, to 'discern' oneself than face the prospect of being judged negatively by the Lord.

There is, however, a difference between being 'judged', that is, to incur the Lord's displeasure, and being 'condemned with the world'. The recent illnesses and deaths in Corinth were evidences of the Lord's displeasure (v. 32), but not yet of his 'condemnation'. These acts of his 'judgement' mean that they were 'being disciplined'. The verb (*paideuōmai*) is used of a parent disciplining a wayward child so as to bring helpful correction. Let the Corinthians learn from such discipline and repent, otherwise they will, indeed, be 'condemned with the world'.

5. Final Exhortation about 'Coming Together' (vv. 33-34)

Finally the apostle brings his readers back to the situation which provoked his powerful criticisms of them, that is, their failure to wait for one another when they 'came together'. So he exhorts them to do precisely that. Let the wealthy among them not begin to eat and drink before others arrive, including the poorer members and the slaves who have little to eat. By so doing the offending members have in effect created an elite dinner party, an exclusive faction based on wealth within the wider community of faith.

So, he advises (v. 34), 'if you are hungry eat at home'. Paul is not urging the members to stop eating a meal together as a context for the remembrance meal. He is not necessarily saying that the dinner of the Lord should be separated from communal eating, which in time came to be the practice, as it largely is today. Paul is neither advocating communal eating as the circumstance for the remembrance meal nor urging its discontinuance. Rather, he is saying that, either way, the dinner of the Lord is for all members, rich or poor, slave or free, and it is focused on remembering Jesus through watching the loaf broken and the cup upraised in thanksgiving, listening to his words given on the night he was betrayed, and eating together from that loaf and drinking together from that cup. But do not spoil this act of 'remembering' Jesus and proclaiming his death by allowing the gathering to become separated into the rich at their own affluent dinner party and the poor who arrive late and hungry.

See to it, he says, that your 'coming together' does not issue in the Lord's judgement on you. There are other matters, he hints, but he will set them in order when he comes.

SOME QUESTIONS FOR PERSONAL REFLECTION:

1. Do you agree or disagree with Paul that it is important to preserve the outward appearance of women and men?

2. What then of his concern that married women in expressing their gifts in ministry do so with a sign of their husbands' authority?

3. Can you think of parallels to the scandalous behaviour of the Corinthians at the remembrance meal?

4. What should you be doing as you prepare yourself to participate in the dinner of the Lord?

5. What should you be doing at that meal?

STUDY QUESTIONS:

1. What does Paul mean by man being 'head' over the woman?

2. Is Paul advocating that women should 'know their place' or is there something much deeper? Is he instructing women to not have a place in the church?

3. How was there disunity in the church in the 'Lord's Dinner' as they came together to partake in it?

4. What were the wealthy members guilty of when coming to the 'Lord's Dinner'?

5. What are the three components in the Lord's Dinner? What then, is remembered?

6. Why does Paul see the sickness and death of some of the members as 'God's discipline'? What is the difference between being 'judged' and being 'condemned'?

12

Gifts and Ministries in the Body of Christ
(1 Cor. 12:1-31)

Paul's opening word, 'Concerning' (*peri*) signals that Paul is again responding to questions in a letter sent by the Corinthians (see on 7:1). In this case they are inquiring about Spirit-based ministries as they affect the gathered congregation. Paul's answer will involve him in a lengthy discussion on this subject occupying chapters 12–14. Chapter 11, which was Paul's response to the corruption of his 'traditions' about women ministering and the church's gathering for the Lord's Supper, clearly belongs to the same broad subject touching their congregational life. Thus chapter 11 belongs with chapters 12–14, which together form the longest 'block' of teaching we find in this Letter.

We face an immediate problem of knowing the meaning of his opening statement, 'Now concerning *spiritual gifts*' (RSV; NIV). The difficulty is that Paul doesn't use the word 'gifts' (*charismata*) here, though he does later in the chapter (vv. 4, 9, 28, 30, 31). Rather, he uses another word of which the root is *pneuma*, 'spirit'. The form of the word in verse 1 (*pneumatikōn*) could mean either 'the spiritual *people*' (masculine) or 'the spiritual *things*' (neuter). By 'the spiritual people' (*pneumatikoi*) Paul points to something positive in such people, that is, their spiritual discernment (2:13, 15), maturity (3:1) and ministry (14:37). By contrast, 'the spiritual things' is a neutral term that only occurs again at 14:1 where the explanation in verse 2 determines that 'the spiritual things' means 'speaking in a tongue'. Which of these does Paul mean in the opening title of the section in chapter 12 verse 1. In short, are chapters 12–14 about 'spiritual people' or the 'spiritual things', that is, 'tongues-speaking'?

Opinions differ. My view, however, is that Paul is most likely addressing the Corinthians' question of tongues-speaking. First, as it turns out Paul does not go on to address 'the spiritual people' in these chapters. Apart from the reference in 14:37 the word *pneumatikoi* does not otherwise occur. Second, 'tongues-speaking' is what he is really concerned about throughout chapters 12–14. His general statement about the diversity of various 'spiritual gifts' (12:4-30) and the necessity for love as the motive for their exercise (13:1-3) leads into the climax of his argument, his damaging contrast of 'tongues speaking' with 'prophesying' (14:1-33a). Third, his 'forbid not speaking in tongues' at the end (14:39) would be consistent with a reference to 'tongues-speaking' at the beginning (12:1), thus creating an *inclusio* for the entire section. In short, these chapters are devoted to establishing the limited worth of 'the spiritual things', that is, of 'tongues speaking' in the assembly of believers.

Nonetheless, although he downplays 'tongues-speaking' in these chapters, his presentation is a model of pastoral tact. Furthermore, this entire section is a good example of Paul's approach to the practice of Christianity. Others might have resolved the issue with a few terse comments followed by a string of decrees. But this is not Paul's way. Rather, he patiently pens his sermon on the subject, taking his readers ancient and modern step by step through his reasoning. Above all, he will teach them and us how to think as believers so that we might learn the mind of Christ for the complexities of life. The way of legalism is a tempting option, but it was not Paul's way.

1. By The Power of the Spirit of God: Deliverance and Confession (vv. 1-3)

Paul's opening words, 'Now concerning' signals that he is addressing yet another question in their letter to him (7:1; cf. 7:25; 8:1; 16:1; 16:12). That question relates not to 'spiritual gifts' in general but to 'tongues speaking' in particular (see above), which some had sought to prohibit (14:39). His words, 'I do not want you to be uninformed' are a kind of formula to introduce teaching or information not given previously by Paul whether in person or by letter. This suggests that the practice of or the greater emphasis on 'tongues speaking' was a recent develop-ment in Corinth since his departure from the city three years previously. Paul made no reference to 'tongues speaking' in his letters to the Galatians and the Thessalonians, which were written prior to First Corinthians. This may explain why he devotes so much space to it here.

His use of the word *pneumatika* for 'tongues-speaking' may have been Paul's own creation. Perhaps there is a touch of irony here. On the face of it the word means 'spirit-inspired', by which its devotees would have felt comforted. Yet the word could also mean merely, 'wind-inspired,' a rather deflating nuance.

Having introduced this extended teaching on a subject about which they are 'ignorant' in verses 2-3, Paul immediately launches into something they do 'know', namely the work of the Holy Spirit that made possible their conversion. Since he will be speaking about the Holy Spirit energising the ministry of the members to one another, it is important for them to be reminded of the initial work of the Spirit changing their lives and attitudes.

Previously, as 'Gentiles' as most appear to have been they were in spiritual bondage to the idols in the temples. Paul reminds them:

> You know that when you were Gentiles
> you were continually led about
> wherever those speechless[1] idols were leading you.

The irony is heavy, perhaps echoing Paul's frontal attacks as an evangelist to idolaters. 'How foolish,' we hear him saying, 'rational, speaking people like you, led by the nose as slaves by lifeless pieces of stone'. Yet this is a fitting description of that kind of spiritual bondage.

He adds a dark note. During those temple sacrifices some people (including the priests?) would cry out, '*Anathema Iēsous*', that is, 'A curse on Jesus'. Here is evidence of demonic opposition

---

1   Greek: *aphonos*, literally 'voice-less'.

to Jesus and the preaching of the gospel in apostolic times.[2] Missionaries speak of such spiritual hostility to the word of God. Perhaps some of his present readers in Corinth were among those who previously cursed the Lord, prompting Paul to say later, 'If anyone does not love the Lord let him be accursed' (16:22).

But the gospel of Jesus has come to these same people. As they assemble with fellow believers, diametrically opposite words are heard, namely, 'Jesus is Lord'. When a convert is baptized or the congregation joins in a hymn their frequent cry is, 'Jesus is Lord'.

Paul's point is a simple one. As a result of the proclamation of the gospel the Holy Spirit has come, bringing a total change of attitude to Jesus. Paul forcibly brings this out by the chiasma (cross over) structure of the words following:

No one speaking	
by the Holy Spirit says,	A
'Jesus be cursed.'	B
No one is able to say, 'Jesus is Lord,'	B
except by the Holy Spirit.	A

In this format the Holy Spirit is at the extremities and Jesus is at the centre. The power of the Holy Spirit has broken the chains of idolatry enabling the new believer to declare the Lordship of Jesus. This is no mere mechanical recitation of credal truths, but heartfelt conviction flowing from radically transformed lives.

It appears that some in Corinth claimed that the test of the Spirit was 'tongues-speaking'. But Paul forcibly establishes at the very outset that the only real test of the presence of the Spirit of God is the conviction and the confession that 'Jesus is Lord'. The assembly of members who make that confession is that 'body' where the Spirit is active. That 'body' is diverse in its activities and 'membership'; 'tongues-speaking' is but one among many manifestations of the Spirit.

Thus the primary activity of the Spirit of God is to liberate idolaters and to inspire in them the counter explanation that

---

2   Other alternatives are less likely: (1) That Paul is echoing his pre-Christian experience in synagogues in Jerusalem where Jesus was cursed, (2) that some within the Christian assembly cried, 'Cursed be Jesus', or (3) that he is merely employing a dramatic fiction. It is more likely that Paul is contrasting their pagan past with their Christian present!

Jesus is the ruler of God's world. As temple worshippers the Corinthians previously were swept along by 'gods many and lords many' (see on 8:5). But now they understand that Jesus of Nazareth, crucified but risen and ascended, is the majestic sovereign in the universe and over history. This confession probably derives from Psalm 110:1 by which Jesus explained his coming exaltation. Peter drew attention to its fulfillment on the day of Pentecost (Acts 2:33-36). Thereafter Psalm 110:1 became a basic text for understanding the identity and mission of Jesus as 'Lord'. Remarkably the word 'Lord' (*kyrios*) is Greek for the Hebrew Yahweh, the God of the Old Testament. By saying 'Jesus is Lord' Paul is declaring that Jesus is the revelation of the God of Israel.

A potent implication of this may be seen in Paul's words, 'when you were *Gentiles*'. The opposite of that word is 'Jews'. Paul is saying that because they acknowledge from the heart and with the mouth that 'Jesus is Lord' they are in fact truly 'Jews', 'the Israel of God' subject to the Lord Jesus under the new covenant (see Gal 6:16).

2. Trinity and Diversity (vv. 4-6)
In verses 4-6 Paul teaches that all godly activities within the congregation, though diverse, have one source, God.

This is expressed in strongly trinitarian terms. God the giver is not a monad but a trinity, revealed here as the Spirit [of God], the Lord [Jesus Christ] and God [the Father]. Yet this trinity is not static, like an equilateral triangle. Hierarchy and subordination, as in 11:3 ('the head of Christ is God'), is implied here, but (unlike 11:3) stated in ascending order.

Spirit	[of God].
Lord	[Jesus Christ]
God	[the Father]

Yet each 'person' the Spirit, the Lord and God distributes the 'diversities' (*diaireseis*) of 'gifts' to the people. It is not the Spirit alone from whom 'gifts' come. This was something the Corinthians, who were preoccupied with the Spirit, needed to know.

Although these 'diversities' go under different names, whether 'gifts' (*charismata*), 'ministries' (*diakonoi*) or 'energisings' (*energēmata*), these are merely different and interchangeable 'labels'. 'Gifts' are 'ministries'; 'ministries' are 'energisings'; 'energisings' are 'gifts'. Yet, each is associated with a specific 'person' of the Godhead. 'Gifts' come from the Spirit, the 'gift' giver; 'ministries' flow from the Lord Jesus who is *the* minister; 'energisings' come from God the source of all creative power.

> But there are diversities of gifts   but the same Spirit
> And there are diversities of ministries   but the same Lord
> And there are diversities of energisings but the same God

While each activity has its origin in a person of the Godhead, each is given for ministry to others. These are not bestowed according to one's innate talent, but are 'gifts' from the Spirit of God; they are not bestowed for self-serving ends, but for 'ministry' to others; they are not self-generated, but are 'energised' by God. Each recipient of a 'gift', 'ministry', 'energising' is merely an instrument in the hands of God sent to serve others. No one can take personal credit for 'gifts', 'ministries', 'energisings'. These are for the benefit of others.

By his carefully crafted statement Paul is laying a foundation for the teaching that will follow.

3. The 'Manifestations' of the Spirit (vv. 7-11)

By introducing 'ministries' (v. 5), a word so closely associated with Jesus ('the Son of man came...to minister' Mark 10:45), Paul is deflecting the Corinthians away from their self-centred approach to ministry. He now makes this explicit.

> To each has been given the manifestation of the Spirit for the good [of others].

By 'manifestation (*phanerōsis*) of the Spirit' Paul means the invisible Spirit of God is 'made concrete', actively present in the 'gifts' of each believer. For Paul the Spirit is a 'deposit' anticipating and guaranteeing the fullness of God's blessings in the coming age (2 Cor. 1:22; 5:5; Eph. 1:14). Thus the effect of the Spirit's activity in the people points on to the goodness of God in the end-time, thus strengthening hope.

Paul now gives examples of the 'concrete manifestation' of the Spirit in 'each' believer.

For, indeed,

to one	a word of wisdom	is given through the Spirit
to another	a word of knowledge	according to the same Spirit
to a different one	faith	by the same Spirit
to another	gifts of healings	by the one Spirit
to another	workings of miracles	
to another	prophecy	
to another	discernment of spirits	
to a different one	various kinds of tongues	
to another	interpretation of tongues	

Is there a structure here? Possibly his use of 'to a different one' (*heterō*) which interrupts the repeating 'to another' (*allō*) serves to divide the group into three unequal sections. In the first, the 'word of wisdom' and the 'word of knowledge' probably describe those whose gift is to teach the gospel, bringing the church 'wisdom' about God, 'knowledge' of God and 'faith' in him. 'Faith' probably means ongoing 'faith' in God, perhaps in the face of difficulty, not initial saving 'faith' in Jesus through the gospel (see on 13:2).

The second group appears to describe various activities, which we might call 'miraculous'. This is probably not a distinction with which Paul would have agreed. Each of the nine activities listed is a work of the Spirit and therefore supra-natural and divinely energised. Nonetheless, gifts of healings, workings of powers, prophecy and discernment of spirits appear to have a distinctive quality. They remind us of Paul's words to the Galatians about God 'who pours out his Spirit upon you and works miracles (*dynameis*) among you' (Gal. 3:5).

The 'miracles' in question were probably 'gifts of healings'. Since medical science was primitive and largely ineffective, diseased and disabled people were thrown upon the mercy of God. God gave to some 'gifts of healings' by the 'working of miracles'. Most likely also connected here are 'prophecy' and 'discernment of spirits'. Given the pagan world of Corinth, 'prophecy', the 'discernment of spirits' of those involved in temple idolatry and mystery cults was an important ministry.

The third group focuses on 'tongues speaking', the presenting issue inspiring Paul to write these chapters for the Corinthians. By allocating only two out of nine 'manifestations of the Spirit' to 'tongues-speaking', and by placing them at the end of the list Paul firmly downgrades their importance and puts their use in a broader perspective for the Corinthians. By 'tongues', which he later qualifies as 'the tongues of men and of angels' (13:1), Paul is referring to ecstatic speech within the assembly. He is not referring to foreign languages like Latin, Greek or Hebrew.

These 'manifestations of the Spirit' which are made concrete in particular individuals are not given as a complete list, but only as representative examples. Other and different gifts are conceivable, as for example in Paul's account of ministries set out in Romans 12:3-8. Paul ends the section with a summary statement:

> One and the same Spirit energises all these
> distributing them to each person as he chooses.

Let the readers understand that there are more 'gifts' than 'tongues', of which they were so enamoured. Furthermore, it is the Spirit, not any Corinthian church member, who determines who will be given whatever gifts are given.

If there was a 'message' for the Corinthians then there is also a 'message' for us now. Paul sketches a 'charismatic community' in which each of the members was seen to be concretely 'gifted' by God for ministry to other people. The question for us is: how does our church and the activities of its members resemble or, more probably, radically differ from his portrayal of that apostolic church?

4. One Yet Many: the Human Body and the Church (vv. 12-37)
How then are we to think of the assembly of believers? Here Paul introduces historically for the first time in his writings the human 'body' (*sōma*) as a picture of the church of Jesus Christ.

1. Immersed in the Spirit (vv. 12-13)
Paul employs the analogy of the human body to drive home the points he has been making about ministry in the church (vv. 4-11).

Paul is not alone in his appeal to the metaphor of the human body. Four centuries earlier Socrates[3], in his picture of 'the best governed state', appealed to the example of the hu-

---

3 Plato, *Republic* 5:10.

man body where the pain of one 'member' is suffered by all. During Roman republican days the ordinary 'members' of the 'body' politic were discontented because they worked hard for no other reason than to swell 'the belly', a reference to the rich patricians. Arguing for the *status quo*, Menius Agrippa countered that the 'members' depended on the 'belly' for nourishment; let them be content![4] In the second century AD the philosopher-emperor Marcus Aurelius urged against divisive nationalism using the example of the human body as a picture of the Roman Empire. A hand, once severed, he warned, cannot be rejoined to the body.[5]

How, then, does Paul use this popular analogy of the human body? The most fundamental difference is that while others pointed to the community at large, Paul was speaking about the Christian community.

> Even as the body is one and has many members
> (and all the members of the body being many are one body)
> so it is also with the Christ (v. 12).

Remarkably, he does not say 'as the body is one and has many members so it is with the *body* of Christ', but 'so it is also with *the* Christ'. This is striking, to say the least. 'The Christ' ('the Messiah') probably means 'the people of the Christ', or 'the messianic community'. The congregation of believers and the human body are each an entity-in-diversity.

What, then, is the source of the unity, a unity Paul says transcends 'Jews and Greeks, slaves and free'. The Jew-Gentile and the slave-free divisions were great in the world of that time. His opening words of verse 13 ('For indeed') are emphatic:

> For indeed
>   we were *all* baptised in *one* Spirit into *one* body...
>   we were *all* drank of   *one* Spirit.

At their initiation *all* believers were immersed in the *one* Spirit and drank of the *one* Spirit and so became members of 'the Christ', his assembly. Here the Spirit is not the divine agent who does the baptising but the figurative 'fluid' into which believers

---

4   Recorded in the historian Livy, *History of Rome* 2:32.

5   *Meditations* 6:4.

are plunged and from which each drinks. For this reason each member has a 'manifestation' of the Spirit in 'gifts' which are now expressed by each person.

The Corinthians had things the wrong way around. They believed that the so-called 'more spiritual' gifts like tongues-speaking were evidence of a greater portion of the Spirit. Not so, says Paul. The one test of the Spirit's presence is the acknowledgment, 'Jesus is Lord', noted above (vv. 1-3). From their immersion in the Spirit and their draught from the Spirit, each has 'gifts' from the Spirit, though, as Paul now proceeds to say, those gifts are not the same.

2. The Necessity of Diversity (vv. 14-20)
This passage is an *inclusio* 'framed' between similar sounding sentences:

> ...the body is not made up of one member but many (v. 14)
> ...there are many members but one body (v. 20)

Within this 'frame' Paul begins (vv. 15-16) by thinking aloud the thoughts of lesser members who feel they do not belong to the body, a foot because it is not a hand, and an ear because it is not an eye. Paul replies (v. 17) that the body needs all its parts. With a touch of humour he replies that a body consisting only of an eye could not hear, or a body that was one large ear could not see. Paul's words serve to comfort those who feel inferior while introducing a note of humility for the high-minded. Marcus Aurelius the Stoic philosopher said, 'If you leave you won't be allowed back,' but Paul the Christian said, in effect, 'Don't go, the rest of the body needs you!'

Paul concludes:

> But in fact
> God has appointed the members,
> each one of them in the body just as he decided (v. 18).

English translation cannot do justice to the form of the verb 'appointed' which in Greek[6] has the nuance 'for God's *own purposes*'. Let each 'member' of the 'body', no matter how seemingly unimportant, be encouraged. Each divine person God, the

---

Lord and the Spirit has 'gifted' each member and 'appointed' each 'member' for a distinctive ministry to the whole, 'just as he has decided'. Each has a special place in the body of believers as personally appointed by God.

3. Interdependence of the Members of the Body, Rich and Poor (vv. 21-26)

In the previous section (vv. 14-20) Paul addressed 'members' in terms of being more 'gifted' and less 'gifted'. In verses 22-24, however, he speaks in socio-economic terms of 'weaker members', 'less honourable members', 'unpresentable and presentable members', and 'inferior members'. These are thinly veiled references to disparities of wealth and status within the congregation at Corinth. Paul's language echoes his earlier reference, on one hand, to 'the wise', 'the powerful', 'those of noble birth,' and on the other hand, to 'the foolish', 'the weak', and 'those of lowly birth' (see on 1:26-29). It is clear from the letter that there were 'those who had nothing' but also the wealthy (11:22), slaves as well as free people (7:22).

Again with a hint of humour (see v. 17) he points to 'less honourable' parts of the body around the crutch, one supposes which, he says, we cover up, investing them with greater honour thereby. These words, when read alongside others in the letter reveal the apostle's concern for the disadvantaged and marginalised members of Corinthian society who were part of the 'assembly of Christ'. The majority in the congregation are 'nobodies', he told them, 'to shame the great of this world' (1:26-29). 'Those who have' are to wait until the arrival at the Lord's meal of 'those who have nothing' (11:22, 33). Those who are 'less honourable', 'unpresentable', 'inferior' are to be given greater honour within the gathering of Christ's people. The slave, he told them earlier, is now the 'Lord's freedman' (7:22).

Paul's inversion of values placed on people then and now may reveal something of his own pilgrimage. As a 'free born' and therefore wealthy and educated citizen of Rome, and an eminent younger Pharisee, Paul was located in the upper social, economic and educational echelon. But now, as a man 'in Christ' crucified his care and commitment extended to the 'weak', the 'poor' and the slave (cf. 8:9-12; 11:22; 2 Cor. 11:29; Philem. 15-16). Paul exercised his ministry as an apostle of Christ in the 'meekness and gentleness' of his Master (2 Cor. 10:1). Accordingly, he urged that 'weaker' members are 'indispensable' within the body of Christ and that the 'less honourable' are to be treated with 'greater honour'. Paul does not advocate a 'levelling' of the rich and poor, but rather an attitude of respect and honour by those who were exalted towards those who were lowly.

Paul gives a twofold purpose, one negative the other positive, in urging the great to respect and honour the little.

That there should be no schism in the body,

but

that the members should have the same concern for one another.

Negatively, Paul is determined that there should be 'no schism in the body' (v. 25) based on wealth, status or education. But this is, in effect, what he had been so concerned about when the wealthy members failed to wait for the poorer members at the gathering for the Supper of the Lord (11:17-22, 27-34). Paul's was a deep concern for the spiritual and practical unity of the local congregation. Positively, he urges that the members, whoever they are and in whatever 'station', should have the same 'anxiety' (literally) for one another.

How revolutionary these words are. The poor and the weak are not inclined to feel any concern for the rich and powerful, but rather to resent them. Equally, the powerful tend not to spare too much thought for the weak. Moreover, they would find it remarkable if the poor and weak felt or showed 'anxiety' for them. The divide between wealth and poverty, power and impotence was great in antiquity and, despite all the efforts of modern political idealism, remains great. But Paul will not allow that divide to separate member from member in the body of Christ.

Such is to be that unity in the people of the Messiah that

...if one member suffers,   all the members suffer
if one member is honoured,   all the members rejoice together.

Socrates said something like this was a mark of his ideal society, but with one major difference. In Socrates' *Republic* slaves were not citizens. In the community of Christ the king, however, the free, eminent and powerful were to respect those 'below' them and to demonstrate, but also reciprocally accept, concern, so that the sufferings of one, whoever he or she might be, would become the suffering of all.

Readers must decide whether Paul's portrayal of life together 'in the body' has been true to their experience. From my understanding of Christian history I express some doubts in this regard. Whatever the truth has been, however, we can be in no doubt as to Paul's charter for relationships between believers, rich or poor, clever or dull, powerful or weak. The truth of the gospel of Christ crucified and risen is to find a Christ-like pattern of expression socially within the gathering of believers.

It happens to be the case, also, that Paul's vision for the society of Christians is also a worthy vision for society at large. How much to be preferred is that society where the lesser members find respect from the greater, where the sufferings of the one become the sufferings of the whole, where the strong care for and offer protection to the weak. However, modern societies are now set on another course, away from Christ and his kingdom and its values. Uncannily the *mores* of the Graeco-Roman world of apostolic times are re-emerging. Sadly we can expect deepening rifts within society based on money and power. But that will only provide the people of the King with an opportunity to show the nature of a true society in the patterns of their life together.

4. Gifts in the Church (vv. 27-30)
What has Paul been saying to this point? A brief recapitulation is necessary lest we lose the thread of his argument.

Throughout the whole of chapters 12–14 he is addressing the vexing question of 'the *spiritual things*', that is, 'tongues-speaking'.

i.   He began (12:1-3) by reminding them of their previous bondage to 'voiceless' idols in the temples where they heard the cursing of Jesus. But by the power of the Holy Spirit they have now been set free in the Christian assembly to confess that 'Jesus is Lord'.

ii. Then he expanded their understanding about godly activities (12:4-11). These issue from *three*-sources, corresponding with the active involvement of the Spirit, the Lord and God, and not the Spirit alone. Above all, these activities are from *God* (not from one-self) and they are 'ministries' exercised for *others* (not for one-self).

iii. To explain how each 'member' is 'gifted' by God for ministry Paul uses the image of the Spirit of God as a bath into which all have been plunged and from which each has drunk (12:12-13).

iv. Lest the readers lapse into free-wheeling individualism in their use of 'gifts', Paul teaches that each believer is a 'member' of the one body, 'the congregation of Christ' (12:14-26). To encourage the lowly while humbling the haughty, Paul insists that *God* appoints the 'members', each and every one of whom is indispensable. Furthermore, in this messianic body, the weak are to be honoured and the pain of one is to be the pain of all.

Now, having hinted that some 'gifts' are 'higher' than others, he proceeds to set out a statement of their relative importance. But first he must insist upon the fundamental unity of the 'members' in the one 'body':

> But you are the body of Christ
> and each one of you a member of that body (v. 27).

The plural pronoun 'you' appears for emphasis at the beginning of the sentence. In other words, you Corinthians are not to think of yourselves first of all as separate, *individual* 'members'. Rather, first and foremost *you* are 'the body of Christ', a plural entity which is 'one', a unity. This is the divine reality which they are to grasp and live by. They are to become in practice what they are by the grace and mercy of God.

Now follows his list setting out his evaluation of the relative importance of various ministries within the church (vv. 28-31). In passing we must note that the list is by no means complete, as is evident in his words, 'God has appointed *some* in the church...' Other edifying activities are readily imagined. Nonetheless, the three leading 'gifts' which are specifically numbered should be regarded as critical to the health of any church at all times and places (v. 28 a,b,c).

First	apostles
second	prophets
third	teachers

By 'apostles' Paul means that select band of the Twelve plus others like himself and James (see on 15:5-11). These are the 'ambassadors of Christ' (2 Cor. 5:20) who first preached the gospel and established churches like the one in Corinth. Such an 'ambassador', however, also bore the 'authority' of the Lord (2 Cor. 10:8; 13:10) to instruct in true doctrine including correcting error, a ministry we see Paul exercising in this present letter. For us now we have the 'apostles' in their writings preserved in the New Testament whose words, borne by the Spirit, must continue to rule our churches. Apostles belong to that brief generation following Jesus. After that, apostleship in persons ceased but was transferred to the canonical texts of the New Testament.

'Prophets' and 'prophecy' articulated the word of God by evident fervent inspiration of the Spirit (cf. 1 Thess. 5:19-20). The prophet was a man (or woman cf. 11:5) of strong faith (Rom. 12:6). The impact of the prophets' words brought 'upbuilding, consolation and comfort' to members of the assembly (14:3), but also the radical conversion of the visiting outsider (14:24-25). Prophets also recognised and discerned alien spirits in others (v. 10). 'Prophets' and 'prophecy' did not cease with the apostolic age, though it seems to me God only raises up such inspired leaders occasionally.

'Teachers', however, are the staple of ongoing Christianity. The teacher 'pastors' the congregation as he teaches the faith 'once delivered to the saints', whether to the new convert or to the long-term member. Initially the teacher was a catechist who explained and reinforced the oral tradition in the time prior to access to written texts (cf. Gal 6:6). As such scriptures became available the teacher's work was to read, apply and teach those texts to the people (see 1 Tim. 4:13). So important is this ministry, that of the various charismas in the church the teacher alone (apart from the apostle) is expected to lay aside his employment and be paid for his work (Gal. 6:6; 1 Cor. 9:3-14; 1 Tim. 5:17-18).

Although Paul stops counting with, 'third, teachers', his following ministries are prefixed with 'next...next', implying, nonetheless, a sense of sequence.

next miracles
next gifts of healings

These were mentioned earlier (see on vv. 9 and 10), where they were also bracketed together. Most probably the 'miracles' included 'gifts of healings'. These come immediately after the 'word' ministries 'apostles', 'prophets' and 'teachers' and begin a set of 'practical' activities for the needs of others. In a pre-medical era nothing was more 'practical' than ministering to the sick. It is likely that Christians were driven to prayer in the face of illnesses and disease. It may have been the case that, in response, God chose to work 'miracles...of healings' among his people. Such miracles were recorded in the centuries following. In the mid-third century Origen wrote:

> 'Traces of those signs and wonders are still preserved among us who regulate their lives by the teaching of the gospel.'[7]

At the same time believers applied themselves to 'healings', to simple nursing care and practical health and, in time, to the development of hospitals. In the next two centuries Christian numbers grew dramatically while the population of the wider Roman Empire declined. This was due to Christians' concern for care of their sick members so as to preserve life, on the one hand, and the lack of such care by others within the Empire, on the other hand.[8] Paul's words here are a good reason to regard medical care as a high calling for Christians.

Although the following items are unnumbered we assume that Paul continues to rank them as to priority. Paul may have thought that to continue numbering them or adding 'next...next' would be tedious. Although the next two are close to the bottom of the list they are by no means unimportant. 'Helping', by which Paul means 'helping others', is a means of great blessing to fellow-members in some kind of trouble, which all of us face at one time or another. The gifts of companionship to the lonely and of pre-cooked casseroles for a family in need are just a couple of practical examples of 'helping [others]'. Implied in 'helping' is a sensitive awareness of others, especially in times of duress.

---

7   *Against Celsus* i.2.

8   This is, in part, the thesis of R. Stark, *The Rise of Christianity* (San Francisco: Harper Collins, 1997).

'Government', or 'administration', is also listed as a ministry. This is a 'gift' that only some have. It is, however, critical for the effective operation of a local church, a denomination or organization. Such a ministry must not be looked down upon by more 'spiritual' believers.

Finally Paul comes to 'various kinds of tongues'. It is well to be reminded that Paul's sermon in chapters 12–14 was necessitated by the Corinthian preoccupation with 'tongues-speaking' as the clearest or even the only evidence of the presence of the Spirit. Pointedly, however, this 'gift' is but one of many 'gifts' and it is the last one in the list. In passing, Paul's pastoral method must be noted. The inference just made by me is there to be drawn and is probably correct. But Paul leaves the readers to draw that conclusion themselves. He does not rub their faces in it, as it were.

A series of rhetorical questions brings this section to an end. Having stated that 'God appointed *some* to be a, b, c, etc'. (v. 28), he now asks, 'Are *all* a, b, c, etc.?' The point is all the sharper when we note that Paul preceded each question with the small Greek word *mē*, which grammatically demands an answer, 'No', to each question.

Are all apostles?	Indeed, no!
Are all prophets?	Indeed, no!
Are all teachers?	Indeed, no!

So Paul proceeds down his list given in verse 28, omitting reference to 'helpers' and 'governments'. He concludes his list:

Do all speak in tongues?	Indeed, no!
Do all interpret?	Indeed, no!

Thus Paul reaffirms the diversity of 'gifts' in the 'members' of the one 'body'. 'Tongues-speaking' is, indeed, one such gift. But it is only one, and it comes at the bottom of the list.

5. The Greater Gifts and A More Excellent Way (v. 31)
This is one of those 'bridge' passages used by Paul to take the reader from one part of his reasoning to the next. The first part of the verse looks back to what he has just been saying.

Be zealous for the greater gifts.

'Zeal' for 'tongues-speaking' was evidently a mark of some of the members of this congregation since later he observes that they are 'zealous for spirits' (*pneumatikōn* 14:12; cf. 14:1). But instead Paul urges 'zeal' for 'greater gifts', that is, in his list given above (v. 28) 'first, apostles', 'second, prophets', 'third, teachers', 'next, miracle workers', 'next, gifts of healings'. Since 'apostleship' was not open to those beyond the original chosen few the leading 'gift' in the list to aspire to is 'prophecy'. The bottom of the list is 'tongues-speaking', a 'gift' for which Paul does not want them to be 'zealous'. In chapter 14 Paul will sing the praises of 'prophecy' while systematically showing up the deficiencies of 'tongues-speaking'.

The second part of the verse points on immediately to his words about 'love', the subject of the next passage.

I will point out a yet more excellent way.

'Love', as he will now demonstrate, is the only true motivation for the exercise of 'gifts' for others. Indeed, in the absence of 'love', anything we do is futile. But then, as he will reason in chapter 14, the most fruitful expression of this 'love' within the congregation is not 'tongues-speaking' but 'prophecy'.

SOME QUESTIONS FOR PERSONAL REFLECTION:

1. How can I be assured that I have the Spirit of God?

2. What am I to conclude by the words, 'gifts', ministries', 'energisings'?

3. What is the origin of the 'gifts' and what is their purpose?

4. Reflect on the 'honouring' of members. Who is to be 'honoured'?

STUDY QUESTIONS:

1. What does Paul say is the test of the Spirit in a believer? What did some believers in Corinth say the test was?

2. What is the Trinitarian understanding of 'Gifts' that Paul is instructing the believers in?

3. What is the source of unity which transcends 'Jews and Greeks, slaves and free'?

4. What is the diversity which is needed in the Body?

5. What 'schism' is Paul addressing with his 'body' analogy?

6. What are the 'greater gifts' to be zealous for?

13

The Way of Love
(1 Cor. 13:1-13)

This is a justly famous hymn-like passage, a favoured reading at weddings and other occasions where the theme is 'love'. Paul at his most poetic, we might say. Yet Paul would be disappointed to know that his 'praise of love' had been removed from his original setting. His references to 'tongues' and 'prophecy' anchor his words in this chapter to the chapter preceding and the chapter following. Indeed, this chapter is critical to the whole sermon on 'tongues-speaking' that occupies chapters 12–14.

However, other 'gifts' are mentioned here alongside 'tongues-speaking' and 'prophecy'. He speaks of 'knowing all mysteries', '[having] all knowledge', 'having all faith', 'selling all possessions', and 'handing over his body' in martyrdom. Once again Paul is reminding them that there is a range of 'gifts' beyond their special interest, 'tongues-speaking'. Indeed, no matter which 'gift' is exercised, if it is not inspired by 'love' of the fellow-member, it is useless.

1. 'Gifts' without Love (vv. 1-3)
There is a simple format here.

If	I do or have	X
but	I have not	love
	I am	Y.

Paul repeats this, either fully or abbreviated, no less than seven times.

In each case the 'If' clause introduces a 'gift' used in and for the congregation. But where a 'gift' is not inspired by 'love' for the persons who are the recipient of 'ministry', the exercise of that 'gift' is futile since it fails in its object to 'build up' others (see on 8:1; 14:12). By 'love' (*agapē,* pronounced 'agapay') Paul means a quality of others-centred concern that looks to the genuine needs and welfare of a person or persons beyond oneself. But this is to anticipate. Paul describes 'love' in the next stanza of his great hymn.

The first 'gift' is 'speaking with the tongues of men and angels' (v. 1). It must be admitted immediately that we can only speculate as to the meaning here. Most likely such 'speech' was ecstatic, and believed to be the dialect of the angels in heaven. Paul's inclusion of 'tongues-speaking' as one of the 'gifts', even if the last on his list (see on 12:28) together with this rather exalted description, serves to confirm it among the approved ministries within the church. But, in the absence of 'love' such speech is like 'a noisy bronze or clanging cymbal'. Again, we can only guess at the precise original meaning. Corinth was famous for its bronzes which were an alloy of copper and tin, manufactured (like Coca Cola!) to a secret formula. Most probably such gongs and cymbals were locally made bronzes. So, even 'heavenly tongues', if not uttered from 'love' for the listener, were just the 'speechless'[1] noise of gongs and cymbals. Worse, such musical instruments may have been used in the pagan cults and processions of Corinth. In this case a loveless articulation of tongues meant, in effect, a return to the metallic noises of the godless temples of Corinth from which the members had recently been converted.

In verse 2 Paul abbreviates the format given in its full outline in verse 1. Here the second 'gift' ('prophecy') appears to be connected to the third ('know all mysteries') and the fourth ('[have] all knowledge'). Because prophets had been given 'knowledge' about the 'mysteries' of God they spoke *prophetically.*[2] By 'mysteries' Paul is using the apocalyptic

---

1 This may be Paul's aural wordplay between *lalo* ('I speak') and *alalazon* ('wailing').

2 See 2:1-13 where Paul uses rather similar language.

language then in vogue among the Jews. But it is clear that such prophetic insight and utterances were not 'free wheeling' but circumscribed within what had been authoritatively and finally revealed in the word of God, the gospel, as proclaimed by the apostle and written down in a Letter like this one. In short, the prophet's 'knowledge' and 'speech' is an interpretation of, but is limited by, the apostolic word (see on 14:36-38). Perhaps the prophet spoke chiefly about the hope of the Kingdom of God so as to strengthen the believers' confidence in that great hope (see on 14:1-4).

A fifth 'gift' is then given by way of example. It is 'faith' such as can 'move mountains'. Here Paul seems to be echoing Jesus' words encouraging Peter that the end of the 'fig tree' cursed by Jesus (the Temple) was not the end of God's good purposes. Jesus said:

> 'Have faith in God.
> Truly I say to you, whoever says to this mountain,
> "be taken up and cast in the sea,"
> and does not doubt in his heart,
> but believes what he says will come to pass,
> it will be done for him.' (Mark 11:23)

This is not that 'faith' which responds to the gospel and which makes one a 'believer' (as opposed to an unbeliever). Rather it is that 'faith' which is directed towards the impossible (see on 12:9). Such 'faith' is, indeed, a 'gift' that not all believers enjoy. But it is 'given' to individuals to strengthen the confidence of others in God's purposes, especially in times of testing. The early persecuted Christians were not strangers to serious trials. The 'gift' of 'faith' as shared in ministry to others was a powerful source of perseverance and comfort.

The sixth 'gift' (v. 3) like the fifth, 'faith' in God for the impossible, is stated in exaggerated terms, 'If I give *all* my possessions...' Like the fifth 'gift' this also seems to have been inspired by words of Jesus, in this case those spoken to the rich man who inquired about eternal life. To that man Jesus said:

> 'Go, sell what you have, and give to the poor' (Mark 10:21).

Yet, in Paul's words, 'If I sell all my possessions...but I do not have love, I am nothing profited'. There is no reference here to giving the proceeds to the poor, but that is probably implied. It seems likely that the Corinthians knew of the teachings of the Lord Jesus relating to 'faith' and 'selling all'. Furthermore, they may have been acting on Jesus' words, but in loveless ways.

The seventh 'gift', 'If I hand over my body',[3] relates to martyrdom. Details are lacking but Paul's words make it likely that precisely this had occurred among the early Christians, whether in Corinth or elsewhere. Perhaps Jesus' example whereby he was 'handed over' provided a model that some felt they must imitate. But self-sacrifice can be self-seeking. Unless genuine 'love' for others underlies the act of martyrdom there is no profit, says Paul. If that applies to something as extreme as the confessor's death, it must also apply to lesser acts of sacrifice. A loveless 'martyr mentality' can be a selfish form of attention seeking.

Before leaving this section we should notice that Paul portrays these 'gifts' in superlative terms. It is 'speaking in the tongues of men *and angels*'. The word 'all' appears next to four of the 'gifts' *all* mysteries, *all* knowledge, *all* faith, *all* my possessions. When this is read alongside verses 8-12, where all these gifts are exercised 'in part' and will be 'abolished' in the Kingdom, it becomes clear that Paul is speaking ironically to bring a little humility and realism to the Corinthians.

Paul has given seven examples of 'ministry' exercised without 'love'. But what is love?

2. 'Love' Described (vv. 4-7)

The word 'love' (*agapē*) was relatively rare before New Testament times and of rather uncertain meaning. A concordance of the New Testament shows us pages of entries for the noun 'love', its verb and adjective. Jesus' teaching on love, his demonstration of love in life and death, led to an explosion of references in the apostolic writings. Furthermore, the meaning of this rare word of vague use now becomes clear. The word *philia* meant 'friendship', *storgē* meant 'family affection', *erōs* meant 'sexual passion', but *agapē* meant 'others-centred concern, expressed at great personal cost'. This special word

---

3   There is textual uncertainty whether Paul's original words were: 'If I hand over my body to be burnt' or 'If I hand over my body that I may boast'. While the former may have a stronger case, the meaning is relatively unaffected.

agapē, which through Christ takes on a unique meaning in the history of ideas, matches the uniqueness of his Incarnation and Atonement. The word 'love' perfectly fits the person, Christ. Just as the word 'radar' was coined to name a new reality, so the writers of the New Testament began to use the word *agapē* to describe the new and radical kind of 'love' manifested in Jesus. The Christian is to show the Master's love to believer and non-believer alike. The gathered congregation is to be the place where *agapē* ('love') is to be most clearly seen. But it was precisely at this point that the 'gifted' Corinthians failed. They exercised their 'gifts', not for the good of their fellows, but for themselves and their own egos.

In verses 4-7 the word 'love' is the subject of various verbs, positive and negative. 'Love' does this, does not do that. In fact, Paul appears to be speaking about 'love' *as a person*. Who is that 'person'? Most likely Paul is thinking of Jesus himself, who is 'love' personified. Remember, Paul introduced this passage with the words, 'I will point out a yet more excellent *way*' (12:31). Jesus is that 'way', the 'way' of 'love'.

Once again Paul's format is interesting. Like other writers of that era Paul wrote primarily for his words to be heard as they were read publicly and aloud. If a word play may be permitted, silent reading was 'unheard of' until the seventh century when spaces between words and punctuation began to appear. Until then all reading, whether alone or with others, was *aural*. Conscious of the *listener* Paul is careful to break up his words for strongest effect.

First, he makes two affirmations about 'love' (v. 4a):

Love shows long-suffering.
Love acts kindly.

'Long-suffering' (*makrothumia* 'slow to anger') is a quality of God, closely connected to 'mercy' (see e.g., Ps. 103:8). It is a metaphorical word, literally 'long burning', as of a decent log burning for many hours in an open fire, as contrasted with light pine kindling that fizzes and sputters, sending showers of sparks in all directions. It is similar to 'patience', though not the 'stoical', 'resigned' kind so much as an active and deliberate determination to await the hand of God's intervention. God is also called 'kind' (*chrēstos*), as in Psalm 34:8 'Taste and see that the LORD is *kind*'.[4] Several times Paul connects 'patience' and 'kindness' as qualities of God (Rom. 2:4) and they are also Holy Spirit-inspired qualities in believers (Gal. 5:22; 2 Cor. 6:6). 'Love' expresses its innermost character as being 'long-suffering' and 'kind'.

Then, follow eight negative attitudes that do not spring from 'love' (vv. 4b-6):

> It is not jealous.
> It does not 'show off.'
> It is not haughty.
> It does not behave unseemly.
> It does not seek its own.
> It is not hot tempered.
> It does not keep account of evil.
> It does not rejoice in wrongdoing, but rejoices in truth.

Moral ugliness is suggested by this list of human qualities. It is by no means a random catalogue, however, but very pointed in terms of the unsavoury behaviour of the Corinthians which has emerged already in the course of this Letter.

The first, 'jealousy' (*zeloō*), recalls his earlier 'there is *jealousy and strife among you*' (3:3), referring to their factions. The second, 'showing off' (*perpereuomai*) echoes their 'boastful' attitudes related, among other things, to their 'pride' in their party leaders (e.g., 4:7). The third, literally 'puffed up' (*phusioō*), depicts haughtiness, which earlier in the Letter was specifically given as a counterpoint to 'love' (8:1). The many other references to this 'inflated' attitude suggest this behaviour was a Corinthian characteristic (4:6,18,19; 5:2). The fourth, 'unseemliness' (*aschēmoneō*) has a parallel in his call that everything in the assembly be done 'decently' (*euschēmonōs* –14:40). This is not merely aesthetic, however, but an implied rebuke to prophets and tongues-speakers who want to parade their 'gifts' with chaotic consequences as they speak while others are still speaking. The fifth, 'seek its own' (*zēteō*), has an exact parallel in those

---

4   The similarity of spelling between Cristos and crhstus was exploited in a wordplay in 1 Peter 2:3-4 where Cristos, the 'Living stone' to whom the believer has 'come' is the 'Lord' who is crhstus, 'kind'. It is unlikely that Christ was proclaimed as crhstos, 'kind'. This may help explain the misspelling in the Roman writer Suetonius, that in AD 49 Claudius expelled all the Jews from Rome on account of disturbances associated with Crhstus (Suetonius *Claudius*, 25.4).

Corinthians who seek not their neighbours' 'good', that is, their salvation, but who pursue their own selfish interests (10:24, 33). The latter three words find no explicit verbal antecedent within the letter. Based on what has emerged so far in Paul's admonitions to them, however, 'hot tempered', 'keeping account of evil' and 'rejoicing in doing wrong not right' are readily imaginable in this strife-torn community of competing leaders.

Notice that Paul does not accuse the Corinthians 'head on' of these eight kinds of selfish behaviour. Rather, by asserting that 'love' does not do 'this' or 'that', when clearly the Corinthians have been doing precisely 'this' and 'that', he not only reminds them effectively of such behaviour but, more to the point, he shows them what 'loving' actions will be. This is Paul the diplomat and pastor, who by his method of raising objectionable conduct points the way to acceptable behaviour.

By contrast with the eight attitudes or actions that 'love' *is not* or *does not do*, Paul now provides four positive expressions of 'love', each strengthened by the word 'all' (v. 7).

It bears	all things.
it believes	all things.
it hopes	all things.
it endures	all things.

Because of sin there are always 'things' in others to 'bear', 'believe', 'hope' and 'endure'. Their behaviour always tests our patience, trust and hope, just as our behaviour tests theirs. Clearly 'love' requires decision making and effort; it is not at all just a feeling or emotion. Indeed, it is a test of character.

Paul is not merely moralizing, however, merely suggesting that we 'make allowances' for others. Rather, it is a call to act positively towards others because our God is a redeemer, a God of positive intent and of glorious eventual outcomes (vv. 8-12). Here, then, we hear the distant echoes of Paul the pastor. But we also discern here his silhouette as exemplar of loving behaviour. Earlier in the Letter he applied the first of these four words to himself: 'we *bear* anything rather than put an obstacle in the way of the gospel of Christ' (9:12). Indeed, these four words sum up Paul's own concrete and positive attitude towards the brittle Corinthians for whom *he* 'bears all things', 'believes all things', 'hopes all things', 'endures all things'! Let them follow his implied example and love one another in the Corinthian assembly.

3. 'Love' Remains (vv. 8-13)

Having declared, '[Love] endures all things' he adds immediately, 'Love never falls'. This serves to introduce a contrast between this age and the coming age (v. 8). In regard to 'this age' Paul's key-word is 'abolished' (*katargeō*). When God draws down the curtain on history 'prophecy' will be 'abolished', 'tongues speaking' will 'cease' and [words of] 'knowledge' will be 'abolished'. When a boy becomes a man he will 'abolish' childish ways. By contrast 'love', the only true motive for the exercise of these 'gifts', will 'never fall' but 'endure' throughout history into the coming age.

Indeed, such 'knowing' and 'prophesying' are only 'in part' (v. 9 *ek merous*) since they belong within this age and suffer the limitations of this age. Likewise the 'understanding' that issues to the hearer from the word of prophecy or knowledge is also only 'in part' (cf. 2 Cor. 1:13-14). When 'the perfect (*to teleion*) comes', that is, the 'perfection' of the new age, all that was 'in part' now will be 'abolished'. The need and the opportunity for the exercise of these 'gifts', even the highest of them, will have passed. Holy Spirit-inspired utterances and helpful for edification they may be (see on 14:3,5,12), but they are also human interpretations of the gospel. Insofar as prophetic words are true to the gospel they will be of great spiritual value. At the same time, being human interpretations of divine truth, they can only ever approximate to the ways of God. Perhaps Paul's words are quite pointed here. After all, the Corinthians had the highest opinion of their spiritual gifts whose exercise may have misled them to think that 'the perfect' was a present reality in their midst (see on 14:37)!

In the two illustrations following Paul teaches that our knowledge of God *now* compared to our knowledge of God *then* is quite limited. First, he reflects on his life as a boy (*nēpios*) with that as an adult (*anēr* v. 11). *Then* he 'spoke', 'thought' and 'reasoned' as a young child but *now* he does so as a man. Second, he contrasts the very limited vision from a mirror of those times, which was made of polished metal, with 'face to face' seeing. The one is indistinct and approximate, the other is crystal clear, a direct encounter.[5]

---

5   Paul may have in mind God's manner of speaking to Moses which was not 'in riddles' (*dia ainigmatōn*), as it had been to prophets by dreams and visions, but 'face to face' (LXX Num. 12:6-8).

Paul is using these analogies to contrast the knowledge of God we have now, in this age, with the knowledge of God we shall have, 'when the perfect comes'. Paul expresses it this way (v. 12b):

> *Now* we know in part,
> but *then* we shall know,
> even as we are known [by God].

When 'the perfect comes' our knowing of God *then* will be like his knowing of us *now*, which is indeed 'perfect' (see on 8:3). Based on the gospel and the Scriptures we have a way of knowing God during this age, a 'knowing' that is good and true. For example, God had made himself known as 'one God, the Father from whom are all things...and one Lord, Jesus Christ, through whom are all things' (8:6). Yet this 'knowing' of God *now*, true as it is, compared with our 'knowing' of God *then*, will prove to be merely 'in part'. When 'the perfect' comes we shall know God as we have been known by God and we shall love God as we have been loved by God.

Few have captured this vision better that Charles Wesley:

> Changed from glory into glory,
> till in heaven we take our place;
> till we cast our crowns before thee,
> lost in wonder, love and praise.

Here a cautionary observation is appropriate. It is that preachers and theologians are sometimes over-confident that their ideas coincide exactly with all that can be known of God. 'Knowing' and 'prophesying', however, are only ever 'in part' in comparison with what will be known of God in his Kingdom. The proud theologians, prophets and 'tongues-speakers' of Corinth needed to be reminded of this and so, perhaps, do we.

Paul rounds off this chapter with his justly famous, 'Now remain faith, hope and love, but the greatest of these is love'.[6] But what does he mean by 'now'? Is 'Now...' a reference to this age ('At this present time...') or to the future age ('Then...')? A future meaning would not make sense, since neither 'faith'

---

6   Faith, 'hope' and 'love' often appear together in the New Testament (Rom. 5:1-5; Gal. 5:5-6; Eph. 4:2-5; Col. 1:4-5; 1 Thess. 1:3; 5:8; Tit. 2:2; Heb. 6:10-12; 10:22-24; 1 Pet. 1:3-8).

nor 'hope' will be needed 'then'. Furthermore, the whole passage has shown the necessity for 'love' to be shown *right now*, within the community of believers in Corinth. Clearly, Paul is urging the exercise of 'faith', 'hope' and 'love' to 'remain' throughout the present age.

But why is 'love' greater than 'faith' or 'hope'? 'Faith' and 'hope' are immensely important, as our primary response to the gospel. We must 'believe' the word of God and entrust ourselves to Jesus Christ as Lord and Saviour. Only by so doing will we find the vindication of God's declaration of acquittal 'in Christ' crucified and risen. The certain 'hope' of God's kingdom based on the resurrection of Jesus from the dead nourishes and sustains us for courageous godliness in the face of peril. 'Love' among the brothers and sisters is the practical outworking in the age of 'faith' and 'hope' (Gal. 5:6; Col. 1:4).

Two closely connected relationships specially mark 'the perfect' when it 'comes'. One is that then we shall know God as perfectly as he knows us now (v. 12). The other is that then we shall 'love' God as he loves us now (cf. 8:3). Thus 'the perfect' will be the pristine vision of God, unspoiled by sin and unbelief, and utter love for God.

'Love' is *who* God is, Father, Son and Holy Spirit. 'Love' (*agapē*) has been and is the great motive for all the actions of God and the basis of our relationship with him. 'Love' is different from 'faith' and 'hope', however, because 'love' will carry on into 'the perfect', the coming age, when we will see Christ, not in a mirror dimly, but face to face. Then 'faith' and 'hope' will be no more. But 'love' will 'remain' forever, his for us, ours for him, and ours for one another.

Did the Corinthians mend their ways, learn the 'more excellent way' of 'love'? Some perhaps, but not all. On Timothy's return from Corinth to Paul in Ephesus the apostle was so alarmed at the state of the church that he paid an urgent unscheduled visit to the Achaian capital. This proved to be very disturbing indeed. Paul later speaks of their 'jealousy, anger, selfishness, slander, whisperings, conceit and disorder' during that visit (2 Cor. 12:20), referring both to their hostility towards one another, but also their hostility towards him. In a follow-up letter which has not survived ('the letter written in tears' cf. 2 Cor 2:4), it appears that Paul gave them an ultimatum, namely, if they did not repent of such behaviour he would not return to them (cf. 2 Cor. 7:8-12). Paul's eventual third and final visit is evidence of repentance in Corinth. Such change, however, may have been shallow. Half a century later Clement, a church leader in Rome, also wrote to the Corinthians. The burden of his letter was to call on the Corinthians to resolve their differences and to show love to one another.[7] The Church at Corinth never amounted to much in the unfolding years of church history. It is quite likely that their lovelessness towards one another was a major obstacle to their impact on their city and province.

SOME QUESTIONS FOR PERSONAL REFLECTION:

1. Why is the exercise of 'gifts' without love for others 'futile'?

2. How can I show 'love' to my fellow-believer?

3. Why is 'love' greater than 'faith' and 'hope'?

4. How might the prospect of 'the perfect' inspire and motivate 'love' now?

STUDY QUESTIONS:

1. Were the believers at Corinth 'obsessed' with having the 'right' gifts of the Spirit?

2. Why does Paul seem to use 'extreme' gifts as examples? How do they counter the lack of love?

3. How does 'agape' love differ from other kinds of love? What are its distinctives?

4. How is 'agape love', personified?

5. How does love's 'long-suffering and kindness' overshadow the eight negatives Paul lists? How do the four positive expressions of love counter the eight negatives?

6. What is the knowledge of God which we have now and what is the knowledge of God we shall have?

---

7   See *1 Clement* 49:5.

14

Tongues-Speaking and Prophecy
(1 Cor. 14:1-40)

In this chapter Paul narrows his focus to the presenting issue, 'tongues-speaking', a phenomenon which may have arisen in the Corinthian church since his departure from the city. For the greater part of the chapter he sets up a contrast between 'prophecy' and 'tongues-speaking' (vv. 1-24). Beyond that he addresses more general questions relating to 'decency and order' within the gatherings of the congregation (vv. 25-40).

We need to be reminded of the careful foundation Paul has laid to this point now that he is directing the Corinthians towards his conclusions. After all, these three chapters belong together as one tightly argued sermon on the exercise of 'gifts' within the church. First, since he was dealing with an activity called 'the spiritual things' ('tongues-speaking' see Introduction to chapter 12) he needed to establish the basic truth that all who had broken free from idolatry to declare that 'Jesus is Lord' had done so only by the power of the Holy Spirit (12:1-3). Conversion, not 'tongues-speaking', is *the* evidence of the Holy Spirit. Second, the same Spirit along with the Lord and God distributes a 'diversity' of 'gifts' to the 'members' of 'the body' of confessors (12:4-11). 'Gifts' to individuals are for the 'common good'. Third, as in a human 'body' there is no one 'member' or organ; all are needed (12:12-21). As in a human 'body' where 'weaker' parts are given greater honour, the 'members' of the 'body of Christ' honour the weaker members and together share one another's joys and sufferings (12:22-26). Fourth, there is nonetheless a hierarchy of 'gifts' graded for their value to the church, of which the last in the list is 'tongues-speaking' (12:27-30). Fifth, 'tongues-speaking', like all the gifts, expresses temporary approximations of truth against the time of the coming of 'the perfect', when knowing God is immediate and complete and love is full-orbed. In the meantime the exercise of 'gifts' which are not 'love'-driven in 'ministry' to and for others are useless (13:1-13).

Now that this carefully planned foundation has been laid Paul is able to get down to teaching about prophecy and 'tongues-speaking'.

1. 'Love' through 'prophesying' 'builds up' others (vv. 1-5)

Paul's guiding principle for all that he will now say, which is derived from the previous chapter, is stated baldly:

> Pursue love (NRSV).

Other translations like 'Make love your aim' (RSV), 'Follow the way of love' (NIV), are rather insipid. Paul's verb elsewhere means 'persecute', as in, 'I persecuted the church' (15:9). He is saying, 'Pursue, *go after* love'. Moreover, it is a command. 'Love' is not an option, but an obligation. In short, nothing in the life of the people of God is worth doing unless it is motivated and informed by 'love' of other members.

To this he adds,

> Be zealous for 'the spiritual things' (*ta pneumatika* 'tongues-speaking'),
> but much rather
> be zealous to prophesy.

Side by side he places an activity he concedes ('tongues-speaking') with one he strongly prefers ('prophesying'). This is because 'prophesying' 'builds up' *others*, and therefore fulfils the necessity to 'love' (see on v. 12).

His explanation now follows (vv. 3-4):

> For
> he who speaks in a tongue speaks not to men but to God
> no one [else] hears him; he speaks mysteries by the Spirit.

But he who prophesies	[speaks]	to men
		upbuilding
		and encourage-
ment		
		and consolation.

Verses 2 and 4 help solve several riddles. One is to identify 'the spiritual things' of the previous verse. It is pretty clear (at least to me) that 'the spiritual things' of verse 1 are now defined as 'tongues-speaking...speaking mysteries in the Spirit' in verses 2 and 3, something Paul earlier called 'tongues of men and of angels' (see on 13:1), a heavenly dialect. Another riddle is: what is 'prophecy'? 'Prophecy', although not defined as such, may be able to be identified by the outcomes it achieves, namely, 'upbuilding', 'encouragement' and 'consolation', which are all blessings of the coming age, the time of 'perfection' (see on 13:10). Life in this age is always marred by sin, suffering and death, with periodic times of severe testing of believers through persecution. The prophet points beyond these to the Kingdom of God, its certainty and blessings. The Christian prophet, therefore, teaches the gospel of Christ out of a pastor's concern for the present sufferings of the people, yet with a special emphasis on the 'hope' of the Kingdom of God, as yet unrevealed to the naked eye. The prophet's language was probably highly poetic and symbolic, as in the Book of Revelation (see on 2:6-10).

The 'tongues-speaker', like the prophet, may also have lifted his eye in hope to God and his Kingdom. Surely since 'tongues' are directed to *God* they will be superior to any other 'gift', including the gift of 'prophecy'? But no. The apostle's stated priority for the gathering of God's people is that they be 'built up', 'encouraged' and 'consoled'. Prophecy will achieve these ends because it comes in a known language, but 'tongues' (unless interpreted) will be of no help since it is 'speech' that will not be 'heard', that is, 'understood' (RSV).

Paul makes an outright contrast between the two activities in verse 4.

He who speaks in a tongue	builds up himself.
But he who prophesies	builds up the church.

Clearly Paul is not opposed to 'tongues-speaking', though we have even less understanding of it than we do about prophesying. 'Tongues-speaking' 'builds up' the speaker (provided there is understanding vv. 13-15) but 'prophesying' 'builds up' the gathered assembly and is accordingly an expression of 'love' towards the 'members' of the 'body'.

The apostle now rounds off the discussion with an interim conclusion which also serves as a 'bridge' into the next part of his sermon (v. 5). Yes, he is glad for 'all' to 'speak in tongues' (though he knows that only *some* have this 'gift' 12:17, 28-29), but his overwhelming preference is that they should 'prophesy' (v. 5a). Paul's words, '...but rather that you prophesy' from verse 1, repeat exactly in verse 5a, framing verses 1-5a as an *inclusio*. This rhetorical device points to his very strongly held desire for 'prophesying' 'rather than' 'tongues-speaking' within the church.

In short, 'prophesying' is 'greater than' 'tongues-speaking' because it enables the church to receive 'upbuilding'. Here we note his introduction of the great principle of intelligibility of speech that Paul will now tease out in the passage following (vv. 6-25).

2. Intelligible 'Speech' : The Principle (vv. 6-12)

Paul appeals to their common sense (v. 6). He asks them to imagine how they would profit by a visit from him when he spoke in tongues unless he also gave a 'revelation', '[a word of] knowledge', 'a prophecy', or a 'teaching'. The first three seem to be future-oriented, pointing to the Kingdom of God. The fourth, 'a teaching' suggests an explanation of some aspect of the received tradition or of some Scripture passage, whether from the Old Testament or from a New Testament text. At the same time these four verbal activities have in common that they are *intelligible*, thus bringing 'profit' to the hearers. On the other hand, his conditional 'unless' shows that there would be no profit to the people in hearing 'tongues' uninterpreted, whether as 'revelation', 'knowledge', 'prophecy', or 'teaching'.

Paul uses three analogies to make his point. First, if a 'lifeless' musical instrument like a flute or a harp does not give distinct sounds, the music will be unidentifiable (v. 7). Second, if another 'lifeless' instrument, the military bugle, sounds an indistinct signal, it will fail to rally the troops to the captain's command (v. 8). In the same way when you 'speak in tongues' you do not give a clear message, but merely speak into the air (v. 9). Third, if you do not know the meaning of another language the speaker and hearer will be like 'Barbarians' to one another (vv. 10-11). Possibly Paul means us to infer something deeper in each of these analogies of unintelligibility. In the first, he may be implying that the tuneless noise of flute and harp reflect a confused babble of tongues-speaking in the church. In the second, he may be saying that muffled and ambiguous tongues-noise is no substitute for the piercing chord of the military trumpet calling for advance in evangelism, for example. In the third, he may be saying that hearing 'tongues' that are not comprehended effectively alienates member from member in the assembly.

Paul concludes this short section with a strong application (v. 12).

> Since you are zealots for 'spiritual things'
> seek to overflow in building up the church.

Apparently the 'tongues-speakers' portrayed themselves as the men and women of the Spirit *par excellence*. Perhaps with some irony Paul addresses these super-spiritual ones as 'zealots for the things of the Spirit'. To this point, in my view, Paul has used this word (*pneumatika*) for 'tongues-speaking'.[1] Now, however, he appears to be turning it back on them in their terms as *spiritually alive* Christians. Paul seems to be saying, 'If you are truly Spirit-filled people you won't be obsessed with "gifts" that begin and end with you, as "tongues-speaking" does. Rather, you will want to exercise those "gifts" that build up the church, which prophesying above all does'. Furthermore, the 'spiritual' man or woman is, first and foremost, a *loving* person. And 'love', as he has eloquently written in chapter 13, is not self-centred (as 'tongues' is), but others-centred (as 'prophesying' by its very nature is).

3. The Mind (vv. 13-20)

In this section Paul has a simple structure:

> Exhortation to do X
> Because if not, then Y and Z will be true.

---

1 The unusual word *pneumatika* also appears in 12:1 and 14:1. In 14:1 it appears to mean 'tongues-speaking' as in 14:2. Hence my view that the term in 12:1 introduces his three chapter long pastoral sermon on this topic.

Paul's strong 'Wherefore' introduces the necessary consequence based on his careful reasoning in verses 6-12. That consequence is stated as an exhortation, a moral appeal to the mind and conscience of the reader. It is that the 'tongues-speaker' prays that he may be able to 'interpret' his unintelligible 'language,' that is, to put that 'speech' into words he can understand.

If he fails through prayer to 'interpret' his 'tongue' it will be unhelpful both to himself and to the hearer. Paul knows what he is talking about; he, too, is a 'tongues-speaker'. In the verses following Paul uses the first person singular ('I') to assume the role of the 'tongues-speaker' so as to teach the Corinthian 'tongues-speakers' what to do.

> If I pray in a tongue my 'spirit' prays but my mind is unfruitful. What shall I do?
> I will pray in my spirit, I will also pray in my mind.
> I will sing psalms in my spirit, I will also sing psalms in my mind. (vv. 14-15)

The problem for the speaker of an uninterpreted 'tongue' is that his 'mind' is detached from his 'spirit', which I think means his 'emotions'. As a result his 'mind' is 'unfruitful' and has no understanding of the sounds coming from his lips. But the 'mind' is critical to human well-being, including 'spiritual' well-being. The 'mind' must not be separated from the 'spirit'. So he asks, rhetorically, 'What will I do?' His reply fills out our picture of 'tongues-speaking'. The 'tongues-speaker' prays in a 'tongue', 'sings psalms' in a 'tongue'. But, as a result of answered prayer, Paul will also pray and sing with his 'spirit' and his 'mind'. In passing, we should note Paul's pastoral method. He identified himself as a 'tongues-speaker', but states his own good practice so as to encourage other 'tongues-speakers' to do likewise.

But now Paul goes back to addressing other 'tongues-speakers', drawing to their attention the effects of uninterpreted 'tongues' on an 'outsider'[2] who happens to be present (vv. 16-17; see also on v. 23). Clearly, it was not unusual for 'outsiders' to attend meetings of the Christians; the first believers were not 'exclusive brethren'. But if the speaker offers a 'thanksgiving'

---

2 Greek *idiotes*, 'uninitiated', 'unlearned'. Our English word 'idiot' is derived from this word which in Paul's day was used of someone unskilled and untrained who was not a member of trade guild, a 'layman'.

(*eucharistia* yet another 'tongues' activity along with 'praying' and 'singing') in a 'tongue', the 'outsider' will not be able to give his '*amen*' to the prayer. (This 'eucharist' may have been a prayer of thanksgiving to God or, equally, a 'eucharist' within the Lord's Supper see on 11:24). Yet because the 'outsider' does not understand the 'tongue' he is not 'built up' in his grasp of the gospel (see on vv. 24-25). Again we hear Paul's concern for the place of the 'mind', previously the speaker's (vv. 14-15) but now also the hearer's.

Paul returns to an 'I' reference in this hyperbole, which is very pointed (vv. 18-19):

> I thank God I speak in tongues more than all of you.
> But in the church I prefer to speak five words with my mind
> that I might teach others
> than ten thousand words in a tongue.

By identifying with them as a 'tongues-speaker' Paul is able to drive home the need for 'tongues' to be made intelligible in church. Otherwise 'tongues' begin and end with the speaker. It is not an 'others-centred' ministry and it is not, therefore, an expression of *agapē*, 'love'. It does not 'build up' others by 'teaching' as 'prophesying' does, that is, as intelligible information about the Kingdom of God is transmitted from one 'mind' to another 'mind'. Just five words spoken 'by the mind' are to be preferred to 10,000 words 'spoken in a tongue'. In short, uninterpreted 'tongues-speaking' has no place in the church.

A proverb-like exhortation based on childish and adult behaviour concludes this section.[3] Paul appears to be picking up his earlier contrast: 'when I became a *man* I gave up *childish* things' (see on 13:11).[4] Now he urges 'grown up' (or 'mature' *teleioi*) attitudes, except in matters of evil.

Brothers [and sisters]

		in your minds do not	be children,
(but	in evil	be children);
	in your minds	be adult.

---

3   While most translations locate verse 20 as the beginning of the next section its references to the 'mind' effectively locate it within a paragraph devoted to the 'mind'.

4   The repetitions 'perfect' (*teleion* 13:11) and 'mature' (*teleioi*); 'infant' (*nēpios*) 'to be an infant' (*nēpiazo*) strengthens this likelihood.

Paul may be giving the Corinthians a broad hint. In the preceding verses Paul spoke about the importance of the 'mind' and 'knowing' (vv. 14, 15, 16, 19), which are not 'built up' by unintelligible 'tongues' but only by intelligible words. Is he now saying that 'tongues', because they have no ministry to the 'mind', are 'childish' and contribute nothing to our 'maturity'? Is he saying that 'prophesying', because it is intelligible, 'builds up' our 'minds' to spiritual adulthood? In this allusive language Paul seems to be criticizing uninterpreted 'tongues-speaking'. In short, he appears to give preference to adult 'prophesying' over childish 'tongues-speaking'.

4. 'Tongues', 'Prophecy' and the 'Outsider' in Church (vv. 21-25)

The apostle now considers further the effects of 'tongues-speaking' and 'prophesying' on the 'outsider' who 'enters' a gathering of 'the whole church'.[5] He begins by quoting from the 'Law' (Is. 28:11) where Isaiah the prophet warns unrepentant Israel of the judgement of impending Assyrian invasion. Because the people refuse to hear the word of God from the mouth of their prophet they will hear only 'strange tongues...through the lips of foreigners'. The tramp of the invading enemy and their harsh guttural sounds speak only of doom.

> Thus
>   tongues   are a sign not for believers   but for
> unbelievers
> but
>   prophecy [is a sign] not for unbelievers but for believers.
> (v. 22)

Critical to this text is the word 'sign' whose meaning becomes clear in the example Paul gives of an 'outsider' (or 'unbeliever') who visits the gathered assembly of believers (v. 23). Paul imagines what will happen if, on the one hand, all the believers 'speak in tongues' or if, on the other hand, all 'prophesy'.

If all the visitor hears is a babble of tongues he will conclude that the assembly of Christians is little different from cults like Dionysius or Cybele where people 'raved' in unintelligible

---

5   Usually the believers were distributed among various house meetings. We do
     not know how often or with what regularity they assembled as a 'whole church'
     though it appears they ate the Lord's Supper on those occasions (see on 11:18,
     33-34).

language. Thus 'tongues' will be a 'sign' not pointing to and urging 'belief' but 'unbelief.' For the visiting 'outsider' this babble will be an omen of judgement just as the foreign language of the invading Assyrians was an omen of judgement to the people of Israel.

If, however, the 'outsider' hears the intelligible words of 'prophecy', his response will be quite different (vv. 24-25).

> If all prophesy
> the outsider/unbeliever will be convicted   by all
> judged   by all.
> The secrets of his heart will be laid bare
> and thus
> falling on his face he will worship God he will declare,
> 'Truly, God is among you'.
> (vv. 24-25)

'Prophecy' is nowhere defined by Paul, except he describes it as intelligible. We only know its effects, given earlier as 'upbuilding', 'encouraging' and 'consoling' (v. 3) and in these verses as bringing a sense of the judgement of God issuing in the worship of God. It seems, therefore, that 'prophesying' relates to Kingdom-related matters of the future, whether the last judgement or the blessings when 'the perfect comes' (cf. 13:10). When 'all prophesy' (as opposed to when 'all speak in tongues') it is a 'sign' to encourage people to become 'believers'.

Paul's words, 'God is among' them, fulfil Zechariah's prophecy that in the last days God will gather his people to his Holy City where he will dwell with them. By way of climax he declared that the nations will come to Jerusalem seeking the Lord, where they will say to the Jews, 'God is with you' (Zech. 8:23). Paul is saying that the words of Zechariah are fulfilled in these, the end times, when the 'outsider' visits the Christian assembly, hears the word of God and falls down before God.

With this section Paul brings to a conclusion his sermon on 'tongues-speaking'. Apparently a new phenomenon since his departure from Corinth, Paul has sought to diminish the importance this 'gift' had been given in the church. In particular, in this chapter Paul has engaged in a lengthy contrast between 'tongues-speaking' and 'prophesying'. His words stand as a strong, theologically based and pastorally realistic affirmation of the centrality of the ministry of the prophetic word of God in the church.

Despite all efforts to devise 'programmes' for evangelism and outreach, the gathered congregation, in its life and ministry, remains a potent force for gathering in the 'outsider'. Churches and their ministers, however, must ensure that the word of the Lord is intelligibly and powerfully taught so that the visitor will indeed say, 'God is with you'.

5. Order in the Assembly! (vv. 26-35)

Having reached his conclusion as to the relative worth of 'tongues-speaking' and 'prophecy', Paul now gives some firm directions to bring order out of the chaos in the church meetings in Corinth. Why else does he observe that 'God is not a God of upheaval but of peace' (v. 33)? In setting limits to the numbers of 'tongues-speakers' and 'prophets' speaking at a meeting (vv. 27, 29) we must assume the need existed for such measures. Moreover, his insistence that 'tongues' may not be spoken unless there is an independent 'interpreter' suggests that the assembly had become 'tongues' dominated. Furthermore, only one tongues-speaker or prophet is to speak at a time (vv. 27, 31) and they are not to speak over the top of another, as they appear to have been doing. Paul's silencing of wives' questions in the meetings (vv. 34-35) points to a further source of disorder.

We must ask, 'What is happening in Corinth?' Perhaps they were merely acting out of hot-blooded Mediterranean temperament, something that puzzles cool Anglo-Saxons. More probably, unruly behaviour by tongues-speakers, prophets and women speaking over the top of one another flowed out of heightened eschatological excitement. Did they believe that the local outbreak of 'tongues-speaking' was evidence of the outpoured Spirit of God, meaning that the day of the Lord had arrived?

In verse 26 Paul gives us a window into the 'meeting together' of this apostolic congregation. He does not say that these elements also occurred at the Lord's supper (see on 11:17-34), though it is a reasonable assumption that they did. When he observes that 'each has a hymn (to Christ?)...a teaching (an exposition of scripture, or the apostolic tradition)...a revelation (from a prophet)...a 'tongue'...'an interpretation', we are struck by absence of reference to a church leader or presbyter. Evidently Paul looked to a free-flowing movement of the Spirit. Although there does not appear to have been a liturgical order, as in the synagogues but also in the churches within the next century, there were recurring elements like those mentioned here. In addition we find reference to 'intercessions', 'benedictions', 'blessings', 'graces', some of which had arrived at relatively fixed forms, as echoed within Paul's letters. The letters of the apostle and writings from other apostolic figures were also read in the assembly.

Some modern commentators, while recognising that the 'revelation' mentioned here is not the revelation of God found in the Bible, nonetheless invest that 'revelation' with greater importance than is warranted. In some churches prophets claim that their 'revelations' dictate who should or should not marry whom, and on other matters which belong within the province of personal decision making. The text as it stands gives no encouragement for such practices. 'Revelations' or 'words of knowledge' must be tested by the scriptural revelation, and direct admonition of a member is only in order if some principle or practice clearly taught in the Bible is involved. Otherwise 'revelations' that intrude are inappropriate. 'Revelations' are for the 'upbuilding' of the members gathered as the church, not for detailed directions to private individuals.

Now, however, Paul is seeking to impose some order on what appears to have been a church that was getting out of hand. He limits 'tongues-speaking' to two or three, who must speak 'in turn' (v. 27). Furthermore, one of the 'tongues-speakers' is to interpret the meaning to the congregation (see on vv. 13-16). If there is no interpreter the 'tongues-speaker' is to be silent. In short, Paul will not permit uninterpreted 'tongues' within the church.

'Prophesying', too, is to be restricted to two or three speaking, with the remaining prophets listening in silence and 'discerning' what has been said (v. 29). If a 'revelation' comes to a listening prophet the speaker is to be silent (v. 30). This was to allow for 'only one at a time' to speak (v. 31), but possibly also to protect the congregation from long-winded prophets.

A prophet is able to withhold speaking since 'the spirits of the prophets are subject to the prophets' (v. 32).

Now follows Paul's instruction that 'the women be silent in the churches' where 'they are not permitted to speak' (vv. 33a-35). Did Paul establish this rule for his churches of the Gentile provinces or did it apply to all the congregations of the apostles? His injunction, 'let them be subject' finds an echo in Peter's, 'Wives be subject to your husbands' (1 Pet. 3:1) and suggests this wife-to-husband submission to have been the norm within the churches of the New Testament.

This restriction is puzzling given his earlier permission allowing a woman to 'pray or prophesy' provided she bore the 'sign of authority on her head' (see on 11:5,10). Is Paul contradicting himself? Our problem is that we do not have a complete picture of church life then nor all of Paul's instructions for the ordering of the churches. This has led to various conjectural reconstructions, 'filling in the blanks'.[6] Our proper method, however, is to stay close to the original text as we have it, and to suggest only those reconstructions which are justifiable.[7]

First, we must resist the temptation to downgrade Paul's earlier permission for women to prophesy (11:2-16). There is no good reason to relegate a woman prophet to some kind of private, non-public setting (as Calvin saw it). Women did prophesy in the public, plenary meeting of believers. Nonetheless, even that permission was given against the background of a current problem, namely, the discarding of her head covering, the contemporary cultural expression of a husband's 'authority'. Paul could have taken the easy option to forbid a woman prophesying altogether, but he did not do this.

---

6   Various attempts to 'fill in the blanks' so as to explain the problem between 11:5 and 14:33b-36 include: (1) the women prophesying in 11:2-16 were unmarried and the silenced women in 14:34-35 were married (Elisabeth Schüssler Fiorenza); (2) the earlier permission was a transitional concession leading to the absolute prohibition to which Paul had been moving (Antoinette Wire); verses 33b-36 are Paul's quotation of the Corinthians' words, not Paul's own viewpoint.

7   Based on the incongruity of 11:5 and 14:34-35 Gordon Fee (pp. 699-705) purposed that the present words are an early interpolation, prior to the copying of our earliest manuscripts. The stubborn fact, however, is that all our earliest manuscripts support the versions of this text as they appear in our standard translations (though some later manuscripts locate vv. 33b-35 after our v. 40).

Second, when we seek to make sense of his line of thought in 14:26-35, 39-40 it becomes clear that various groups, women among them, were contributing to disorder within the meetings of the church. He admonishes them in turn: first, 'tongues-speakers' (vv. 27-28); second, prophets (vv. 29-31); third, women (vv. 33b-35). These admonitions are undergirded by his injunctions that punctuate the passage: 'Let everything be done for upbuilding' (v. 26); 'God is not a God of upheaval but of peace' (v. 33); 'Let all things be done decently and in order' (v. 40).

Third, we note that in 11:2-16 Paul speaks of 'a woman' (singular) praying or prophesying, but that in 11:33b-35 he enjoins 'women' (plural) to be silent and under submission. Evidently, Paul is now addressing women as a *group*. His direction that wives ask their 'own' (*idious*) husbands their questions at home (v. 35) suggests that women were seated separately from their husbands, as in the synagogue.

My suggested reconstruction[8] of the situation Paul sought to correct is as follows: a prophet has spoken and a time of silence should have ensued before the next prophet rose to speak. Instead, however, various women seated together were breaking the silence by calling out questions to the prophet. Furthermore, it seems likely that the wives in question were addressing the questions to husbands who were prophets. Thus their action suffered from two faults. On one hand, it was disruptive of congregational 'silence' following the prophetic word, but on the other, it failed to express wifely submission to a husband in public. This explains Paul's, 'Let them be in submission', and, 'it is shameful for a wife to speak in the church'.

By this reconstruction the integrity of both texts 11:2-16 and 14:33b-35 is preserved. The issue in both texts was but differing aspects of the one problem current at that time in Corinth, namely, the submission of wives to husbands in the public life of the church. In the first, a woman may prophesy, but she may not do so (as some were doing) without the 'sign' of a husband's authority on her head. In the second, she must not subvert her husband's role by unseemly public questioning of his prophetic utterances (as some were doing). While the 'subjection of wives

---

8   Depending on E. E. Ellis, *Pauline Theology* (Grand Rapids: Eerdmans, 1989), pages 67-71, with refinements.

to their husbands'[9] is uncongenial to many in modern western societies, it is a clear teaching of the apostles.[10]

Paul was deeply concerned that the gathering of believers in Corinth be orderly. Meetings had become dominated by the babble of 'tongues-speakers' and the oracles of many prophets, both of whom failed to wait until others had finished speaking. Wives were breaking the silence by calling out questions to husbands across the assembly, contributing to the din and upsetting the order of the sexes. Such chaos did not reflect the character of the 'God of peace' in whose name they were assembled, nor did it facilitate the purpose of their meeting together, their 'upbuilding' (v. 26). Not least, such behaviour may have brought the Christians into disrepute locally. After all, 'outsiders' did visit these meetings and doubtless reported what they had observed to the wider community. Paul had good reason for concern about disorderly conduct in meetings of his fledgling group on the margin of suspicious Corinthian society.

6. The Authority of the Apostle (vv. 36-38)

Paul's questions (v. 36) give an indication as to the desperate point to which church life in Corinth had come. Their many words whether from 'tongues-speakers' or even of prophets appear to have led them to think they were some kind of 'fountainhead' from which the word of God gushed forth. Equally, in their thinking they were the only church the word of God had reached, allowing them to hive off doing their own thing at their meetings.

Paul must reassert his authority as an apostle (v. 37):

If anyone thinks he is a prophet or a spiritual man
let him understand that
what I am writing to you is the commandment of the Lord.

Let such 'gifted' ones understand that all the churches established by Paul are subject to his authority, Corinth included! The

---

9   Paul's appeal, 'Even as the Law also says' is unclear, whether by 'Law' is meant the Old Testament as a whole or just the Pentateuch. The problem is that this form of the verb 'be subject' is not found in the Old Testament. One Old Testament text possibly in Paul's mind is LXX Genesis 3:17 where God addresses Eve: 'Thy submission (*anastrophe* 'way of life') shall be to thy husband, and he shall rule over thee.'

10   Cf. Eph. 5:22; Col. 3:18; Tit. 2:5; 1 Tim. 2:11; 1 Pet. 3:1.

words written in this Letter by the apostle are the 'command-ment of the Lord [Jesus]' to which this church must submit, including the public order of their meeting together. If any prophet or inspired person does not recognise Paul's authority, let him or her not be recognised within the church.

Important lessons are still to be drawn from these words. First, it was 'the word of God', the gospel, that brought salvation to this group of people. Only by that word did they come into existence, or will they continue to exist as a true church (see on 15:1-2). The gospel does not come *from* the church but *to* a people whom it forms and shapes as the church of God.

Second, only as they confessed Jesus as Lord were they plunged into the Holy Spirit, becoming 'gifted' with utterance of 'tongues' and 'prophecy'. Such 'prophecy', however, is derived from, dependent upon and to be measured by the gospel (see on 15:3-8, 11). 'Words of knowledge' and of 'prophecy' bring 'upbuilding' to the congregation through 'teaching' by 'encouragement', 'consolation' (14:3) and conversion (14:24-25). Yet they are not absolute, but only 'in part' (13:9). Pastors, preachers and theologians take note. Your words, despite the assurance with which they are spoken, can never coincide exactly with the reality of the Kingdom of God. Humility is appropriate!

Third, the written words of the apostle determine what we believe and how we order our lives inside and outside the church throughout this age. Like the Corinthians, we are called upon to bend stubborn necks and wills carefully to read the will of God out of the text of the apostle.

7. Finally, My Brothers and Sisters....(vv. 39-40)

With verses 39-40 Paul rounds off all that he has said in this extended pastoral sermon on 'tongues-speaking' and 'prophesying' spread over three chapters. In verse 39 he summarises 12:1 to 14:25 where he sought to divert their energies away from 'tongues-speaking' to 'prophesying'. To be sure, they are not to 'forbid tongues', although this ministry is much less valuable than other 'gifts', and its use in church is to be limited. Let there be no misunderstanding. Since it is an expression of 'love' in seeking the upbuilding of the church, they are to be 'zealous' in their pursuit of 'prophesying'.

In the final sentence (v. 40) he catches up his directions setting right the disorder within the church in Corinth (14:26-35), 'Let all things be done decently and in order'.

SOME QUESTIONS FOR PERSONAL REFLECTION:

1. Why is the 'mind' of the speaker as well as the hearer so important?

2. How can I assist in the 'upbuilding' of the church?

3. How important are the needs of the 'outsider' in shaping church practice?

4. What has 'the God of peace' to do with 'things being done decently and in order'?

STUDY QUESTIONS:

1. Why is 'prophesying' greater than 'tongues speaking'?

2. Why is Paul concerned with 'tongues-speaking' being 'intelligible'? Does it not edify?

3. How might 'tongues-speaking' affect outsiders who covenant the assembly?

4. Why does there need to be some 'order' in the church concerning tongues-speaking? What about prophesying?

5. What attitudes may have contributed to the disorder in the congregation at Corinth?

6. Why does Paul have to return to reminding them of the authority of his spostleship?

15

The Abolition of Death
(1 Cor. 15:1-58)

We come now to the last of Paul's great pastoral sermons in this Letter. Once again Paul has taken advantage of a theological or moral problem in Corinth to write expansively on that subject, far beyond the original boundaries of the problem.

Reports from Corinth had come to him in Ephesus that 'some' in Corinth were denying a future resurrection of the body (v. 12). As a result others in the church were being 'led astray', (v. 33), 'shaken' in their faith, 'moved' from their firm 'seat' as Christians (v. 58). This unbelief by some of the members was 'corrupting' the whole body (vv. 33-34).

Paul has addressed a sequence of serious current difficulties in Corinth through the pages of this Letter, but none so critical as this. He has kept the most potentially dangerous matter to the end so that his words will have greatest impact on the assembly as they sit listening to his letter being read to them.

1. A Reminder about Basics (vv. 1-11)

1. The gospel I preached to you (vv. 1-2)
Paul introduces his teaching on 'the resurrection of the dead' with the words, 'I *remind* you, brothers...' This is not new material but a reminder of what they already knew. By contrast the opening words of the previous sermon (12:1 on 'Tongues-speaking'), 'I would not have you *uninformed*', signalled the introduction of teaching that was new to them. But this was not the case here.

v. 1 I remind you, brothers and sisters
         of the gospel   which I proclaimed to   you
                          which also   you received
                          in which   you stand
                     through which also   you are saved

v. 2 by which words   I proclaimed to you
                                       if you hold fast to it
                           unless you believed in vain.

Paul is reminding them of his initial visit five years earlier, that is, in AD 50 when he began his year and a half ministry in Corinth.

As his teaching unfolds (see vv. 3b-8) he will recall for them 'by which words' he preached the gospel to them at that time. But how can we be sure that Paul will remember *exactly* what he told them five years earlier? For two reasons we can be confident that the words Paul will quote were spoken by him then. First, as we will see, they are in the form of a rote-learned summary of the gospel detailing the elements that are 'of first importance' (v. 3). In addition, they are introduced by the words 'I handed over...you received' which were technical terms used by the rabbis for 'handing over' to their disciples a body of teaching. At that time people were more accustomed to memorizing than we are today.

This 'gospel' (*euangelion*) which Paul 'handed over' and which they 'received' is very important. That church and every other church 'stands *in* it', that is, exists *by means of* it. The gospel is the very 'means' of a church's existence. It may have a noticeboard bearing the word 'church', but unless that assembly is founded on the gospel it is a church in name only. Furthermore, it is this gospel 'through which' the church and its members 'are *being* saved'. The present tense tells us that 'salvation' is a continuing process as well as an accomplished fact (cf. 'you *have been* saved' Eph. 2:8). As the gospel continues to be echoed and re-echoed in the assembly in hymns, creeds, prayers, thanksgivings, testimonies, readings and teachings, the people continue to believe in Jesus and continue to hope for their resurrection of the dead.

Here, however, Paul sounds a pastoral note. His words, 'If you are *holding fast* to it, unless you believed *in vain*', are really a probing exhortation. They did not 'believe in vain' at the beginning, though he is concerned that they may not be 'holding fast' what they initially believed. 'Drifting' from the gospel is a continuing concern (cf. Heb. 2:1). Clearly Paul is urging them to *continue* to hold tenaciously and purposefully to the gospel.

2. Paul 'receives' and 'hands over' the gospel (v. 3a)

The entire passage (vv. 1-11) is autobiographical. Paul touches on his own experience between the resurrection of Jesus (in AD 33[1]) and his arrival in Corinth (in AD 50).

We should notice the sequence of events:

AD
33	Christ's death, burial, resurrection and appearances	(vv. 3b-7)
33	Paul persecutes the church of God	(v. 9)
33	The risen and exalted Christ appears to Paul	(v. 8)
33	Paul 'receives' the gospel in Damascus	(v. 3b)
50	Paul 'hands over' the gospel in Corinth	(vv. 1, 3b)

Paul's arrival in Corinth for the gospel is anchored in earlier historical realities the resurrection of Christ, Paul's persecution of the early church and the exalted Christ's 'Damascus Road' call to Paul to become, instead, his apostle (see Gal. 1:1,13-17).

Verse 3a, however, focuses on just two critical 'moments', first when Paul *received* the gospel and second when he *handed over* the gospel in Corinth. But *when* and *where* and *from whom* did Paul 'receive' the gospel? Here we are dependent on the book of Acts, where we learn that Paul was taken to the house of Judas in 'Straight Street', Damascus, where he was ministered to by Ananias and subsequently baptized (Acts 9:11-19; 22:16). Since Paul immediately began preaching Jesus in Damascus (Acts 9:20; 26:20) it is reasonable to assume it was *then, at Damascus* and *from the mouth of Ananias* that Paul 'received' the form of the gospel he later 'handed over' to the churches.

Now follow the four 'dot point headings' of the gospel, the matters 'of first importance'.[2] It is assumed that Paul expanded

---

1 There are two possible dates for the crucifixion-resurrection of Jesus, AD 30 and 33. I hold to the latter.

2 Greek *en protois* is capable of several possible meanings: (1) The gospel Paul 'received' 'at first' at Damascus; (2) the gospel Paul 'handed over' to the Corinthians 'at first'; or, more probably (3) the 'main points' of the gospel Paul handed over to the Corinthians (as preferred by Fee, page 722).

on these initial summary points in his ongoing pastoral teaching of the congregation.

3. The gospel: A Seamless Robe (vv. 3b-7)
The format of the gospel outline should be noted.

1. Each of the four lines begins with 'that' (*hoti*) introducing words in quotation[3] marks by way of a reminder of his initial teaching.

2. Grammatically speaking 'Christ' is the centre of this gospel summary: *Christ* died, *he* was buried, *he* was raised, *he* appeared.

3. The critical first and third elements ('he died'...'he was raised') are each 'according to the Scriptures'.

4. The first and the third lines are supported *historically* by the second and the fourth lines. He died *and he was buried*; he was raised *and he appeared* alive to a sequence of persons. The *burial* confirms the fact of the death and the *appearances* confirm the fact of the resurrection.

5. The word 'and' (*kai*) joins the lines together forming one complete statement: Christ died *and* was buried *and* was raised *and* appeared. No part of this garment can be cut out otherwise the whole robe unravels.

Line 1: that

> Christ died for our sins according to the Scriptures.

Here 'Christ' is Jesus' title, the Greek form of the Hebrew 'Messiah'. The coming of the Messiah/Christ was a great hope of the Old Testament, focused on a new David, his 'son' who will reign from his throne forever, the Lord's 'anointed', 'Immanuel', 'born of a virgin', called 'mighty God...prince of peace', 'the shoot from the stump of Jesse' on whom 'the Spirit of God will rest'.[4] Jesus was confessed by Peter to be 'the Christ', addressed by Bartimaeus as 'son of David', and inquired of by the High Priest as to whether he was 'the Christ', to which Jesus replied, 'I am'

---

3   There were no quotation marks in Greek at that time.

4   See 2 Samuel 7:12-16; Psalm 2:2; Isaiah 7:14; 9:6; 11:1-2.

(Mark 8:29; 10:47-48; 14:61-62). The New Testament throbs with *Christology*, the conviction that Jesus was the One 'anointed of the Lord', 'his Christ'.

The death of Christ 'for our sins' fulfils another hope of the Old Testament, the advent of the Servant of the Lord who was to die 'for' the sins of others (Isa. 53:8).[5] Isaiah connects the new 'David' or 'Christ' *and* the Suffering Servant; both are anointed with the Spirit of God (Isa. 11:2; 42:1). Thus the coming of a Spirit-anointed 'David' and the suffering for the sins of others of the Spirit-anointed Servant are both 'according to the Scriptures'. These great and central promises of the Old Testament converge on the 'Christ who died for our sins'.

Paul's preposition 'for' (*hyper*) most probably derived from Jesus' own interpretation of the meaning of his death given at the Last Supper ('my body given *for* you' Luke 22:19-20). He 'died for our sins' in the sense that he 'stood in' for us, suffering in our stead the just condemnation of God due to fall on us because of our sins.

As Paul will say later, 'The sting of death is sin' (v. 56). But Christ has removed that 'sting' by dying for our sins.

Line 2: and that

     he was buried.

The burial of Jesus is important.

First, it must be regarded as a historical fact.

1. Each gospel refers to the burial of Jesus (Matt. 27:57-61; Mark 15:42-47; Luke 23:50-56; John 19:38-42).

2. The circumstances of the burial are consistent with Jewish beliefs. Jesus died on the cross late on the afternoon of Good Friday, that is, shortly before the beginning of the Sabbath which began at sunset. According to Jewish Law, however, a deceased person must be removed from the cross and buried prior to nightfall to avoid defiling the land.[6] It was critical that Jesus be buried in

---

5   Isaiah has four 'Servant Songs' 42:1-4; 49:5-6; 50:4-11; 52:13–53:12.

6   According to Deuteronomy 21:22-23: 'If a man guilty of a capital offence is put to death and his body is hung on a tree, you must not leave his body on the tree overnight. Be sure to bury him that same day, because anyone who is hung on

the remaining hours of the Friday prior to the Sabbath when no work was permitted.

3.   Jesus was buried in the tomb of an eminent man. The urgent task of burying Jesus before the Sabbath fell to Joseph of Arimathea, a member of the Jewish Council and secret follower of Jesus, the disciples having fled. Joseph, assisted by Nicodemus, took Jesus' body down from the cross and prepared it for interment in Joseph's own tomb, which was in a garden close to Golgotha where Jesus had been crucified. Jesus' burial was not in a grave or hole in the ground, however, but in a vault hewn from the rock face, whose mouth was sealed with a large rolling stone.[7] Jesus was not buried in a grave but 'entombed' in a 'tomb'.[8]

4.   The witnesses of his 'entombment' in Joseph's vault were identifiable (Mary Magdalene, Mary, mother of James the Less), one of whom was the wife of a high official (Joanna, wife of Chusa, the head steward of Herod Antipas, Tetrarch of Galilee). Thus the burial of Jesus in the tomb of an eminent member of the Sanhedrin as witnessed by identifiable persons, one of whom was prominent, are details that were readily verifiable. This is not the stuff of myth and legend but of history.

Second, the burial of Christ as a fact of history is connected to another such fact, that the tomb was empty. The tradition Paul quotes implies that the tomb was empty. Since Christ died *and* was buried *and* was raised *and* appeared to many witnesses, how could the tomb not have been empty?

The Gospels tell us that these named women came to Joseph's tomb early on the morning of the 'first day of the week' and discovered that the body of Jesus was no longer there. Upon

---

a tree is under God's curse. You must not desecrate the land the LORD your God is giving you as an inheritance.'

7   Numerous tombs from this period with entrances sealed by a large wheel-like stone are to be seen in Jerusalem to this day, for example, in a park close to the King David Hotel.

8   One of the words for tomb in the Gospels is *taphos* (Matt. 27:61, 64, 66) which resembles Paul's verb *etaphe* 'buried' (from the verb *thaptein*, 'to bury').

inquiry the temple authorities also found the tomb empty and the body gone (Matt. 28:11-15). Since both the supporters and opponents of Jesus asserted that the tomb was empty we must assume that the tomb was, in fact, empty. The 'tradition' Paul 'received', to which he is presently appealing, assumes this too.

Third, the burial of Jesus underscores that fact that he had, indeed, truly died. At the same time, his 'buried' body did not decay, as his buried forefather David's did, but was raised alive, pristine and perfect. Thus his burial, but non-decay, was the evidence he was the promised son of David, one whose body would not decompose, the Messiah, the Saviour and the Son of God (see below).

Line 3: and that

> he was raised on the third day according to the Scriptures.

We must note the subtle changes in the verbs in this pre-formed tradition. Christ died by his own volition, but he was 'raised' *by God*.[9] God did not allow death to hold him but in vindication of the promised Messiah raised him alive as Lord for the duration of history before the End, and beyond the End forever (see on vv. 23-24). This is the greatest miracle of God since the creation of the world.

Christ died on Friday afternoon and 'was raised' sometime on the Saturday evening, so how are we to understand the words 'he was raised on the *third* day'? The tradition Paul quotes does not say, 'He was raised three days later', that is, seventy two hours later, but rather 'he was raised *on*[10] the third day'. The Jewish day began at sunset. Thus Christ died and was buried on Friday afternoon (day one); he remained in the tomb Friday sunset to Saturday sunset (day two); he was raised

---

9 Two points of grammar must be noticed about *egegertai*, 'he was raised': (1) The form of the verb here is Divine Passive indicating that *God* raised Jesus, as Peter says directly in Acts 10:40. The passive form of *egeiro*, 'I raise' also occurs when the women found the tomb empty: 'He is raised (*egerthe*); he is not here. See the place where they laid him' (Mark 16:6). The verb *egegertai* is also cast in the Greek Perfect Tense, used to indicate a past event with continuing consequences. Thus (1) and (2) combine to indicate that God raised Christ but that act will have continuing effects, notably his 'Lordship' over all things and his reappearing at the end of the Age when he will finally abolish Death.

10 The literal translation 'he was raised on the day the third' is unusual Greek, suggesting an underlying Aramaic original.

alive sometime during Saturday night before the arrival of the women on Sunday morning (day 3).

This 'he was raised on the third day' seems to be a different tradition stream from the 'first day of the week' traditions of the four Gospels when the women found the body gone and the tomb empty. Yet it is significant that both traditions innocently intersect. Christ being 'raised on the third day' explains why the body was gone from the tomb when the women came 'on the first day of the week'.

But how is Christ's resurrection 'according to the Scriptures'? Which Scriptures? Both Peter and Paul appeal to Psalm 16:10, written by David, as prophesying God's raising of Christ:

> You will not abandon me to the grave,
> nor will you let your Holy One see decay.

Both Peter and Paul point out that when David died *his* body did, indeed, 'see decay' but that the body of his 'seed', Jesus, *did not* 'see decay'. Peter said that David's body was in his tomb in Jerusalem (Acts 2:29), so his Psalm prophesied beyond himself to the resurrection of his descendant, the Messiah (Acts 2:31). Paul also contrasted David with his descendant Jesus, both of whom died and were buried. But God raised Jesus from the dead so that 'his body did not see decay', as David's did. This was God keeping his promise to David that a descendant was to be the Saviour and the Son of God (Acts 13:23,29, 32-38).

But how are we to resolve the problem that there is no specific Old Testament text prophesying the resurrection of the Christ 'on the third day'? The answer may be in consideration of two related facts:

1. The Old Testament speaks generally of salvation occurring after 'three days' (e.g., Hosea 6:2 'After two days [God] will revive us; on the third day he will restore us, that we may live in his presence');

2. Jesus often speaks of his resurrection occurring after 'three days' (e.g., Matthew 12:40 'For as Jonah was three days and three nights in the belly of a huge fish, so the Son of Man will be three days and three nights in the heart of the earth' ; Mark 8:31 'The Son of Man...must be killed

and after three days rise again'; cf. John 2:19 'Destroy this temple and in three days I will raise it'). In short, 'Christ was raised on the third day' may be a 'shorthand' way of speaking of a great saving act of God, which as it turned out, occurred historically 'on the third day'.

Line 4: and that

	he appeared	to Cephas
next		to the Twelve
then		to more than 500 brothers at one time
		of whom the greater number remain until
		this day but some have fallen asleep[11]
next	he appeared	to James
then		to all the apostles.

The force of line 3 ('he was raised') and line 4 ('he appeared') considered together emphasizes the objective reality of Christ's bodily resurrection. A merely 'spiritual' resurrection is shut out by these words.

The Christ who was raised on the third day appeared to various people in a known sequence on five occasions, as implied by 'next...then... next...then'. The Gospel of John also notes a specific sequence of three occasions when Christ appeared to his disciples 'after he was raised from the dead' (John 21:14; cf. 20:19, 26).

Nonetheless, neither Paul's 'tradition' nor John's account is complete. There are omissions from Paul's list the various women witnesses (John 20:14-18; Matt. 28:9), the two men going to Emmaus (Luke 24:13-35), the disciples apart from Thomas (John 20:19-23), the seven disciples at the lakeside (John 21:2) and the Twelve in Jerusalem before his ascension (Acts 1:4-8). If the various accounts in the Gospels and in the pre-Pauline tradition are set side by side it appears there were at least twelve separate occasions when the risen Lord appeared to many hundreds of people over a thirty seven day period between the resurrection and the ascension (Acts 1:3; cf. 13:31).

It is not known precisely what is meant by 'he appeared to all the apostles'. Presumably 'the Twelve' were their core but

---

11   The words 'of whom the greater number remain until this day but some have fallen asleep' are probably a Pauline addition to the briefer summary.

other 'apostles' were included. It may be significant that reference to James (most likely the Lord's brother) precedes 'all the apostles' in this list. James was an apostle though he was not one of 'the Twelve' (Gal. 1:18-19; Acts 1:13, 21-26; cf. 1:14). So are we meant to infer, 'He appeared to James (the apostle), then (he appeared) to all the (other) apostles'? Almost certainly there were others 'apostles' beyond James. Paul mentions his 'kinsmen' Andronicus and Junias who were 'outstanding' apostles and who were believers before him (Rom. 16:7). Most likely Junias was a woman, as the early church commentator Chrysostom believed.[12] If so, Junias most probably would have been wife to Andronicus. Perhaps, too, various members of the seventy two (Galilean?) missioners were among 'all the apostles' (Luke 10:1-24). 'Apostles', however, were not only witnesses of the resurrected Christ. They had also been 'sent' to preach, as the word 'apostle' indicates.

Where did these 'appearances' occur? It was in Jerusalem that Christ appeared to Cephas and the Twelve, and most likely it was in Galilee that he appeared to more than 500 brothers (and sisters) and to James. Most likely he appeared to 'all the apostles' in Jerusalem.

We must note that the names of those to whom Christ 'appeared' are either given or made readily ascertainable. In myth, details are either missing or given in vague terms, but this is not the case here. This is a historical statement, not a mythological one.

4. Christ Appears to Paul (v. 8)

The Risen Christ appeared alive on five separate occasions according to verses 5-7. These 'appearances' occurred within the period of a little more than a month prior to Christ's ascension (Acts 1:2-3). After Christ appeared to 'all the apostles' there were a sequence of closely related events in Jerusalem, as related in the book of Acts:

> Christ ascended to heaven
> The Spirit was given at the Feast of Pentecost a few days later
> Peter begins to preach that Jesus was the Christ
>
> The Hellenists led by Stephen separated from the 'Hebrews'

---

12   C. E. B. Cranfield, *Romans* II (Edinburgh: Clark, 1979), page 788.

led by Peter
Stephen is arrested, tried by the Sanhedrin and stoned
Saul begins his persecution of believers

Saul sets out for Damascus to extradite fugitives for punishment back in Jerusalem.

These events together probably occupied less than a year. Their climax was the appearance of the Risen Christ to Saul the persecutor as he travelled to Damascus.

Paul's words appear to answer the criticism that he was not a true apostle because he belonged neither to 'the Twelve' nor was he among 'all the apostles' who had seen the Risen Christ and been commissioned by him (see on 9:1-6). This barb had probably been directed at Paul in Jerusalem by believers of intense Jewish conviction who were offended by Paul's preaching of a circumcision-free gospel to Gentiles. But the opinion that Paul was not a true apostle seems to have reached the ears of the Corinthians.[13] To this Paul makes a reply:

> But last of all
>> as to the one abnormally born
>> he appeared to me also.

By 'last of all' Paul means that Christ's appearance to him was the 'last' in the sequence of separate appearances of the Risen Christ. Paul belongs to that sequence, though he comes 'last' in that sequence. If Cephas was the first to whom Christ appeared Paul was the 'last'. Like those listed before him Paul, too, saw the Risen Christ, 'last of all'.

But 'last of all', which immediately follows 'all the apostles' (v. 7), may also mean that Paul was also the 'last' of the apostles to be appointed. Since there would be no more 'appearances' of the Risen Christ there would be no more apostles. Thus, to those who denied or questioned his credentials as an apostle, let them be clear that Paul is an apostle even though he was the 'last' of 'all the apostles', to whom Christ appeared 'last of all'.

It was a matter of difficulty for Paul that he did not belong to the original group of disciples and that his 'call' occurred a year or so after Christ's resurrection appearances to 'all the apostles'. But Paul's case was different and special. He saw

---

13   Perhaps also from Peter who had visited Corinth in recent times (1:12; 9:5).

Christ who was *both* resurrected *and* glorified. This was no mere vision, however, since the glorified Christ also *spoke* to him, commissioning him to be his apostle to the Gentiles (Gal. 1:15-16; Rom. 1:5; Acts 22:21; Acts 26:17).

Paul's self-description of himself 'as to one abnormally born' (*hōsperei tō ektrōmati*), while difficult to understand, is probably also part of his rejoinder to his critics. This is a medical term originally applied to premature birth but also to someone 'freakish' in appearance. In my view, it is unlikely that Paul is hinting at some physical abnormality that had been noticed by the Corinthians. Rather, it is more likely that he is making a virtue of being later than 'the Twelve' and 'all the apostles' to whom Christ appeared. Unlike those before him who only saw the resurrected Christ, Paul also glimpsed the *glorified* Christ, that is, in his parousia brightness, *prematurely*, as it were. Unlike any others Paul 'saw' the risen Christ whom he also previewed as the returning Christ. And he received his 'call' to be an apostle *at that time*. So far from discrediting his credentials as an apostle, Christ's unique encounter with Paul made him a special apostle, his apostle to the Gentiles.

5. Paul the Persecutor is, nonetheless, an Apostle (v. 9)

Nonetheless, he will admit to being 'the least of the apostles' who does not 'deserve to be called an apostle'. But this is not at all because Christ 'appeared to' him later than and outside the time frame of the appearances to the other apostles. Rather, it is because he 'persecuted the church of God' that he is not fit to be an apostle.

This historical reference to himself as 'persecutor who became apostle' serves to confirm the accuracy of the narrative in the Acts of the Apostles, whose historicity is routinely discounted by many scholars. Paul himself tells us firsthand that initially the risen Christ appeared to his original disciples (v. 5); then, Paul persecuted the church of God (v. 9); next, on the Road to Damascus Paul as 'prematurely born' saw the resurrected but now glorified Christ (v. 8), where by the 'grace of God' he was commissioned to be an apostle (v. 9); finally, that 'grace' enabled Paul to work harder than the other apostles in the twenty or so years since the Damascus Road 'call' to the time of writing this present Letter (v. 10). The historical information briefly and gratuitously given in this Letter innocently corroborates the accuracy of the intentionally written history of the book of Acts.[14]

6. The Grace of God on Damascus Road and Since (v. 10)

Paul was deeply ashamed that he had attacked the followers of Jesus (see 1 Tim. 1:12-16). Yet, equally, he was aware of the 'grace of God' that had been shown to him on the Damascus Road. Christ's call to proclaim him to the Gentiles was an expression of the Lord's 'mercy' which Paul humbly received at that time. As he will tell the Corinthians in a later letter, 'Therefore since through the mercy of God we have this ministry...' (2 Cor. 4:1). Christ showed his 'mercy' and 'grace' to Paul in his 'call' to him to be his 'apostle'.

That 'grace' was not shown 'in vain', or 'emptily'. As a result of 'grace' shown to him Paul has laboured strenuously for the past twenty years, indeed, more strenuously than 'all of them', that is, the other apostles of whom Paul was historically the 'last' and, because he had been a persecutor, the 'least'. Yet, as he emphasizes, it was not he who worked, but the 'grace of God that was with' him. 'In myself', as he says later, 'I am nothing' (2 Cor. 12:11).

7. The Apostolic Faith (v. 11)

Paul now expresses the 'grace' which he had been shown and which continued to work in him. While others sought to 'de-apostolize' him, he actually affirmed the ministry and the message of those who rejected his apostleship. At the same time he firmly locates his ministry with theirs, as a true apostle.

> Therefore
> > whether it was I or they
> > thus we preach
> and   thus you believed.

Reject him as the Corinthians may have done, his preached message is the same as the other apostles. Here he refers back to the four point proclamation summarized in verses 3b-7, that Christ died for sins, was buried, was raised on the third day, and appeared alive to a sequence of verifiable witnesses. The

---

14   See P. W. Barnett, *Jesus and the Logic of History* (Leicester: Apollos; 1997), pages 39-58.

persons to whom the risen Christ appeared, as listed by Paul, preach exactly the same message as Paul. Emphatically Paul belongs to that apostolic list and emphatically he preaches the same message as they do.

The implications of this are momentous for the ongoing life of the church. The apostolic message is definable as in verses 3b-7, namely, that Christ died for our sins and was raised bodily from the dead on the third day, both in fulfilment of the Old Testament Scriptures. This is the 'core' message that needs to be held to, proclaimed and heard in our churches, but also in the wider community. Matching this preaching, however, is what *is* and is *to be* 'believed' within the churches, that is, the self-same message whose summary has now been set out above. The apostolic gospel is to be the faith of the church. The church of Jesus Christ 'stands' because of this gospel and is 'saved through' this gospel (v. 1). There is no other 'gospel' and there is no other 'faith'.

But why has it been necessary for Paul to repeat the gospel message, especially with so much emphasis on the resurrection appearances of Christ? Why did Paul need to reaffirm his apostleship? Answers will emerge as we read on.

2. 'If Christ has not been Raised...' (vv. 12-19)

The key to chapter 15 is found in verse 12. 'Some' among the Corinthians were saying, 'There is no resurrection of the dead'. We infer that these persons were denying the general resurrection of the dead at the end of history.

But for what reason? Did their experience of the full flood of spiritual gifts in the church tell the Corinthians that the end of the age had (somehow) 'already' come, so that no future resurrection would occur? Or, were they expressing the Greek belief in the immortality of the soul as against the resurrection of the body? Remember how the Athenians mocked Paul when he spoke of the resurrection of Jesus (Acts 17:32). Were Greek beliefs inspiring doubts about the resurrection in Corinthian hearts? This explanation is plausible since Paul goes on to answer the Corinthians' questions, 'How are the dead raised?' and 'With what kind of body do they come?' (v. 35). A third possibility, which seems likely, combines the previous two, that is, their *present* dramatic experience of the Spirit strengthened their pre-existing Greek disbelief in the resurrection.[15] In this case their Greek worldview was reinforced by religious experience. Whatever the explanation, 'some' among them repudiated the resurrection of the dead.

The apostle now confronts the Corinthians with the logical consequences of their doubts. It makes no sense for them to be denying the resurrection of the dead when the resurrection of Christ is being preached by all the apostles including Paul, and believed in the churches (v. 12; cf. v. 11). The resurrection of Christ is *continually* being preached, but some in Corinth are *continually* saying that there is no resurrection of the dead.[16]

Paul confronts the Corinthians with the logical consequences of their denial. His argument can be summarized as follows:

If the dead are not raised   (v. 13)
then Christ has not been raised
But if Christ has not been raised   (v. 14)
        Then: our preaching is empty
                 and your faith is empty
Result: We are false witnesses of God   (v. 15)

But if Christ has not been raised   (v. 17)
     Then: Your faith is in vain
          you are still in your sins
          deceased believers are 'lost'   (v. 18)
Result: We would be the most wretched of people (v. 19)

Paul's argument falls into two parts. The first relates to his ministry and the second to their faith.

First, if Christ has not been raised then Paul's preached message (*kerygma*), which earlier he called 'the gospel' (v. 1), is 'empty' (v. 14). This is because that gospel's content is centred on, 'he was raised...he appeared'. Take out Christ's resurrection and the message is now void of content, as empty as a bucket with no water. Paul, however, has 'witnessed' to the Corinthians that God has raised Christ, based on Paul's own encounter with the risen Lord. If this is false it means that Paul has been 'found' to be a 'false witness' to God's raising of Christ if, in

---

15   In Aeshylus' play *Eumenides* (647-648) Apollo says, 'When the dust hath drained the blood of a man, once he is slain, there is no resurrection.'

16   The present tense *legousin*, 'they are saying' pointedly matches *kerussetai*, 'is continually being preached' (present passive).

fact, Christ was not raised. We sense that Paul the devout Jew shrinks from this, awestruck at the very possibility of giving false testimony about God. 'Found' *(heuriskometha)* is a divine passive indicating *God* will 'find' Paul guilty of such a crime on the Day of Judgement.[17]

Second, if Christ has not been raised, there are grave consequences for Christian faith. In verse 14 he has already introduced the idea that their faith would be 'empty' if his message is 'empty' of reference to the resurrection. Now he expands on that 'emptiness'. Faith in an un-resurrected Christ is, he says in verse 17b, 'futile', 'senseless', 'pointless' *(mataia)*. This word is used of the worship of carved idols that are no gods, that have no existence. Faith in a dead man is just as futile. What help can a corpse give?

If Christ died for our sins, but was not raised by God in vindication, then his death by itself achieved nothing and so our faith is 'senseless'. Paul illustrates this in two ways. First, the Corinthians, and all believers, would be 'still in their sins', remaining unforgiven (v. 17c). On the day of judgement those who have passed their days believing they have been forgiven through Christ's death will discover how cruelly mistaken they have been, facing only the wrath of God. Second, those who have 'fallen asleep', that is, who died 'in Christ' (i.e., as Christians), will prove to have been 'lost'. Instead of the comforting hope for deceased loved ones who died in Christ, that we will see them again in the Kingdom, we will find to our horror that like us they, too, are 'lost'.

Paul's conclusion, 'If we are hoping in Christ only in this life, of all people we are the most to be pitied' (v. 19) may be a pointed reference to the Corinthians' super-spirituality. Did their preoccupation with spiritual gifts lead them to think that 'this life' in the 'here and now' was all that mattered, so that it was immaterial whether or not Christ was raised? Were that the case their assurance of forgiveness is a delusion and their hope for the salvation of the deceased would be a delusion. What pathetic creatures they would be, living a life based on assurance and hope, if there was no basis for that assurance and

---

17 'Found' is often used in this sense in the New Testament (see e.g. 1 Cor. 4:2; 2 Cor. 5:3; 1 Pet. 1:7).

hope, the resurrection of Christ from the dead. Paul is saying that there is no true faith without genuine hope and there is no hope without Christ's resurrection from the dead.

When we turn Paul's words around positively, however, we find that Christian believers are, on the contrary, the 'most blessed' of all people. Because Christ died for our sins and has been raised alive by God we are, indeed, forgiven. Furthermore, we who have lost loved ones who died in Christ are assured that they are not 'lost' but are 'safe in the arms of Jesus'.

3. The Abolition of Death (vv. 20-28)

The Corinthian doubters were saying that because Christ was dead he was, in effect, 'finished'. God might 'be there', but Christ lay dead, un-resurrected and decaying somewhere. But this could not be further from the truth, says Paul in the passage following. Rather, the risen and exalted Christ rules history as King, defeating his enemies until his return when he 'hands over' his rule to God, his Father.

Many aircraft display a screen for passengers tracing the origin, progress and destination of the flight. Verses 20-28 display where history has come from, where it is going and who is in control. Paul's history, however, is not about the rise and fall of the Egyptian, Greek, Roman, British and other empires. Rather, it is a short history of Death.

1. Adam and the Christ (vv. 20-22)

In verses 20-22 Paul contrasts Christ with Adam. Through the first man Adam, Death entered history. The 'seed' of every man and woman in history was present in Adam, so that all people owe their life and their physical descent to that man. But because of his sin, Adam's 'seed' was infected with the fatal virus called 'Death' so that all people must die. The man Christ, however, has been raised from the dead, making possible the resurrection of the dead for others.

For			
just as	in Adam	all	die
so also	in the Christ	all will be made	alive

(v. 22.)

Paul refers to the extremities of the history of Death, its beginning and its end. Adam introduced Death, but the Christ will abolish Death.

And the reason? It is because *Christ* has been raised from the dead on Easter day that *all* will be raised alive on the last day. Here Paul uses the language of the 'first-fruits' reaped early in anticipation of the whole harvest. Christ as raised from the dead was the historic 'first-fruits' of a 'harvest' of the dead that will be raised on the last day. With the resurrection of Christ the harvest was begun, but it has been temporarily 'put on hold' to allow opportunity for more and more people to be 'reaped' for the Kingdom.

In this passage, and indeed, in this whole chapter, Paul is not addressing the question of the judgement of all people at the general resurrection (see, e.g., 2 Cor. 4:14; 5:10). Rather, Paul is ignoring the future of the unbeliever and concentrating on the abolition of Death for those who are 'in Christ'. For those who are 'in Christ' his resurrection has already defeated Death, at least in principle. Those who have died 'in Christ' are said to be 'asleep', ready and waiting to be roused from sleep by the Lord at his coming (v. 23).

2. Each in his own order (vv. 23-24a)
Paul sets out the sequence of events that will culminate in the abolition of Death.

> But, each 'in its own order' (v. 23-24a):
>
>> Christ, the resurrected 'first-fruits'.
>> *Then*, at his coming,
>>> the resurrection of those who belong to the Christ.
>> *Then*, the end when
>>> he hands over the kingdom to God his Father, and
>>> he abolishes every dominion.

There is a divine 'order' here. 'Christ the resurrected ... *then* ... *then* ...' Christ, the 'first-fruits', has already been raised, at the First Easter, as Paul reminded them (see on v. 4). This is an accomplished fact of history. But still in the future is another historical event, Christ's 'coming' (*parousia*). This word, which is regularly used of Christ's return,[18] was often employed for

---

18　See e.g., Matthew 24:3, 27, 37, 39; 1 Thessalonians 2:19; James 5:7; 2 Peter 3:4; 1 John 2:28.

the grand appearing of an emperor or other high dignitary. At his 'coming' those who belong to the Christ, that is, those who are 'asleep in him', will, as he was, be raised from the dead (see v. 20). Then follows 'the End' (*telos*), a word for 'goal' or 'end-point', but which has the idea of 'perfection' (see on 13:10; cf. 1 Pet. 4:7). In the verses following Paul explains what will happen then.

3. The Kingdom of Christ (vv. 24b-26)

When he was raised from the dead and exalted Christ assumed his kingly rule.

> He must reign as king
> until he has put all his enemies
> under his feet.   (v. 25)

This kingship is expressed in the language of Psalm 110:1, the Old Testament text most quoted in the New Testament:

> Yahweh said to my Lord [= the Christ],
> 'Sit at my right hand,
> until I make your enemies your footstool.'

Paul identified the 'enemies' of the Christ as various malevolent spiritual forces, whom he calls 'all rule', 'all authority', 'power' and 'death' itself. These are the 'enemies' over whom Christ must reign as king until they are all finally 'abolished'. Christ exercises his kingly rule and abolishes these 'powers' through the preaching of the gospel of himself crucified and risen. Through this gospel sins are forgiven and those formerly in bondage are set free from the powers of darkness and, in the power of the Holy Spirit, brought under the dominion of Christ (Col. 1:13-14).

According to an advertisement for a funeral company, 'Death is just a natural part of life'. This is not the way death is viewed by ordinary people. Death brings the one precious life we have to its end. Death takes loved ones and friends from us. Nor is the advertisement the view of Paul the apostle. For Paul death was *un*natural, a malevolent spiritual 'enemy', a blight caused by sin, the 'last' and most formidable 'enemy' of God.

> The last enemy being abolished is death.

Death 'is being abolished' (present tense)[19] because the risen Christ is 'reigning as king' (present tense) as men and women who hear the gospel of his death and resurrection begin to 'belong to' him. But Death will be finally and visibly removed at the coming of Christ.

4. The End of Kingly Rule (vv. 27-28)

The risen Christ rules throughout this age until his coming (*parousia* v. 23c), the arrival of the end (*telos* v. 24a), when all his 'enemies' will have been 'abolished', Death in particular. At that time Christ will 'hand over' his kingly rule to God his Father (v. 24 b).

Indeed, it was God who placed all things under Christ's feet (v. 27). It was only ever a *delegated* rule, not an autonomous one. Here Paul appeals to Psalm 8:6:

> Thou [God] hast set him [the Son of Man]
> over the works of thy hands.

Paul does not quote, but rather echoes this text in his own words, 'All things *are put* in subjection to him', that is, by God. God is not among the 'all things' that are subject to Christ. Rather, *God* placed Christ over the works of God's hands.

Once the 'enemies' of God including Death are finally vanquished by the Son, he will 'hand over' his kingship to the Father and be subject to him (v. 28). The humility and obedience of Christ shown in his incarnation and dreadful death (Phil. 2:5-8; cf. 2 Cor. 8:9; 10:1) is shown also in his voluntary subjection to the Father once his work of ruling is completed.[20] From that moment God will be 'all in all', which is Paul's idiomatic way of saying that God will reign supreme over all that is evil and that has been opposed to him. Then we will 'see God face to face' and we will 'know him as we have been known' (13:12).

No human commentary on Paul's words can equal the inspired text of John in his book of Revelation:

---

19 *katargeitai*, 'is being destroyed', is present passive. Death is being abolished by God.

20 Though equal in deity to his Father, Jesus is at all points subject to him.

And I heard a loud voice from the throne saying,
'Now the dwelling of God is with men,
and he will live with them.
They will be his people,
and God himself will be with them and be their God.
He will wipe every tear from their eyes.
There will be no more death or mourning or crying or pain,
for the old order of things has passed away.'

(Rev. 21:3-4)

4. 'Do Not be Led Astray' (vv. 29-34)

Paul returns to the doubters in Corinth, peppering them with two questions, each beginning, 'Why...?' Furthermore, each question addresses 'a life or death' issue.

First, he asks the Corinthians 'why' they are 'being baptized on behalf of the dead' (v. 29). This is most unusual and a deep puzzle, since its meaning is unclear and there is no parallel reference in the New Testament to cast light upon it. We are helped a little by the verses following, where Paul speaks of 'danger' to him (v. 30) and of being 'forced to fight with wild beasts', metaphorically speaking (v. 32). Life was precarious for the apostle and, we infer, for the local church people also. Our best guess, therefore, is that some believers in Corinth have lost their lives under persecution before an opportunity arose for baptism, and that others have been baptized 'in their place' (*hyper*), by substitution. Presumably this was done for pastoral reasons, to assure surviving believers including family members that all that baptism signified was true for the deceased.

It deserves to be noted that Paul merely refers to this practice and does not prescribe it. It is to be doubted that Mormon baptism for the dead can be sustained by this reference. Their practice of baptizing thousands of deceased persons vicariously and maintaining their records in disused rocket silos in the USA is bizarre in the extreme!

But the point Paul was then making is that their practice of being baptized on behalf of deceased members is utterly irrational where the resurrection of the dead is doubted, as it was by 'some' within the church in Corinth.

A second question is directed to Paul himself (v. 30-32). As an apostle who preached Christ crucified and risen, his own life was exposed to constant danger (v. 30). 'Why do I die every hour?' To this he adds (v. 31[21]), 'Such is my pride in you, which I have in Christ Jesus our Lord, that I die daily' (see on 16:9). Paul amplifies this with dark comments, that 'humanly speaking, he is forced to struggle with wild beasts in Ephesus' (the city from which he is writing this letter). But what profit or advantage is there for Paul if the dead are not raised and if Christ has not been raised (v. 32a)? Why would he choose to live so precariously if the resurrection of Christ is not historically true? Paul's concerns about the dangers of Ephesus proved to be well founded. He narrowly escaped death from a riot, forcing him from the city (Acts 19:23-20:1; 2 Cor. 1:8-10).

'If the dead are not raised' (v. 32b), as some of them are saying, the only sensible course would be to make the most of this life, circumscribed as it would be by birth and death, with nothing beyond. As an example of living just for 'the here and now' Paul quotes Isaiah 22:13:

> Let us eat and drink
> for tomorrow we die.

Of course, eat and drink we must. But is eating and drinking all there is to human existence? 'Surely there must be more', our consciences cry. The resurrection of the dead, however, immediately introduces an element of accountability. For I will be caught up in that resurrection to give account to God my judge as to how I have lived this one life that was assigned to me.

Paul concludes this short section by directly admonishing the Corinthian Christians not to be led astray by the doubters among them (vv. 33-34):

> Do not be led astray.
> Bad company corrupts good habits....
> For some are ignorant of God.
> I say this to your shame.

Paul is not speaking generally here. Rather, he is still addressing the precise situation where there are 'some who say there is no resurrection of the dead' (v. 12). First, he speaks to the congregation as a whole. 'Don't *you* be led astray...', he urges.

---

21   The Greek text appears to have been dislocated and is not easy to understand.

Hold firmly to the gospel, whose core belief is the resurrection of Christ from the dead (see on vv. 4-5). Second, he refers obliquely to those who deny the resurrection as 'bad company' that 'leads astray' and 'corrupts' others. Third, he also speaks indirectly of another group, those who are 'ignorant of God' (*agnōsian...theou*). It is a matter of 'shame' that some among them are so 'ignorant of God' and vulnerable to corruption. Here is a call to teach the gospel clearly and effectively.

Sadly, it has to be said that 'some' in the church today continue to dispute the resurrection of the dead and the resurrection of Christ. Among these are some prominent church leaders who exercise a 'corrupting' influence among Christians. Paul's advice continues to shine like a beacon, 'Do not be led astray' by them. Hold fast to the gospel as the measuring rod for the teachings of all ministers, including those who hold high office.

5. The Resurrection Body is a Transformed Body (vv. 35-41)
The questions, 'How are the dead raised?' and 'With what kind of body?' most likely come from those who are doubting or denying the resurrection of the body. It is the second question, however, that Paul will answer. The first requires no reply. God will raise the dead by his irresistible power.

The second question ('What kind of body?') is echoed by many today. Some, for example, simply cannot imagine a 'dead man walking', that is, a re-animated corpse. Paul anticipates that question by insisting that resurrection means *transformation*. Others who raise objections, however, are really latter day Gnostics who, as mystics, do not believe that 'the word became *flesh*' (John 1:14) nor that Christ was raised *bodily* from the dead (see on vv. 4-7). For them, as with the Gnostics of the second century, God is 'up there' and cannot be conceived of as having dirtied his hands as the Son of God who 'for us and our salvation' came 'down here'.

Paul rather abruptly addresses the one who asks such question as 'Fool, the answer to your question stares you in the face'. In an agricultural age, when everyone depended on sowing and reaping, two things were obvious. On the one hand, the seed you sow 'dies' in the ground before it sprouts with life (v. 36), and on the other, the plant that rises from the soil has a *different* 'body' from the 'naked' seed that was sown. The self-same seed that 'dies' in the ground is 'raised' in a transformed 'body'. The same is true of the resurrection of the dead. I who die will be raised alive, but changed into a different form.

He further illustrates the difference between the seed and the plant by two sets of contrasts, between various kinds of 'flesh' and between 'earthly' and 'heavenly' 'bodies'. The seed has one 'body', the plant another 'body', just as there are different kinds of 'flesh', whether of humans, animals, birds or fish (vv. 38-39).

Paul also raises ideas here which he will develop later. To prepare us for the promise that the resurrection body is 'raised in glory' (v. 43), he contrasts the 'glory' of 'earthly bodies' with the 'heavenly bodies', the sun, moon and stars, which have 'different glory' (vv. 40-41). Furthermore, 'earthly bodies' and 'heavenly bodies' anticipates 'the man from the earth' and the 'man from heaven' (v. 47).

6. The Resurrection of the Dead (vv. 42-50)
Two connected contrasts follow: (a) between the 'body' that is 'sown' in death and the 'body' that is 'raised' in resurrection, and (b) between Adam and Christ.

1. 'Sown Soulish, Raised Spiritual'
In verses 35-41 Paul has given the analogy of a seed that is 'sown' (and 'dies' v. 36) yet which is 'raised', though as a different 'body'. This is the principle of 'continuity and transformation'. Paul now uses the words 'sown' and 'raised' in a rapid fire sequence of contrasts that springs from the second analogy, the distinction between 'the earthly' and 'the heavenly' (v. 40).

The 'body' of a deceased believer is the antecedent of the repeated pronoun, 'it':

> It is sown in corruption, it is raised imperishable;
> It is sown in dishonour, it is raised in glory;
> It is sown in weakness, it is raised in power;
> It is sown a 'soulish' body, it is raised a spiritual body.
> If there is a 'soulish' body, there is also a spiritual body.

Believers share with other descendants of Adam the frailties of life in this present age, its corruption, dishonour, weakness and 'soulishness'. Nowhere is the 'fallenness' of this age more apparent than in the feebleness and powerlessness of death as evident at funerals. From this fallible 'fallen' existence, however, believers will be 'raised' alive into the imperishability, glory, power and spirituality of the coming age.

A word of explanation is necessary for my word 'soulish', used above. 'Soulish' translates *psychikos* which is related to *psychē*, 'soul'. 'Soulish' is not ideal but is to be preferred to the various translations ('physical' in RSV and NRSV; 'natural' in NIV). The word *psychikos* occurs earlier in First Corinthians (2:14), the only other place in the New Testament where it is found and where the context makes its meaning clear enough.

> The *psychikos* man does not receive the things of the Spirit of God for they are folly to him and he is not able to understand them because they are spiritually understood.
> But the spiritual man understands all things...

In that passage a *psychikos* or 'soulish' person is an unbeliever in contrast with a 'spiritual' person, a believer. When used in chapter 15, however, the contrast is between the 'soulish' body as death-bound and the 'spiritual' body which lives forever in the kingdom of God. Because of our descent from Adam, the man of dust, every person, including the believer, is 'sown' *soulishly* in death. Unlike the unbeliever, however, the believer will be 'raised a spiritual body', fit for the new age. This is because, while all are children of Adam, believers really belong to Christ, the man from heaven.

Thus the contrast in verse 44 is not between 'physical' and 'spiritual', but between 'soulish' and 'spiritual'. Had the contrast been between 'physical' and 'spiritual' it would have suggested that the 'spiritual body' is somehow not a true 'body' but *unphysical*. But a 'spiritual body', in truth, is a *body*. That is, it is a 'body' transformed from death through resurrection and filled with the Spirit of God for the kingdom of God.

Were this not the case the door would be opened to two serious theological errors, both of which have their modern advocates. One is that the 'body' is not resurrected at all, so that the afterlife is merely a 'mystical' mode of being. This is very close to the Greek idea of the 'immortality of the soul' that Paul is rebutting in this chapter, as urged by the doubters of Corinth. A resurrected 'body', however, is the total *person* mind, emotions and 'appearance', not a disembodied phantom.

The other deeply insidious error, which is a related one, is that Christ himself was not resurrected bodily, but only spiritually. In other words, he remained dead, but the disciples experienced an inward, mystical 'resurrection' experience.

Paul's whole case, as argued methodically throughout this lengthy pastoral sermon on the resurrection of the dead, is that Christ truly *died* (and was *buried*) and was truly *raised* alive at a precise moment (and *appeared* alive to many people). The resurrected body of Christ, as narrated in the Gospels, was transformed so that he passed through solid walls and merely reappeared among the disciples. Yet he was no phantom. He conversed with his disciples, ate with them, and had a body that was touched by them. In the coming age, the believer's body, too, will be in genuine continuity with his former body, but will be transformed by resurrection into a spiritual body.

2. Adam and Christ

Paul, by his contrasts, 'It is *sown*...it is *raised*', has been comparing death in this age with resurrection in the coming age. He continues by contrasting the 'First Adam' whom God created 'a living *soul*' (*psychēn zōsan*, 'as it is written' Gen. 2:7), with 'the Last Adam' who became 'a *life giving Spirit*' (v. 45). We who are 'a soulish body' (because of the First Adam) will become 'a spiritual body' (because of the Second Adam), but according to the God-ordained sequence *first* the 'soulish', *then* the 'spiritual' (v. 46).

This 'First Adam' and 'Last Adam' Paul now calls 'the First *Man*' and 'the Second *Man*' (v. 47) to align them with the sequence of 'soulish' and 'spiritual' of the previous verse. His contrast between the two picks up and expands his earlier contrast between 'earthly bodies' and 'heavenly bodies' (v. 40).

The First   Man was of the earth, a man of dust.
The Second   Man is of heaven.
As was the man of dust,   so are those who are of the dust.
As is the man of heaven,   so are those who are of heaven.
                                              (vv. 47-48)

Adam, 'the First Man', was 'of dust' (Gen. 2:7), like those who belong to him in this present age. He and we *are* dust, that is, what we *are* in essence. The Second Man, Christ, is, by contrast, 'of heaven', a different essence, like those who belong to him in the coming age.

The 'earthly' body, composed as it is *of dust*, will be transformed into a body that is *of heaven*. We who descend from the First Man bear his 'image' (v. 49), the outward shape and form of the 'man of dust', which means that to dust we must return. In the coming age, however, we will bear the 'image' of the Man of Heaven, Christ. But, as Paul will say elsewhere, this transformation has already begun here and now, since 'beholding the glory of the Lord *we are being transformed* into the same image' (2 Cor. 3:18).

Paul now rounds off his lengthy response to the questions (v. 35), 'How are the dead raised? With what kind of body do they come?'

This I say:		
Flesh and blood	cannot inherit	the kingdom of God
Nor	[can]	
the perishable		inherit the imperishable.

(v. 50)

In short, 'flesh and blood', that is, the 'soulish' (vv. 44-46), those who are 'of dust', the 'perishable', cannot *un-transformed* inherit the Kingdom of God. The 'body' that belonged to this age must be 'changed' prior to its entry into the coming age, as Paul will now explain (vv. 51-54).

They are wide of the mark who claim that since 'flesh and blood cannot inherit the kingdom', therefore the resurrection is not a resurrection of *the body*. On this premise they conclude that neither Christ's resurrection in the past nor ours in the future is a bodily resurrection. But in no way is Paul saying this. On the contrary, 'flesh and blood' describes human mortality which is dust-like and 'perishable'. The resurrected body is a true body but it is *transformed* 'flesh and blood', an 'imperishable' body.

7. A 'Mystery': All Must be Changed (vv. 51-54a)
We overhear Paul telling a 'mystery'. A 'mystery' is not a 'secret' being revealed for the first time, as to initiates in the 'mystery religions' of that period. Rather, Paul is expanding further on a now-open 'secret', that is, what will happen at the resurrection of the dead.

Look, I am telling you a mystery.
We will not all sleep,
but we will all be changed

                 in a moment
                 in the blink of an eye
                 at the last *trumpet*.

For the trumpet   will sound
and the dead   will be raised incorruptible
and we   will be changed.

Paul is not speculating what will happen but is expanding on Jesus' own 'revelation' of the end-times:

[The Son of Man] will send his angels with a loud *trumpet* call,
and they will gather his elect from the four winds,
from one end of the heavens to the other.   (Matt. 24:31)

Trumpets make a loud and piercing sound and were employed as signals in ancient battles (cf. 14:8). The prophets speak of the 'last trumpet' as announcing the end, God's final moment of intervention (Zech. 9:14; Is. 27:13). Jesus' reference is repeated by both Paul and John (1 Thess. 4:16; Rev. 8:2). When that 'last trumpet' blast is sounded all whether 'asleep' or alive will be 'changed' (divine passive, 'changed *by God*') in a moment (*atomō*, literally, 'in an atom' that is, something too tiny to be 'cut') and in an eye's twinkle. God's irresistible power is such that we, whether dead or alive, will be 'changed' immediately.

When Paul says, 'We will not all sleep...when the trumpet will sound and the dead will be raised', he could be saying one of two things. So, is he saying, (a) that he expects to be alive at the time of the general resurrection, or (b) that not all humanity will have 'fallen asleep' when that final moment comes? Option (b) is to be preferred since Paul's point is that 'all', whether dead or alive, will be indeed, 'must be' 'changed'. Had (a) been Paul's chief concern we might have expected more urgent passion at this stage of his argument. On the contrary, he moves on immediately to insist that our bodies must be transformed for life in the coming age.

The 'change' that all must submit to is now spoken of metaphorically as 'clothing' (v. 53):

The corruptible	must be clothed	with incorruption.
The mortal		with immortality.

Because 'flesh and blood cannot inherit the kingdom of God' the present corruptible and mortal frame '*must* be clothed' (divine passive, 'clothed *by God*'). Paul comments further on this in his Second Letter. At the onset of the new age God will graciously 'clothe' his people with new bodies (2 Cor. 5:2, 4). Such is God's kindness that we will be neither found 'naked' in death nor left standing in the old rags of this existence, but 'clothed' with a pristine new body covering the old.

Charles Wesley has captured the spirit and the sense of Paul's words here:

Changed from glory into glory,
Till in heaven we take our place;
Till we cast our crowns before Thee,
Lost in wonder, love and praise.

8. The Victory of God (vv. 54b-58)
Paul's words, 'Death is swallowed up in victory' (cf. 2 Cor. 5:4) speak of 'battle' and remind us of his earlier reference to death as 'the last enemy' (v. 26). Here the apostle echoes Isaiah's prophecy (25:8):

[God]	will swallow up death forever.
The Sovereign Lord	will wipe away the tears from all faces.

When the last trumpet is sounded for the last battle God will be victorious over the last enemy. God will stand victorious with Death at his feet, defeated forever.

So Paul flings two challenges at Death who, until now, always defeated every man and woman in history (v. 55). First:

Where, death, is your victory?

Death is like a schoolyard bully before whom other children cowered, until a Stronger One came along and defeated him, giving all others freedom and hope. At the last day Death will be finally vanquished.

His second question is:

Where, death, is your sting?

The 'sting' (*kentron*) was a poisonous and painful sting as of a scorpion or snake. Naturally we dread pain at death, whether the last throes of cancer or heart failure. Rightly we apply palliative care for those in such pain. Paul, however, is speaking of another pain at death. This is the 'sting' of unforgiven sins, sins which are shown for what they are by God's law, his ten commandments. Such is our innate rebellion against God that his law, which is 'good', has actually inspired and inflamed our evil behaviour (see Rom. 7:7-25).

> The sting of death is sin and
> the *power* of sin is the law (v. 56).

What is the ultimate 'pain' of Death? It is to die unforgiven. But Christ has 'died for our sins' (v. 3) and has been 'raised on the third day' (v. 4) so that, on the last day, Death will fall defeated forever.

God won the victory over sin and death, through Christ crucified and risen, at the first Easter in AD 33. That is an accomplished fact of history. We do not know when God will sound the last trumpet, but we do know that whenever it will be, God will give us the victory over sin and its accompaniment death which he has already won. We humans could never win that victory ourselves. It had to be won for us and won for us, indeed, it has been through Jesus Christ our Lord. Thus Paul offers deep and heartfelt thanks for God's power and kindness to his people (v. 57).

So he exhorts them, 'Be steadfast' (*hedraioi*, literally, 'firmly seated'), immovable (*ametakinētoi*, literally, 'unshaken'). They must not be moved from their firm foundations of the faith by the folly of doubters among them. Paul's word applies to many modern church leaders who have become skeptics and who spread their unbelief far and wide, often through accommodating media. Rather, he says, 'be always overflowing in the work of the Lord' (v. 58). That 'work' (*ergon*) Paul does not specify here, but since the same word is also used of Timothy we take it to mean spreading the gospel among unbelievers as he was doing (cf. 16:10). Paul adds, 'Knowing that your toil (*kopos*) is not in vain'. Our 'work' is not to be passive or half-hearted, rather we are to 'toil', to 'labour', as we do the 'work of the Lord'. We are partners with our great God who has won the victory over sin and death and who will share the fruits of that victory with us at the end. Our 'work' done in his name will never be wasted, since it was done in light of the reality of the eternal kingdom of God.

Paul brings to a conclusion his majestic pastoral sermon on the resurrection of the dead. It was made necessary by the doubters and deniers among the Corinthians who were disputing the resurrection of the dead at the end of history in favour of some alternative doctrine. Paul, however, does more than rebut their erroneous teaching. He shows how the historical reality of the resurrection of Christ, on which the church is founded, demands the future resurrection of those who belong to Christ. Indeed, none of the fundamental benefits of Christ's death and resurrection the assurance of forgiveness or our hope for the deceased have any meaning or content if this teaching is overturned.

But Death has been deposed from his throne by the resurrected King, Jesus, whose kingship is made effective through the proclamation of the gospel delivering prisoners from bondage to evil principalities, the 'last', the most evil and the most powerful of which is Death. In the course of his engagement with their questions, Paul shows us that our 'flesh and blood' bodies inherited from Adam, bodies which are 'soulish' and not 'spiritual, cannot inherit the Kingdom of God but they must be 'changed'. But 'changed' they will be in an instant by the power of God when the 'last trumpet' is sounded.

Thus the mundane fact of some doubters in the Corinthian assembly all those years ago has drawn forth from Paul his timeless and Spirit-inspired teaching about the 'victory of God' in the death and resurrection of the Messiah, Jesus, who has secured the 'abolition of Death'.

SOME QUESTIONS FOR PERSONAL REFLECTION:

1. Read this chapter and note the benefits to us of Christ's resurrection from the dead.

2. Now look at this in reverse, as if Christ had not, in fact, been raised.

3. How meaningful for us are Paul's words about the 'changed' nature of the resurrection body?

4. Reflect as to your current 'labour' as you do the 'work of the Lord'. Is it half-hearted or full-blooded?

STUDY QUESTIONS:

1. Why does Paul 'outline' or 'bullet point' the gospel for the believers in Corinth before he begins his argument for the resurrection?

2. What does Paul mean by calling himself 'the least of the Apostles'?

3. Why has it been necessary for Paul to repeat the gospel message, especially with so much emphasis on the resurrection?

4. What are the results of the believer if Christ is not raised from the dead?

5. What is meant by Christ being the 'first-fruits'?

6. What is the 'mystery' which Paul reveals?

16

Future Plans
(1 Cor. 16:1-24)

In this chapter Paul answers two remaining questions from the Corinthians' letter. One related to arrangements for the 'collection' (v. 1), the other to Apollos' return to Corinth (v. 12). It seems that Paul kept these answers until the closing stages of the letter to allow him to raise related matters, in particular about Paul's own plans to return to Corinth (vv. 5-9), the need to respect Timothy when he came (vv. 10-11), and the importance of submitting to Stephanas, Fortunatus and Achaicus (vv. 15-18). Finally, Paul takes the pen from his amanuensis and concludes the letter with four sentences written in his own hand (vv. 21-24).

1. The Collection (vv. 1-4)

1. 'The collection': what was it, and why did Paul arrange it? (v. 1a)

This is the fifth occasion Paul introduces a section of his letter with the words, 'Now concerning', signalling that he is about to reply to a question in a letter from the church in Corinth (see also 7:1, 25; 8:1; 12:1). The subject of their inquiry was 'the collection', or, more exactly, 'the act of collecting' (*logeia*). Since the Corinthians were seeking clarification about 'the collection' we must assume that Paul is not raising the matter for the first time. Indeed, strong hints found in the Second Letter suggest that Titus had already been to Corinth to establish 'the collection' (2 Cor. 8:6, 10).

So what was this 'collection'? It was a 'collecting' of money from the missionary churches of the Gentiles established by Paul in Galatia, Macedonia, Achaia and Asia for the mother church, Jerusalem. The historical origin of this 'collecting' was probably the gift of money sent by Christians in Antioch to the church in Jerusalem at the time of the severe drought which began c. AD 46 that affected the eastern Mediterranean (Acts 11:27-30; Gal. 2:1-10). The famine and its effects lasted for many years and brought great hardship to Judaea and its capital, Jerusalem. Queen Helena of Adiabene in Mesopotamia, a convert to Judaism, sent substantial relief to Jerusalem at this time. Paul's 'collection' from the Gentile churches for the 'saints' in Jerusalem must be understood as an expression of practical compassion in the face of great distress (2 Cor. 8:4, 14, 19-20; 9:12; Rom. 15:25-26, 28; Acts 24:17).

There is, however, more to 'the collection' than this. So far as we know, the Gentile churches were not continually send-ing relief to Jerusalem throughout the years of famine (but cf. Gal. 6:7-10). Rather, the 'collecting' was for a special gift co-ordinated by Paul to be sent once by appointed delegates from these churches who were to travel together to Jerusalem as a group (v. 3; 2 Cor. 8:19; Acts 20:3-4). For some time Paul had been hoping to move to Rome for ministry but had been pre-vented from doing so due to the Emperor Claudius' expulsion of Jews from the Eternal City in AD 49 (Acts 18:2). Claudius' death in 54, however, opened a door of opportunity for Paul the Jew to go to Rome. Paul saw this as closing the chapter of ministry in the provinces of Galatia, Macedonia, Achaia and Asia where he had been establishing churches for the past six years (Rom. 15:19). But he would not go directly to Rome but instead pay a final visit to Jerusalem to bring the fruits of 'the collection' (Rom. 15:22-25, 31).

So what was Paul's purpose in establishing and adminis-tering this complex 'collecting' in these Christian assemblies scattered across four Roman provinces? First, it was to be a confirmation of the genuineness of their acceptance of the gospel of Christ (2 Cor. 9:13). Faith in Christ is to be expressed in love towards others, especially to those in deep need. Second, since the Gentile churches had received 'spiritual blessings' from the 'saints in Jerusalem', it was right to repay this 'debt' by sending in return their 'material blessings' (Rom. 15:27). Third, the bonds of fellowship between congregations expressed in practical compassion are to be upheld regardless of geographical remoteness. Paul is saying, 'You meet their need at this time, as they may meet yours at another time when the circumstances are reversed'. There is to be a practical 'equality' among Christ's people wherever they are throughout the world (2 Cor. 8:14; 9:13). Fourth, as a consequence, those who receive are knit together in 'fellowship' with those who have given as they offer thanks to God and pray for brothers and sisters who have cared for them (2 Cor. 9:12, 14-15).[1]

2. 'Collecting' in Corinth (v. 1b-2)

The arrangements Paul laid down for the Corinthians' 'collecting' was to be the same as in the churches of southern Galatia, that is, in Antioch of Pisidia, Iconium, Lystra and Derbe. Paul had established these churches in *c.* A.D. 47 and revisited them in *c.* A.D. 52 as he travelled overland from Jerusalem to Ephesus (Acts 18:23). Most likely he set in place the details for 'collecting' at the time of the second visit. Yet we note that Paul's letter written some years earlier (*c.* 48) laid the theological groundwork for generous giving, including to believers in Jerusalem (Gal. 6:7-10; cf. 2:10).

These arrangements were (v. 2):

> Every first day of the week
> let each one of you at home put money aside
> however each has prospered
> so there will be no collecting when I come.

In line with Genesis 1 Jews *numbered* the days of the week, but did not name them. By contrast, our names for days often derived from paganism, e.g., 'Monday', the 'day of the moon god'; 'Tuesday', the day of the old German god 'Tiwes', and

---

1 Historically, Paul may have had a further intention. He may have seen the 'gift' and the Gentile believers who brought it to Jerusalem as a tangible evidence to help the 'saints' in Jerusalem understand that God was, indeed, 'including' the Gentiles among the true people of God (cf. Rom. 11:12), fully and equally 'justified' in Christ crucified and risen. The related belief, that Paul intended this 'gift' and its Gentile bearers somehow to precipitate immediately the return of Christ, is conjectural and rendered unlikely by Paul's plans to visit Rome en route to Spain for longer term ministry in the western extremities of the empire.

so on. The 'first day of the week' was the day Christ was raised from the dead, which appears from the beginning to have become a day when the first disciples gathered (John 20:19, 26) and 'broke bread' (Acts 20:7). Evidently the Lord's Day had become the focus of meeting in early Christianity (Rev. 1:10).

Each member of the congregation was to store the money at home according to good financial circumstances (*euodoomai*, literally, 'to travel well'). Paul's extended teaching on 'the collection' in the Second Letter insists that such giving was to be voluntary, a matter of 'grace' (2 Cor. 8:3-4). While the contributions were eventually sent on from the church they were really the gifts of individual members (so too Acts 11:29).

Paul gives no guidance as to the amount to be set aside. There is no hint that it was to be a 'tithe' or tenth of income. Presumably the 'collecting' was to occur over a considerable period of time to enlarge the ultimate amount sent to Jerusalem. We can only wonder at the practical problems of storing money at home over many months. There were banks of sorts associated with pagan temples, but Paul does not suggest these as a means of securing the funds.

3. Sending the money to Jerusalem (vv. 3-4)

Paul now mentions his return visit to them, which he will expand upon in verses 5-7 (see also on 4:18-20). Let the usurpers in Corinth (see on 4:18-21) understand that he will remain there for some time, even for the duration of the winter (v. 6). Furthermore, if *he* then decides that the delegates from Corinth are to travel to Jerusalem at the same time he does, they will accompany *him*. The crisis in Corinth called for strong leadership from the apostle.

We should note carefully Paul's practical concern for the proper administration of the money. Listen to his assurance in the Second Letter (8:20-21):

> We want to avoid any criticism of the way we administer this liberal gift.
> > For we are taking pains to do what is right,
> > not only in the eyes of the Lord but also in the eyes of men.

Paul set out those provisions in the First Letter, as follows:

> Whoever you approve
> I will send with my accompanying letter.[2]

Again we see Paul insisting on his leadership in Corinth; *he* will accredit them. At the same time the church had the prior responsibility to choose its delegates.

A word on the historical background may help us. Each year the tens of thousands of Jews living outside Israel sent a 'gift' for the upkeep of the Temple in Jerusalem. Surviving records tell us that the most eminent members of the synagogues were entrusted with the responsibility of accompanying this money to Jerusalem.

> At stated times there are appointed to carry the sacred tribute
> envoys selected on their merits, from every city,
> those of the highest repute....[3]

A rather different qualification was to guide the choice of those whom the church would send with the money. They were to be men whose faith in Christ had been 'tested' and 'proved' in the crucible of hostility (see 2 Cor. 8:22; cf. Rom. 16:10; 1 Tim. 3:10; 2 Tim. 2:15; 1 Pet. 1:7).

2. Paul's Final Visit to Corinth (vv. 5-9)

Certainly Paul tells the Corinthians here of plans to go to Jerusalem (v. 3). But there is no hint in this letter of his larger plan, that is, his intention to travel on from there to Rome which we know of only from other sources (Rom. 15:24; Acts 19:21). Perhaps the Corinthians already knew of it or, alternatively, Paul expected Timothy to tell them when he came.

This short passage is highly informative about Paul's passion for Christ, but also his sense of missionary strategy. His reference to 'Pentecost' (v. 8) and 'winter' (v. 6) allow us to establish a rough time frame but also to notice his carefully laid plans.

---

2   My translation following the sense though not the exact words of NIV. RSV, however, translates as the church accrediting its delegates by letter. While the grammar could support either option, if Paul was to travel independently to Jerusalem it would make better sense for Paul to accredit by letter those whom the church approved as its delegates.

3   Philo, *Special Laws* 1.79.

verse 8	Ephesus until Pentecost	Spring:	April
verse 5	Travel through Macedonia	Summer-Autumn:	April-Nov.
verse 6.	Corinth	Winter:	Nov.-Jan.

It is evident that Paul planned to leave the region in an orderly way, making the most of his ministry wherever he was. 'A great and effective door' for ministry had swung open in Ephesus, so that he will stay as long as possible (vv. 8-9; cf. 2 Cor. 2:12; Col. 4:3). 'But', he adds darkly, 'there are many opponents'. The riot of the silversmiths and Paul's narrow escape from death was to prove the accuracy of Paul's assessment of the danger (2 Cor. 1:8-10; Acts 19:23-20:1).

At the same time Paul was aware of the need to spend a lengthy period in Macedonia (v. 5), where his initial visits to Philippi Thessalonica and Berea four-five years earlier had been cut short by local opposition (Acts 16:39; 17:10, 14). Timothy and Silvanus were able to remain in Macedonia after Paul was forced out. It made good sense for Paul to send Timothy on ahead of him to Macedonia, which he did on Timothy's return from Corinth (v. 11; Acts 19:21; 2 Cor. 1:1).[4]

Corinth was to be the final stage of Paul's withdrawal from the churches of the Aegean provinces (vv. 5-7). Although such a visit may not have been for the best part of a year, Paul earlier made it painfully clear that he would come 'sooner' if the usurpers in Corinth continued in their rebellious ways (see on 4:18-21).[5] After his arrival the Corinthians were to 'send him on his way' to Jerusalem. Here the word (*propempein*) was a term for a congregation providing temporary hospitality, food and money for the Christian worker 'passing through' (Acts 15:3; 21:5; Rom. 15:24; 2 Cor. 1:16; Tit. 3:13; 3 John 6). Paul, however, envisaged an extended stay beforehand, perhaps for the winter, which appears to have happened. The book of Acts mentions that after leaving Macedonia Paul spent 'three months in Greece' before departing for Syria (Acts 20:3).

---

4   We lose track of Silvanus' association with Paul after his arrival with Timothy in Corinth (2 Cor. 1:19; Acts 18:5). Our only other glimpse of Silvanus is as Peter's amanuensis of 1 Peter and possible bearer of that letter to the provinces of Anatolia (1 Pet. 5:12).

5   As it happened, Timothy's report was so alarming that Paul went immediately to Corinth (2 Cor. 1:23–2:1).

Although Paul made these plans yet he adds, 'If the Lord permits' (v. 7; 4:19). It is interesting to reflect on the circumstances the Lord did 'permit' to eventuate. Yes, Paul did leave Ephesus for Macedonia, but not voluntarily or when he planned to do so; the silversmiths' riot brought Paul face to face with death and forced his premature departure. Nor did Paul return to Corinth by the smooth and easy road as indicated in these verses. In fact, his relationship with the Corinthians deteriorated dramatically. Paul was forced to make an unscheduled visit to Corinth on hearing Timothy's report, a visit which proved to be a bruising experience (2 Cor. 2:1,5; 7:12; 12:20-13:2). His follow-up letter from Ephesus (now lost) was misunderstood and brought even more grief (2:3-4; 7:8; 10:10). Meanwhile some Judaizing preachers had arrived in Corinth further undermining Paul's fragile relationships with the church (2 Cor. 2:17-3:1; 10:12-11:6, 13-15, 22-23). Paul's co-worker Titus must engage in many weeks of 'shuttle diplomacy' between Paul and the church before it will be possible for Paul eventually to return. The actual course of events, as opposed to Paul's plans, proved infinitely more complex and painful than he could have imagined. That he stuck to them demonstrates how determined he was to obey the Lord Jesus. It proved to be the Lord's 'will' for Paul to come back to Corinth, but, as things often transpire, in very different circumstances.

3. Timothy and Apollos (vv. 10-12)
Paul now refers to Timothy and Apollos, both of whom were known to the Corinthians.

Timothy had laboured alongside Paul in preaching the gospel not long after Paul first arrived in Corinth (2 Cor. 1:19; Acts 18:5). We cannot be sure why Paul could only say, '*If* Timothy comes...' (v. 10). Perhaps Paul's encouragement that they take care that Timothy was 'not ill at ease' with them (v. 10), that they do not 'despise him' (v. 11), and that they 'send him on his way in peace' (v. 11), point to reasons why Timothy might be hesitant about coming. Was this because of Timothy's relative youthfulness? Had Timothy sustained some bad experience in Corinth during his previous visit there? Was Paul concerned that the troublemakers in the church would make life difficult for him (see on 4:18-21)?[6] When Timothy reported back to Paul in Ephesus, the apostle himself came immediately to Corinth, while he sent Timothy to Macedonia (Acts 19:22). Subsequently Paul sent Titus as his envoy to Corinth.

While Timothy was Paul's 'beloved and faithful child in the Lord' (4:17), Apollos was merely Paul's 'brother' or fellow-Christian (v. 12). The formulaic, 'Now concerning...' points to another answer by Paul to a question the sixth in a letter from them (7:1, 25; 8:1; 12:1; 16:1). Evidently they inquired when Apollos might be returning to Corinth. It appears they hoped he would accompany those who brought Paul's letter of reply to them. Apollos was a formidable figure whose ministry had made a great impact in Corinth (Acts 18:27-28). Although a party had formed around Apollos in Corinth, Paul betrays no hostility towards this eloquent Alexandrian Jew who had become a Christian (1:12; 3:4, 5, 6, 22; 4:6; cf. Titus 3:13). According to Paul Apollos will come to them later, when opportunity arose. Perhaps Apollos recognised that his arrival in Corinth at this time might not help Paul's relationship with the church.

4. Admonitions (vv. 13-14)
Paul now directs a series of pithy admonitions to his readers.

> Be on your guard;
> stand firm in the faith;
> be courageous;
> be strong.
> Let everything among you be done in love.

Similar staccato exhortations are to be found in some other New Testament letters.[7] This, however, is no mere formality or literary convention. Each word is carefully chosen for the particular situation of this letter and its readers.

The first, 'Be on your guard' (or 'be watchful'), is restated in the second, 'Stand firm in the faith'. Furthermore, the second echoes his earlier reference to 'the gospel...in which you *stand*' (15:1). Thus '*the* faith' and '*the* gospel' are to be equated.

---

6   Timothy may have remained in Corinth after Paul's departure (Acts 18:18), perhaps suffering imprisonment there (Heb. 13:23).

7   See e.g., Romans 12:9-21; 2 Corinthians 13:11; Philippians 4:4-9; 1 Thessalonians 5:16-22; 1 Peter 5:6-9.

Christians are to exercise 'faith' (personal) in 'the faith' (propositional), 'the gospel' that 'Christ died for our sins' and 'was raised on the third day'. It will be remembered that 'some' in the church were questioning the resurrection (15:12). Thus they are to be 'watchful' against turning away from 'the faith' while actively and resolutely 'standing firm' in it (cf. 15:58).

The second and the third admonitions, 'be courageous' (literally, 'show yourselves to be *men*') and 'be strong' (literally, 'be powerful'), both address the ever-present danger of persecution for the early Christians. Paul faced 'danger' at every turn (2 Cor. 11:26), including in Ephesus, even as he wrote this letter (15:30-32; 16:9). But because Paul's readers were forced to endure 'the same sufferings' (2 Cor. 1:6) as he did, he encourages them to be 'courageous' and 'strong'.

The final exhortation, that their 'every deed' be done 'in love', is quite pointed in view of their lack of love evident at many points. The theologically strong did not show love to the 'weak brother' (8:1, 9-13). The rich failed to love 'those who had nothing' (11:20-22). The verbally gifted spoke for personal self-display rather than in love to 'build up' the assembled church (14:1,12). Paul's famous 'hymn to love' (13:1-13) was written precisely for this church, to show its members how to love one another. Here, then, is one more reminder for them to love, strategically placed near the end of the letter. In a few moments he will also call on them to 'love the Lord' (cf. 8:3).

This was a church that was rich in 'speech and knowledge', for which Paul gave thanks to God (1:5; cf. 2 Cor. 8:7). 'Speech and knowledge', however, can be very ego-centred and self-affirming, leading to pride and arrogance, even among believers. 'Love', on the other hand, is, by its very nature, directed outwards away from oneself to others and their needs. Where 'speaking' and 'knowing' are exercised in humility, self-forgetfulness and love of others, God will add his rich blessings. But where love is not the inspiration and motivation, then even eloquent 'speaking' which is correct in 'knowledge' is quite without value or profit (13:1-3).

5. The House of Stephanas (vv. 15-18)
This is quite a formal sounding paragraph whose 'weight' is increased by its appearance as the last section in the Letter before the writer's final greetings.

v. 15 I appeal to you, brothers
           you know the household of Stephanas
           that it was the first-fruits of Achaia, and
              [that] they have devoted themselves to
ministry to
  the saints.
v. 16 Be subject to such people, and
           to everyone who works with me and labours.

Having introduced his appeal Paul immediately breaks off into parenthesis to mention, first, that Stephanas' family was the 'first-fruits of Achaia' (cf. 1:16) and, second, that its members had given themselves in ministry to the 'saints'. 'First-fruits' was the choicest part of the early harvest offered in sacrifice to the Lord (Exod. 23:16). Paul uses this imagery for the exemplary quality of the service of this household to others as expressing their special status as the 'first reapings' of Paul's harvest in the province.[8] Accordingly, the Corinthians were to be 'subject' to such people, along with others who worked with Paul, labouring in ministry.

To Stephanas Paul adds the names Fortunatus and Achaicus (v. 17). These were probably manumitted slaves (set free by Stephanas?) bearing the nicknames 'Lucky' (that is 'lucky' to be free!) and 'Achaicus' (after the province where he found his freedom). It was as if the church came with these men, since Paul says they made up for his absence from the Corinthians. He notes appreciatively that these three refreshed his 'spirit' as he expects they will also refresh the spirits of the Corinthians on their return.

Thus it is evident that Stephanas and his colleagues were the sources of some of the reports of troubles back in Corinth. Most probably they were also the bearers of the letter from the Corinthians (see on 7:1). They must have remained in Ephesus for several weeks while Paul wrote his reply, our canonical First Corinthians, which they, in turn, brought back to Corinth.

There is more to these words (vv. 15-18) than appears on the surface. The church in Corinth was in considerable difficulty. Various theological and moral errors were bad enough. Even more serious was their rebellion against the leadership of their

---

8   Epaenetus was the 'firstfruits' of the province of Asia (Rom. 16:5).

apostle, Paul (see on 4:8,14-21; 14:37-38). It seems that there were local leaders who were rising up against him (4:18), although Paul does not mention them directly. Paul responded to this crisis by writing this Letter in which he reasserted his authority as an apostle (see on 3:10-11; 4:14-16). But Paul will also need living supporters in Corinth as well as his letter. For this reason he called on the Corinthians to 'imitate' him as Timothy, his dear 'son', does, who is soon to come to them, and who knows Paul's 'ways' (4:17; cf. 16:10-12). In the meantime, however, let the Corinthians 'submit' to and 'recognise' Stephanas, Fortunatus and Achaicus.

Doubtless Paul prayed that the combined effect of the Letter and the presence of Stephanas and Timothy would be sufficient to 'hold the line' against doubters, disputers and usurpers in Corinth. This, however, proved not to be the case. Timothy did indeed arrive, but probably did not remain long, returning to Paul in Ephesus. Paul himself came immediately to Corinth for what must have been a 'nightmarish' visit. He was opposed and miscalled in a context of very serious disorder within the church (2 Cor. 1:23-2:1; 2:5-11; 12:20-13:3). The church in Corinth was now divided between his supporters and opponents led by a particular individual (2 Cor. 7:12). But that is another story whose threads must be picked up in the reading of his Second Letter.[9]

One further comment is appropriate before leaving this passage. It is that neither here nor anywhere in this lengthy epistle does Paul speak of 'authority' figures or officials such as elders/bishops and deacons. We know that Paul appointed such persons to order and govern the churches (Acts 14:23; Phil. 1:1). Doubtless such leaders were part of the church in Corinth, though there is no hint of them in either First or Second Corinthians. The Corinthians were to 'submit' to Stephanas, Fortunatus and Achaicus on account of their dedicated ministry to the saints. We do not even know if any or all were elders! Likewise Paul could have dealt with so many issues in this letter by simply appealing to the lines of authority which were in place. But he does not do this. Rather, he teaches, teaches,

---

9   See P. W. Barnett, *The Second Epistle to the Corinthians NIC* (Grand Rapids: Eerdmans, 1997), pp. 9-15.

teaches, so that believers will learn to behave based on great principles which can be applied to the manifold circumstances of life. Paul is as concerned that believers know 'how to think' as that they know 'what to believe'.

6. Greetings from Asia (vv. 19-20)

Paul addressed this letter to the church in Corinth but also to others 'in every place', by which he means Christians in other assemblies in the province of Achaia (1:2; cf. 2 Cor. 1:1). In keeping with this a greeting comes from 'the churches of Asia' and not only the church in Ephesus, the city from which Paul was now writing. Where were these 'churches of Asia'?

Apart from Ephesus we know of congregations in Troas, Colosse, Laodicea and the house churches of Aquila and Prisca in Ephesus and of Philemon and Apphia in Colosse. Doubtless there were others. As well as the Pauline churches of Ephesus and Laodicea, John later addressed churches in Smyrna, Pergamum, Thyatira, Sardis and Philadelphia, some of which may also have been in existence in the fifties.

A warm greeting also comes from 'the church in the house' of Aquila and Prisca (called Priscilla in Acts). It will be remembered that Aquila and Prisca were already in Corinth when Paul arrived and that he stayed with them and worked with them as a tentmaker (Acts 18:1-3). They were well known in Corinth.

Finally, Paul sends a 'global' greeting from 'all the brothers and sisters' from the churches of Asia. The assemblies sent their greetings, but so too did the individual members. Such was the sense of fellowship within these communities of faith.

How moving it is to ponder that after just a few years of Paul's ministry there were congregations of 'brothers and sisters' in Roman Asia composed in the main of Gentiles who belonged to Jesus, the Messiah of Israel. This is nothing less than the work of God by his Word and Spirit working through his servant Paul and his co-workers. But God continues his work in the world through the gospel, winning people to himself through Christ and establishing congregations of believers. This is a challenge and encouragement to the ongoing work of evangelism today.

As the church in Corinth receives these greetings from Asia across the Aegean Paul encourages them to 'greet one another with a holy kiss' (v. 20; Rom. 16:16; 2 Cor. 13:12; 1 Thess. 5:26). Was this to remind them that they were 'brothers and sisters' of 'one another' in a 'family' to which they belonged locally, but to which they also belonged internationally? The reference to 'one another', a term that occurs seventy or so times in the New Testament letters, reminds us of the intimacy of relationship of church life in early Christianity, and the apostles' expectations of such intimacy.

Such a 'kiss' must surely have helped transcend and overcome the divisions and difficulties so evident in this church. So long as people can keep talking to one another and respecting one another, there is hope of reconciliation. That hope recedes when people stop talking. Whatever the differences, it is worth working away at them while remaining in whatever relationship is possible.

7. Paul's Signature (vv. 21-24).

The final few sentences of the letter form a postscript and are written in Paul's own hand (see Gal. 6:11-18; Col. 4:18; 2 Thess. 3:17; Philem. 19). The preceding part of the letter was dictated to a scribe who, however, is not identified (cf. Rom. 16:22). Was the amanuensis Sosthenes, the co-sender (1:1)?

Paul then adds four sentences:

> If anyone does not love the Lord, let him be anathema.
> *Marana tha.*
> The grace of the Lord Jesus be with you.
> My love be with you all in Christ Jesus.

1. No love for the Lord

The failures of the Corinthians, which have been so obvious throughout this letter, all stem from one root problem, an absence of love for the Lord. No matter whether it has been proud wisdom, unfettered sexual behaviour, wild litigiousness, self-display or wilful disbelief, a greater sin has inspired all of these, that is, failure to love the Lord Jesus. His love for his people underlay the death he died by crucifixion 'for our sins'. That love is to be reciprocated, to Christ and to God (8:3), and is to be expressed in hearty love for others and in the avoidance of wicked behaviour. Love for the Lord bears good fruit, but its absence produces much evil.

Paul's words, 'If anyone does not love the Lord...' must be read alongside those of 8:6, 'there is...one Lord'. This text completes the earlier one. Both texts echo the great daily prayer-confession, the 'Shema' from Deuteronomy 6:4-5

> Hear, O Israel:
> The LORD our God, the LORD is one.
> Love the LORD your God with all your heart...

These words express the heart of Israel's faith. The LORD (Yahweh) is 'one', that is unique and incomparable. The Israelite is to love Yahweh with all of his being. This is expressed also in Psalm 31:23, 'Love the Lord, all you his saints'.

Do we see what Paul is doing? Israelite though he is, the impact of Christ's resurrection and exaltation are such that he is now identifying Jesus with Yahweh, the God of Israel. Jesus the Lord is to be loved as Yahweh the God of Israel was to be loved. This is, indeed, an exalted Christology. At the same time it underlines the significance of 'love' in this letter, evident also in the closing words two sentences later, 'My love be with you all in Christ Jesus'.

'Anathema' (literally, 'set aside') was used by pagans and Jews for 'accursed'. Earlier Paul appears to be echoing the cursing of Jesus from pagan lips in temple cults (12:1-3). Here, however, Paul may be evoking Jewish synagogue prayers against heretics, including Christians.[10] Paul, however, is not calling for excommunication or even exclusion from the Lord's Table, procedures which applied to overt and public wickedness, for example, the sexual immorality referred to earlier (5:1f.). Rather, Paul is now expressing a strong sentiment with pastoral intent, namely, that those Corinthians who do not love the Lord begin to do so and to demonstrate that love ethically.

2. 'Come back, Lord.'
Embedded in Paul's Greek is his quotation of two Aramaic words, but without translation (cf. Rom. 8:15; Gal. 4:6). These could mean, 'Our Lord has come' (*Marana tha*) or, 'Our Lord, come' (*Marana tha*). The similar prayer in Revelation 22:20

---

10 Benediction Twelve of the Eighteen Benedictions (Palestinian Rescension) prays: 'For apostates let there be no hope ... and may the Nazarenes and heretics perish quickly ...'

('Come, Lord Jesus') probably determines that Paul had the latter in mind.

Marana tha is the prayer of an Aramaic-speaking church, almost certainly the earliest church in Jerusalem. It is addressed to Jesus as Lord, and most likely arose from his appeal to Psalm 110:1: 'The Lord said to my *Lord,* "Sit at my right hand until I make your enemies your footstool"' (Mark 12:35-37; Acts 2:34). Jesus understood this as Yahweh telling the risen Christ to sit next to him in the place of honour *until* all enemies are overcome (see on 15:20-28). After his exaltation to God's right hand and 'until' his enemies are vanquished, the people cry to their Lord, *Marana tha,* 'Our Lord, come back'.

The Aramaic words *Marana tha* within Paul's Greek text are like an archaeological inscription that sheds valuable light on the times from which it came. These words allow us to overhear the worship in the earliest Jewish church after Jesus' resurrection. They make clear that from the beginning Jesus was worshipped as the exalted *Mara,* 'Lord', and that the believers prayed to him, pleading for his return. These words render null and void the claim that only after many years did Christians introduce the idea of the second coming. The prayer *Marana tha* makes such views impossible.

3. First Concluding Prayer

Paul concludes the letter with two prayers. The first is that 'the grace of the Lord Jesus be with' them, a prayer Paul often prayed for his readers near the end of his letters.[11] Paul will expand this prayer along Trinitarian lines in the Second Letter 'The grace of the Lord Jesus Christ, the love of God and the fellowship of the Holy Spirit be with you all' (2 Cor. 13:14).

What does Paul mean by 'the grace of the Lord Jesus'? According to 2 Corinthians 8:9 it is that voluntary, unconditioned mercy by which Christ surrendered his riches in the presence of God to come among us in the poverty of birth, life and death to bestow upon moral paupers the wealth of God's salvation. Paul is praying that they and we will grasp this 'grace of the Lord' but also express it in graciousness to others.

---

11   11 Galatians 6:18; 1 Thessalonians 5:28; 2 Thessalonians 3:18; Ephesians 6:24; Philippians 4:23; Colossians 4:18.

4. Second Concluding Prayer

His second prayer, which is the last sentence of the letter, is that Paul's own 'love be with all' of them in Christ Jesus. Paul is asking God that they will realize within themselves the love their apostle has for them. Why does Paul conclude his letter on this note? Almost certainly it is because the Corinthians were at risk of serious alienation from Paul. Perhaps the major 'message' to emerge from the letter is that only a fragile thread held together the relationship between that church and Paul. It was important, therefore, for them to know within their being that he loved them.

There is a good lesson here for any who are alienated from friends or family. We need to have and express love to those who have wronged us and with whom we seek to be reconciled. Love is essential for healing the wounds of division.

With these words the reader (Stephanas?) comes to the end of the scroll sent from Paul. Did this church heed Paul's words? When Timothy arrived did he find changed hearts and changed behaviour? Doubtless some were chastened by the powerful words of this letter. It appears, however, that many remained stubbornly at odds with Paul, so that he, too, must now come to the city. That visit was followed by two further letters and the diplomatic efforts of Titus before Paul would come for the last time to this city. The Letter to the Romans, written from Corinth, is relatively calm in tone. Perhaps by then this church and its apostle were reconciled.

By the grace of God Paul penned this great letter which was preserved throughout Roman antiquity, the chaos of the Barbarian invasions and the uncertainties of medieval times. Throughout those years millions have been blessed and built up in faith, hope and love by a letter that may have been resisted by its original readers.

SOME QUESTIONS FOR PERSONAL REFLECTION:

1. What is my responsibility to churches in other places where the people face persecution or hardship?

2. Does my church follow best practice in regard to the auditing of the books, for example?

3. What do we learn for our own prayers and plans from Paul's plans and what *actually* happened?

4. How do the examples of Stephanas and his associates help us understand the basis of and importance of Christian leadership?

5. Do we pray *Marana tha*?

STUDY QUESTIONS:

1. What is the 'collection' Paul refers to?

2. What was the purpose in establishing and administering this 'collection'?

3. How might Paul's admonitions remind them of the larger context of his letter? How are the admonitions related to other issues in the church at Corinth?

4. Why does Paul appeal to the believers at Corinth to give respect and honor to Stephanas? What about Timothy?

5. What is the purpose of greeting one another with a 'holy kiss'? What is implied in this custom?

6. In Paul's concluding prayer, what does he mean by 'the grace of the Lord Jesus'?

Subject Index

Scripture Index

FOCUS • ON • THE • BIBLE

2 CORINTHIANS

THE GLORIES AND RESPONSIBILITIES
OF CHRISTIAN SERVICE

GEOFFREY GROGAN

ISBN 978-1-84550-252-2

2 Corinthians

The Glories and Responsibilities of Christian Service

GEOFFREY GROGAN

The second letter to the Corinthians is Paul's personal appeal to the church he founded in Corinth, a church influenced against Paul by false prophets. In describing the type of Church Leader that is pleasing to God, Paul reveals more about himself than in any other of his writings. It is as if we can see into his soul as he lovingly points out the faulty attitudes of the church at Corinth.

In addition to guidance on leadership and on other subjects he also wrote about Christian giving. Paul was eager for the church to participate in the relief fund he was putting together for poor believers in Jerusalem. His rulings on these matters need to be applied to today's church.

Dr Geoffrey W. Grogan was Principal Emeritus of Glasgow Bible College before it became International Christian College, Glasgow. His theological studies were undertaken there and at the London Bible College. He served the College as a full-time lecturer for fourteen years before going south in 1965 to teach at LBC. In 1969 he returned to Glasgow as principal. He has served on four missionary councils, on the Strathclyde Education Committee and the Management Committee for the Cambridge University Diploma in Religious Studies. He has written books on the Trinity, the Person of Christ, Paul, the Psalms and commentaries on Isaiah, Mark and 2 Corinthians. He is now retired and has been a part-time pastor in a Baptist Church.

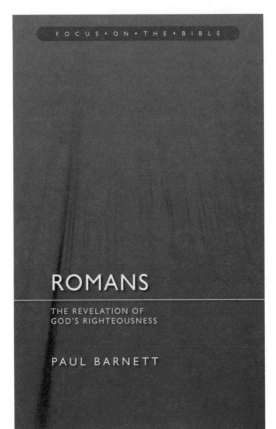

FOCUS·ON·THE·BIBLE

ROMANS

THE REVELATION OF
GOD'S RIGHTEOUSNESS

PAUL BARNETT

ISBN 978-1-84550-269-0

Romans

Revelation of God's Righteousness

Paul Barnett

"Paul Barnett combines a thorough going exegesis which is sane and helpful, as well as lucid and well argued, with a pastor's heart and a good eye for application. This is a brilliant commentary on a key book, which I warmly and wholeheartedly recommend. Every preacher and lay reader should have it and read it!"

Wallace Benn,
Bishop of Lewes, Sussex, England

"Distinguished New Testament historian and pastor, Bishop Paul Barnett, has given us a clearly written commentary on Romans which, while critically conversant with the present debate over the new perspective, is clear and accessible to preachers and Bible teachers. The deft hand of a scholar preacher is everywhere evident in the neat organisation, precision, lucid explanative and warmth of this most helpful work."

R. Kent Hughes,
Senior Pastor Emeritus, College Church, Wheaton, Illinois

'Paul Barnett's refreshing commentary on Romans is marked by warmth, clarity, careful exegesis of the text, and a fine grasp of the historical circumstances surrounding this letter.'

Peter O'Brien,
Emeritus Faculty Member, Moore Theological College, Sydney

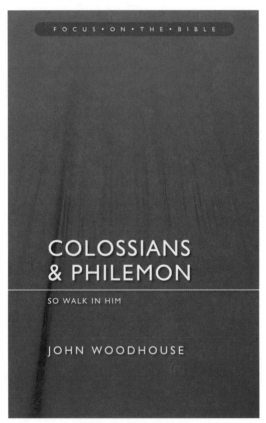

FOCUS • ON • THE • BIBLE

COLOSSIANS
& PHILEMON

SO WALK IN HIM

JOHN WOODHOUSE

ISBN 978-1-84550-632-2

Colossians and Philemon

So Walk in Him

JOHN WOODHOUSE

Come and hear a wonderful story of evangelism, church planting and Christian growth. Colossians was a letter, which would have first been read by Tychicus in Philemon's house in Colossae. People who were to read that letter had been converted as a result of Paul's teaching in Ephesus (Acts 19). As they read they are about to understand better the reality of life in Christ and reading it years later we can understand better too.

"This commentary by John Woodhouse is a rich source of biblical insight on the texts of Colossians and Philemon. This volume is a great resource for the pastor as he prepares to feed his flock, but it is equally helpful for students of the Bible who desire to understand better these magnificent letters. Maybe even more importantly, the text reflects the author's own love for the Savior. I can gladly commend it."

Bill Cook
Professor of New Testament Interpretation,
The Southern Baptist Theological Seminary, Louisville, Kentucky

John Woodhouse is the principal of Moore College, Australia and lectures there in doctrine and Old Testament. As well as writing a commentary on 1 Samuel, he has written various articles based on the New and Old Testament.

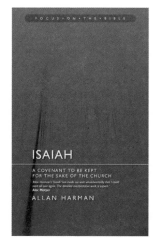
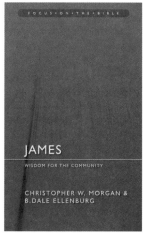

Christian Focus Publications

Our mission statement –

STAYING FAITHFUL

In dependence upon God we seek to impact the world through literature faithful to His infallible Word, the Bible. Our aim is to ensure that the Lord Jesus Christ is presented as the only hope to obtain forgiveness of sin, live a useful life and look forward to heaven with Him.

Our books are published in four imprints:

CHRISTIAN FOCUS

Popular works including biographies, commentaries, basic doctrine and Christian living.

CHRISTIAN HERITAGE

Books representing some of the best material from the rich heritage of the church.

MENTOR

Books written at a level suitable for Bible College and seminary students, pastors, and other serious readers. The imprint includes commentaries, doctrinal studies, examination of current issues and church history.

CF4•K

Children's books for quality Bible teaching and for all age groups: Sunday school curriculum, puzzle and activity books; personal and family devotional titles, biographies and inspirational stories – because you are never too young to know Jesus!

Christian Focus Publications Ltd,
Geanies House, Fearn, Ross-shire,
IV20 1TW, Scotland, United Kingdom.
www.christianfocus.com
blog.christianfocus.com